During the twentieth century the number of people who

speak English as a first or second language has increased dramatically. The covers of

the Voyages series reflect the fact that English is the most widely read language in the world.

This year our Voyages in English book takes us to Europe.

VOYAGES in English

Revised Edition

Carolyn Marie Dimick

General Editor

Marie T. McVey

Revision Editor

Jeanne M. Baker

Maria Byers

Carolyn Marie Dimick

Joan I. Rychalsky

Authors

Loyola University Press · Chicago

Contributors	Michael Lipkin
	Sylvia Foust
	Martina Anne Erdlen
Managing Editor	Juanita Raman (revision)
Project Editor	Janet Battiste
	Kathleen Schultz
Production / Design Manager	Carol Tornatore
	Frederick Falkenberg (revision)
Designer	William A. Seabright

ISBN 0-8294-0760-X

In every grade, language development challenges teachers and students to explore their world through the spoken and written word. Language in all its aspects is essential to the development of the individual on both personal and social levels. We use language as a vehicle for expressing wonder and delight, a tool for exchanging ideas, a medium for transmitting information, and a resource for bridging the differences among peoples. These are the ultimate goals of language and the underlying philosophy of *Voyages in English*.

Integration of the language arts

The revised *Voyages in English* series is designed to include the major areas of the language arts curriculum: writing, grammar, correct usage, mechanics, dictionary and library skills, speaking and listening skills, and literature. These areas should not be considered separate and distinct from one another even though, for purposes of instruction, the skills may be taught in isolation.

The challenge of the teacher is to present the areas as integrated so that the students can perceive the seemingly discrete parts of the curriculum as an interrelated whole. Ultimately, students should view the entire program as essential to building competency and success in other curricular areas.

Parts I and II. Before teaching the material in *Voyages in English*, the teacher should become acquainted with the format of the textbook. There are two distinct sections: writing and grammar. (Literary selections are incorporated into each chapter of the grammar section.) Neither section is meant to be taught in continuity without reference to the other. Familiarity with the chapters in both sections will enable the teacher to move with ease between the two sections.

For example, when working with the students in the proofreading stage of the writing process, the teacher will discover areas of weakness in correct usage and mechanics. At this point it is recommended that the teacher turn to the lesson in the grammar section that corresponds to the particular problem area and teach the concept in the context of the writing activity.

While teaching an area of grammar such as adjectives, teachers may refer to the lessons on word substitution, sentence expansion, or descriptive writing so as to integrate grammar and writing. At all times the instructional goal should be integration, not isolation.

Illustrations. The full-page illustration that opens each chapter relates directly or indirectly to the chapter that follows, but it may often be as appropriately used with other subject matter.

In the writing section of the book, the captions are "lead" questions designed to serve as a springboard for class discussion. The ideas explored through the illustrations can often inspire a composition. Teachers having an overview of the illustrations in the book can refer to a specific one to prompt a writing activity.

In the grammar section a credit line identifies photographs and fine art. Illustrations may inspire a poem, a theme, or different kinds of sentences (declarative, interrogative, exclamatory, imperative). A simple sentence about the picture might be expanded with words, phrases, or clauses—all of which might include various types of figurative language. The inclusion of much regionalist (especially American) and other art from different periods provides opportunities for cross-curricular links.

Practice Power. This feature provides a skill-extension or a writing activity following each grammar lesson. Sometimes it is simply writing sentences or completing a review exercise; at other times it is writing a brief paragraph or poem. With teacher assistance, the students should be led to realize the importance of integrating correct grammar, usage, and mechanics with writing skills.

You Are the Author. This feature extends the integration of the language arts, replacing the final Practice Power activity in each chapter with an assignment related in some way to the literary opener. The students learn to apply the grammatical concept taught in the chapter to writing that draws on the genre, subject, or content of the literature. In addition, students engage in cooperative learning, which teaches them to take pride in sharing both their individual skills and the rewards of group achievement.

The writing process

Exploring and discovering meaning through written language should be part of every child's educational experience. Schools that make the development of writing skills a high priority foster the writing process within the curriculum.

Developing good writing skills is essential at every grade level. The teacher should become familiar with the elements of the writing process. The goal is for writing to be a natural, enjoyable means of expression in which the students engage frequently.

When the writing process is begun in the early school years, children have no fear or anxiety about writing. Instead, building on their ability to communicate through speech, they find writing an exhilarating and happy experience. There is a sense of satisfaction in knowing a piece is well written and has expressed exactly what the writer intended to say. Although research on the composing, or writing, process is ongoing, most authorities agree that the process has four stages: prewriting, writing or drafting, revision, and editing. These are not mutually exclusive, however, so should not be taught in isolation. Writing is a cyclic process; thus its components overlap, allowing the writer to wander in and out of all stages at will.

Prewriting. Observing, discussing, reading, journal writing, note-taking, interviewing, brainstorming, imagining, and remembering are some activities that take place before the writer begins an actual draft. In this stage the writer hones in on a subject, narrows it, and makes decisions about the purpose and audience of the piece. Why is it being written? For whom? (The teacher, parents, principals, other students, and the community are all appropriate audiences.) What form should the writing take? In this stage enthusiasm is generated. Interaction between student and teacher helps attest to the value of the project. Teachers should encourage students to share their ideas so as to "hear" their own ideas and others', ultimately helping them to evaluate their material, to be selective about it, and to make associations.

Writing. During the creation of the first draft, the student puts the information on paper. At this stage the writer should be encouraged to keep the ideas flowing without worrying about sentence structure or correct usage. Maintaining momentum is important, so completing this process at one sitting is the ideal. The first draft is the visible form of what took place in the prewriting stage. It allows the student to see a dim shape of what the material is to become. Teachers should encourage students to write without making corrections—on alternate lines so as to provide room for revision.

Revision. This can be the most difficult stage of writing yet the most vital to its success. Here students look over the work again and again. First drafts are rarely well organized or cohesive. Ideas need clarification, sentences need variety, and vocabulary needs development. Such refining takes more than one revision. Teachers should encourage students to write as many drafts as seem necessary.

Editing and proofreading. In the final stage before "publication," the students must look to the correctness of the piece. Correct punctuation, spelling, capitalization, and usage are important if the work is to be taken seriously. The students should be taught the importance of reviewing their own work for accuracy. Frequently at this stage, however, they can get caught up in refining content, which is not the domain of proofreading, instead of being attentive to mechanical details. The teacher can help control the proofreading process by suggesting four or five areas to check so that all the students proofread for at least those specific prime areas of concern.

Having another student proofread the work is another way to help avoid major revisions at the proofreading stage. To increase objectivity and foster cooperative learning, students should be encouraged to do what real publishers do: select "a second pair of eyes." Teachers may wish to assign a team of students who are good in proofreading to serve as a class resource in this area.

It is important to note again that writers wander in and out of the various writing stages. Many times one begins to revise while writing a first draft. Frequently it may be necessary to return to prewriting in order to gather more information or think about an idea. Bits of proofreading are done while revising. No student should be locked into writing stage by stage, although it is often productive to restrict the critical faculty during a creative time.

Finally, students are ready to publish their work—as close to perfection as possible. The audience has the right to require that finished writing be comprehensible and stylistically consistent. The students can learn a great deal from total involvement in the process of writing. If the audience receives the work well, the students learn to take pride in achievement.

Write Away! This extension of the activities in each writing lesson may or may not be completed by students, depending on their ability to manage the assignment. Some will respond to the challenge. Others may perform better on a version modified to address individual interests, learning styles, or needs.

Grammar, usage, and mechanics

Part II of the *Voyages in English* program offers the students a traditional approach to grammar in a handbook-reference format. Lessons include definitions, explanations, and then exercises that allow for abundant practice in each concept. The activities and recurring features build on learning by providing opportunities for practical application and language-arts integration.

Recalling What You Know. A few review questions in the first lesson of each grammar chapter set the stage for learning and relate loosely to a literary selection in the chapter. The questions are intended not to test students' previous learning but to remind them of what they already know, to show them that they can do the exercises that follow, and so to instill self-confidence.

Chapter Challenge. At the end of each grammar chapter is a paragraph that incorporates all the grammar skills the students have learned in the chapter. Identifying various grammatical structures is more difficult in paragraphs than in isolated sentences. In most cases, therefore, this feature should be teacher directed rather than used as a testing tool.

Literature

New to the *Voyages in English* program is literature-based traditional grammar. The series' ample poetry component has now been expanded to include other literary genres drawn from a broad range of ethnic backgrounds, social contexts, and historical periods. The literature is integrated into the other language arts and suggests many cross-curricular applications as well.

Literary opener. The literature that opens each chapter in the grammar section of the book includes fiction, drama, history, fables, folktales, fantasy, and biography. Topics often relate to other academic subjects. Exciting, thought-provoking subject matter stimulates discussion of current issues, introduces students to new cultural perspectives, and has personal relevance.

The Writer's Craft. This feature relates the literary selection the students have just read to their experience. Open-ended questions stimulate discussion and encourage interpretation, teaching students to think and developing an appreciation for writing style. By eliciting the students' feelings, opinions, and judgments, the reader-response questions create interest and reinforce the literary intent. Subsequent questions highlight the author's application of the grammatical concept being taught in the chapter.

Creative Space. The poetic selections that close each grammar chapter should be enjoyed first and then analyzed. They open up new writing possibilities for students, including using the literature as a model for students' original work.

The Teacher's Edition

The teacher's text sets the objectives and presents directives for the lessons. Some lessons may require two or three days of instruction. The pacing depends on class as well as individual needs.

Enrichment. This section in Part I, to be used at the discretion of the teacher, provides a challenge for more-advanced students. Many exercises in Part II also contain an extended application.

Voyages in English 6 will provide students with a thorough knowledge of English and will lead them to appreciate language as a gift. The textbook, together with a teacher's own love of language and attentiveness to its many nuances, can be a vehicle for growth and development in all areas of the curriculum.

Teacher-student interaction is vital in the writing process. When trust is built up, students readily share their work. The teacher can guide by asking questions: What are you writing about? Should you say more about your subject? Have you expressed what you have written in the best way you can? What part do you like best? least? Deleting, adding, and rearranging ideas are essential to the revision process.

Students should be taught to look for specific things as they examine their own work: Is the opening sentence effective? Is there one topic sentence? enough sentence variety? strong action verbs? Does the ending sentence draw the whole to a close?

Peer response is important, so students should ask these questions when critiquing one another's work too. The more response from others, the better the revision will be. Language at this point is exciting and challenging. Trying to select just the right word in the right place is the challenge of revision.

Likewise, teachers creating original pieces of writing *along with* the students reinforce the feeling that the challenge and effort involved in the writing process are worthwhile.

The satisfaction that comes from creating a good piece of writing is immeasurable. The hard work is well worth the effort.

Contents

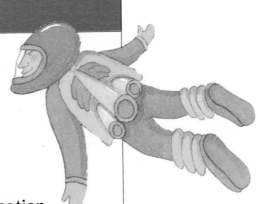

Part I   Written and Oral Communication

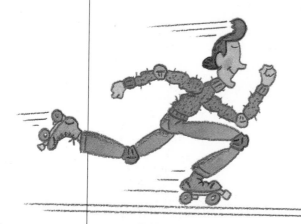

Part II   Grammar, Correct Usage, Mechanics

Exploring Our Language

Part I

Written and Oral Communication

Chapter 1

Building the Paragraph

Lesson 1 Selecting and Narrowing a Topic

A topic is the idea about which a paragraph or a composition is written.

The first step in writing is to decide on a topic. Do you think choosing a topic is difficult? Actually, it is easier than you might imagine. Professional writers usually find topics from their experiences and interests, and you can choose your own topics the same way. You probably will be surprised at how many topics there are for writing!

The best way to find a topic is to *brainstorm* for ideas. Think about some of your interests and about experiences you have had. Then take out a sheet of paper and write down ten topics that come to mind. For example, some of your topics might be "trips," "movies," "sports," or "friends."

As you look over your list, you will see that some of the items are things that are familiar to you. Others are things you like, but about which you need to learn more. Write the headings "Things I Know About" and "Things I Like (But Need to Learn About)" on a sheet of paper and put each topic you listed under the appropriate heading.

Everyone likes to share ideas. If you were in this picture, what thoughts would you be sharing?

For now, concentrate on choosing things familiar to you as paragraph topics. Suppose one of the topics you listed was "trips." That is such a big topic it would be difficult to know where to begin. So before you start to write, you must *narrow* the topic "trips" to one specific idea. That specific idea will become the topic of your paragraph.

Look at the two examples below. What happens to each topic?

> *Topic*: Trips
> *Narrowed topic*: A class trip
> *Narrower topic*: Our class trip to the planetarium
> *Specific idea*: How I got lost in the planetarium

> *Topic*: My neighborhood
> *Narrowed topic*: My block
> *Narrower topic*: People on my block
> *Specific idea*: My best friends on my block

Activity A

In each list below, a topic is narrowed down to a specific idea. However, the items in the list are out of order. Number them in the correct order as follows:

> *topic* (1)
> *narrow topic* (2)
> *narrower topic* (3)
> *specific idea* (4)

1. Movies
   Why _____ is my favorite movie of the year
   Movies I like
   Movies I liked this year
2. Soccer
   My soccer team
   Sports
   How my soccer team almost won the championship
3. Houses of the Algonquian Indians
   American Indians
   The Algonquians
   Indians of our area

The planet Saturn

4. Why I liked *The Left Hand of Darkness*
   The Left Hand of Darkness
   Science fiction books
   Books
5. How I learned to do a cartwheel
   Stunts I learned in gymnastics class
   Gymnastics
   My gymnastics class
6. Some good advice from my older sister
   My family
   Families
   My older sister
7. American history
   Zebulon Pike
   Exploration of Zebulon Pike
   Famous explorers in American history
8. Piano
   Music
   My first piano recital
   Learning to play the piano

Zebulon Pike

Activity B

Narrow each of the topics below to one specific idea. Write each specific idea as a statement.

1. Computers
2. Clothes
3. Food
4. Parties
5. Games

Write Away!

Think of three topics about which you would like to write. Narrow each down to a specific idea. Then discuss with another student what you might include in a paragraph about that specific idea.

Lesson 2 Writing Topic and Beginning Sentences
Topic Sentences

A topic sentence states the specific idea of a paragraph. It is often the beginning sentence.

Has anyone ever asked you "What was that movie about?" If you answered that it was about alien beings coming to earth or about how Egyptians built pyramids, then you have given the specific idea of the movie. When you write a paragraph, it is important to tell the reader your specific idea. The specific idea is expressed in a *topic sentence*.

Here are three topic sentences. What information do you think would be included in each paragraph?
 1. Stickball is becoming a popular sport in our neighborhood.
 2. My bedroom looks like a miniature zoo.
 3. A shower of popcorn signaled my first real cooking disaster.

Now find the topic sentence in the following paragraph.

> Lively monkeys chattered nonstop as they swung about in their roomy cages. Puppies whimpered and made little barks when anyone approached them. Melodious songs came from the quivering throats of sleek canaries, and monotonous chirps were produced by baby chicks. From their perches overhead, brightly colored parrots squawked as if they were determined to be heard above the din. The pet shop we visited last week was an orchestra of competing sounds.

In the paragraph above, the topic sentence is the last sentence. The specific idea is "the noises in a pet shop." The topic sentence states the specific idea. All the other sentences in the paragraph give details about that idea.

The topic sentence is often—but not always—the first sentence in a paragraph. In the paragraph you have just read, the writer put the topic sentence last. All the sentences in the paragraph lead up to the topic sentence. The writer might also have put the topic sentence first to let the reader know the location of the noises immediately. If you had written this paragraph, where would you have put the topic sentence? Why?

Activity

Find the topic sentence in each of the following paragraphs.

<u>1</u>

Making quilts is a traditional American art. It dates back to the days of the American colonies. A quilt results when two layers of cloth are stitched together with a soft stuffing between them. American pioneers often stitched many pieces of colorful cloth together in their quilts. Because all the sewing was done by hand, making a quilt took a long time. To speed the process, pioneers would join in quilting bees. Families would sew quilts in the afternoon, and they would eat and dance in the evening. Quilts were valued by pioneers as warm bed covers and as shields from cold drafts. Their quilts are still valued by Americans today— mostly for the beauty of the quilts as colorful, original works of art.

Traditional American Quilts

2

I felt unsure, but I decided to try anyway. I took a firm grip on the sticks. My first attempt ended with a "plop" and splatter. I looked around to see if anyone in the restaurant had noticed, but no one had. I practiced moving the sticks until I felt more comfortable with them. Gathering my courage and determination, I tried again and managed to get a piece of vegetable into my mouth. My first experience at using chopsticks in a Chinese restaurant started out shakily but ended in success.

3

Why is a porcupine a porcupine? Why is a hippopotamus called by such a strange, hard-to-spell name? The variety in the origin of animal names is almost as varied as the animals themselves. Some animals are named after places. Shetland ponies are named for islands near Scotland. Some animals are named after people. The Doberman pinscher, a large, smooth-coated dog, is named for Ludwig Dobermann, the German who first bred the dog. Some names describe the animal. Often, however, these names are in foreign languages. For example, *porcupine* comes from Latin words meaning "pig with thorns." The Greek words "river horse" make the word *hippopotamus*. Check your dictionary or other word books to learn more about how animals get their names.

Beginning Sentences

A good beginning sentence introduces the topic and tries to interest the reader in the paragraph.

Whenever you write, you are writing *to someone*. You may be writing a composition for your teacher, a note to your parents, or a letter to a friend. You want to make sure that your audience will be interested in what you write. To create interest, you should write a good *beginning sentence*. A good *beginning sentence* will *introduce the topic of the paragraph, arouse the reader's curiosity*, and *encourage him or her to read on*.

Sometimes a beginning sentence may be written as a simple topic sentence, which tells the specific idea of the paragraph.

The day finally arrived for our trip to the wax museum.

Sometimes a beginning sentence may be written in a more interesting and creative way. Such a sentence may still give the specific idea of the paragraph.

How many famous people would greet me on my journey through the halls of the wax museum?

The first example tells the reader that the paragraph will be about a trip to the wax museum. The second example gives the same information, but it does so in a more creative style. The writer uses an interrogative sentence and colorful language so that the reader will want to continue reading to discover more about the famous people in the wax museum.

Below is an example of each kind of beginning sentence. Either one could be used at the beginning of a paragraph about fossils. What is the difference between the two sentences?

Topic sentence: Fossils are records of the distant past.
Creative sentence: Fossils are a kind of ancient photography that captures life as it was millions of years ago.

Here are two more beginning sentences. Think about how they are different and what each one tells you about the topic.

Topic sentence: Autumn is my favorite season.
Creative sentence: When leaves turn to red and yellow and a cool wind blows, I anticipate some of my favorite things—apple picking, the World Series, and jack-o-lanterns.

Activity A

Tell whether the beginning sentences below are simple topic sentences or creative sentences.

1. The family gathered together for Thanksgiving.
2. Will a typical lunch of the future be a "hamburger" tablet?
3. Wow! I never thought all this could possibly happen to me in one day.
4. Christmas is always a great deal of fun.
5. I watched the rain making patterns on my window and wondered if she would find shelter out there.
6. Len's face beamed as he surveyed the delicious dinner spread before him.
7. Owning tropical fish can be a fascinating hobby.
8. Zoom! Our spaceship sped like lightning through the vast empty space of the galaxy.
9. "Oh, no!" Anita cried. "I forgot to study for the math test."
10. An astronaut's training is very difficult.

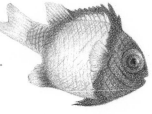

Activity B

Below are five simple topic sentences. Each expresses the specific idea, or topic, of a paragraph. Try writing a creative beginning sentence to go along with each topic sentence. If you do not know enough about a topic, use your imagination.

1. Last year my family took a trip to New York City.
2. Cars of the future will be longer and sleeker.
3. Life was an adventure for King Arthur's knights.
4. My friend Sally had a huge insect collection.
5. Buildings shook as an earthquake rumbled through the city.

Activity C

Supply a beginning sentence for each of the paragraphs that follow. Be sure to write one that is interesting and gives a hint of what the paragraph is about. Decide whether you want to write a simple topic sentence or a more creative sentence. You may write two sentences to begin a paragraph if you need to.

<u>1</u>

_____

My uncle and I sat at either end of the canoe and paddled, and my little brother Jimmy sat in the middle. Jimmy was content to sit still and watch the world go by until he spied a frog resting on a floating log. I saw what he was going to do and shouted, "Jimmy—no!" It was too late. Jimmy reached out to grab the frog, the canoe tipped over, and we all tumbled into the lake. Although it was a frightening moment, luck was with us. We fell onto a sandbar where the water was shallow, and we were safe. I didn't see the frog again, but I'm sure that wherever it went, it was laughing all the way.

2

The typical cowboy of the late 1800s was a short, rather ordinary-looking man. He rarely, if ever, shot his gun, got into barroom fights, or chased desperadoes. Much of his time was spent on long and hazardous cattle drives, where blankets and some extra clothing were all he could bring along. Often, there was not even a tent in which to sleep. If he was injured on the drive, he was likely to be left behind. It was a hard life, and very different from the way we picture it today.

3

Each day I feed him, clean his cage, and let him fly around the house. If he lands on my arm, I say "Hello" in the hope that he will learn to say the same to me. Taking care of Petey is not much trouble, but yesterday I was careless and left a window open. I saw a flash of brightly colored feathers, and Petey was gone. It was such a shock that at first I stood perfectly still. Then I raced to the window and peered anxiously in every direction. There was no sign of Petey anywhere. I turned sadly away and started to walk across the room when suddenly I heard "Hello." Spinning around, I saw Petey perched on the windowsill. He had come back on his own—and announced his arrival!

Write Away!

Write a simple topic sentence for each of the topics below. Then write a more creative beginning sentence for each topic. If you do not know enough about one topic, use your imagination.
1. The flight of monarch butterflies south for the winter
2. My favorite ride at the amusement park
3. Food that astronauts eat on space flights
4. Winning a contest
5. The day I disappeared

Lesson 3 Writing Supporting Sentences

Supporting sentences give details that explain the topic.

You have already learned how to choose a topic, narrow it, and write an interesting beginning sentence. After you write your beginning sentence, you will want to tell more about your topic. *Supporting sentences*, or middle sentences, tell the important details. Each supporting sentence adds information and carries the idea of the paragraph forward.

Read the paragraph below. Notice how the supporting details develop the idea expressed in the topic sentence.

A Useful Plant

The whole life of Egypt seemed to depend on the papyrus plant. The young shoots were eaten, and the juice was made into a drink. Weavers learned how to twist its fibers into a kind of cloth, and shoemakers made shoes of its bark. Boatmakers tied bundles of it together to make small canoes and even larger boats. Out of its stems were made utensils for the house. Last, but not least, paper was made from it! Is it any wonder that the Egyptians valued papyrus so highly?

The topic of the paragraph is "the usefulness of the papyrus plant." The beginning sentence explains that life in Egypt depended on this plant, and the supporting sentences provide the details that show this. The supporting sentences do not tell what the plant looked like or how it was grown. Instead, they keep to the topic and explain how the plant supplied things needed for life.

Papyrus

The diagram below is a *word map* that describes the paragraph about papyrus. At the center of the word map is the topic of the paragraph. Around the center are the supporting details. You may want to draw a word map before you write a paragraph. A word map is a useful tool to help you organize your ideas and decide what details to include.

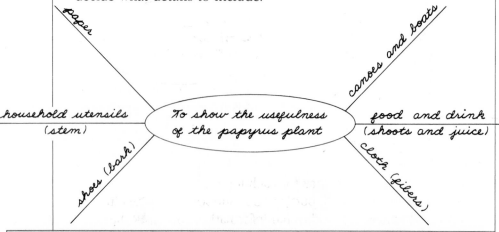

paper

canoes and boats

household utensils
(stem)

To show the usefulness of the papyrus plant

food and drink
(shoots and juice)

shoes (bark)

cloth (fibers)

A painting illustrating a noble Egyptian family's use of the papyrus plant.

Activity A

Read the specific idea in each circle below. Then complete the word maps by giving four supporting details for each topic.

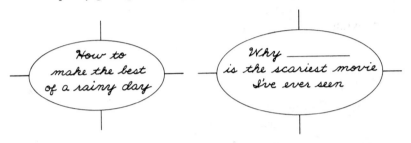

How to make the best of a rainy day

Why _____ is the scariest movie I've ever seen

Activity B

Write a beginning sentence for each topic in activity A. Then complete the paragraph, putting your supporting details in order and adding any additional information you think the reader might need to know. Remember to keep to your topic! Read your paragraph and decide if it makes sense and reads smoothly. If not, move sentences and words around to improve it. Reread your paragraph one more time.

Write Away!

Choose any two of the five topics below. Make a word map with four to six details for each topic. Then choose the word map that has the most ideas and write a paragraph using the word map as a guide. Write a good beginning sentence and supporting sentences that give the details. Put the sentences in the order that seems most logical to you.

1. How to roller-skate
2. Why _____ is my favorite _____
3. An afternoon in the year 2050
4. A punishment I really deserved
5. The best adventure of my life

Lesson 4 Writing Ending Sentences

An ending sentence draws the paragraph to a close.

In lesson 3, you wrote some paragraphs with beginning sentences and supporting details. Perhaps you added a sentence at the end to express your opinion or to sum up the ideas in the paragraph. You might have done this simply to bring your paragraph to a smoother conclusion. If you did, you were writing an *ending sentence*.

An ending sentence, besides just bringing the paragraph to a close, may do several things.

An ending sentence may give a last fact or detail.

> An old red cloth thrown over the cage soon silenced the bird.
>
> Suddenly, the diver emerged from the glistening blue-green water with a handful of gold coins.

An ending sentence may tell what the writer thinks or feels.

> After that experience, I'll never hike in shorts and tennis shoes again.
>
> Now I know that joining the neighborhood swim team was a good idea.

An ending sentence may also draw together everything in the paragraph.

> With all these uses, it is no wonder microwave ovens are part of the modern kitchen.
>
> The magician's fast-paced tricks left Jonathan wide-eyed with amazement.

Activity A

Choose the ending sentence that would best complete each of the paragraphs described below. Explain the reason for your choice.

1. Gary is writing about how he sold the most candy in the candy drive at school and won a prize for his efforts. Which of the following sentences would be an ending sentence that expresses Gary's feelings about the contest?
   a. When the teacher announced a candy drive, I just groaned.
   b. This is the most exciting thing that ever happened to me!
   c. Finally, I sold twenty boxes to my favorite aunt.

2. Tina has just finished writing about a collection of stories by Rod Serling. She is ready to draw the ideas in her paragraph together. Which of the following sentences would be an ending sentence that would do this?
   a. Everyone interested in mystery and suspense should sample a Rod Serling story.
   b. I can't believe I read the whole book in one sitting!
   c. Are you hooked on stories about strange happenings?

3. Hanna is writing a paragraph about her first experience waterskiing. Which sentence could end the paragraph and give a detail?
   a. Waterskiing will be part of my summer activities from now on.
   b. If my little brother could water-ski, so could I.
   c. I let go of the ropes and collapsed into the water, ready to take up the challenge once again.

Activity B

Supply a good ending sentence for each of the following paragraphs. Think of one that is interesting and will really wrap up the story.

1

The flap-flap-flapping noise attracted my attention, so I gazed across the park. What a surprise to see a man in blue jeans and a floppy old top hat juggling silver-colored clubs. Before long, I learned about this unusual young man. He had spent the winter at clown school in Florida where he studied such skills as magic, juggling, gymnastics, and mime. He had not yet found a job as a professional clown, but each evening he came out to practice his new craft. Day by day, more people gathered to watch. _____

2

"I'll never make any friends in this new neighborhood," I thought, as I bounced a ball against the brick wall. The block seemed deserted, and I missed my old friends. As the ball thumped against the wall, I noticed someone standing near me. A dark-haired, freckle-faced girl was watching me. She seemed to be wondering who I was. I didn't know what to say, but suddenly I had an idea and flipped the ball over to her. "Nice catch," I said. _____

3

Shortly after the Civil War, American theatergoers watched a young actress named Belle Boyd give dramatic readings about the adventures of a Confederate spy. It was more than just an act, however, since Boyd had really led the life of a Civil War spy. By the age of seventeen, she was watching the Northern army move through her native South and sending coded messages to Southern leaders. Northern soldiers captured her three times, but each time she was released. One of her guards even fell in love with her, and the two were married. _____

Write Away!

Here are five topics for paragraphs. Write an ending sentence for each paragraph and explain what purpose or purposes the ending sentence serves.

1. My worst injury
2. A troublesome neighbor
3. A surprise birthday party
4. An unexpected friend
5. If I could live in another time . . .

Lesson 5 Paragraph Unity

Paragraph unity means that all the sentences in a paragraph are related to the specific idea.

In the previous lessons, you wrote some paragraphs. Then you reread your paragraphs to see if they made sense. What does it really mean for a paragraph to make sense? For one thing, it means that all the sentences are related to the topic.

Sometimes when you reread a paragraph you have written, one or two sentences just do not seem to belong. These *misfit sentences*, which are not related to the topic, must be taken out. Read the following paragraph and note how one sentence interrupts the thought. Which sentence does not belong? Why is it a misfit?

"Can this thing really play music?" I thought as Willie handed me his electric guitar. It wasn't hollow like other guitars, and when I plucked a string, there was no noise. Willie said that he would explain to me how an electric guitar worked. Willie's group is called the "Soul Rockers." He plugged the guitar in, and when I plucked the string again, there was a rich, loud sound. "The strings don't really make the music," he explained. "When you play a string, it gives an electrical signal to the amplifier and to the loud speaker. That's where the music comes from!"

Such a journal entry might give you an idea for a poem like the following.

It's time for bears to yawn and stretch
To open their eyes, look outside, and watch
Birds chirp and chatter
Trees and bushes turn green
Worms rise and squirm
Crocuses and snowdrops bloom
Winds warm and play
Kites bob and jerk
Because it's finally SPRING!

★ Buy a spiral notebook, and begin to keep your own journal. Here are some ideas about which you might like to write.

My idea of the perfect day/friend/meal
The most difficult thing I have ever done
The best/scariest/funniest thing that has ever happened to me
My favorite place/season/movie/hobby/music
I wish I could meet . . .
I wish I could learn to . . .
What I think life as a doctor/zookeeper/TV star would be like
What would happen if there were no TV
What would happen if I could be in two places at once
What would happen if I could change places with Mom or Dad
A country that I would like to go to and why

Prefixes

A prefix is a syllable (or syllables) added to the beginning of a word that changes the meaning of that word.

You already know many prefixes. If your teacher tells you to *re*write a paragraph or *re*read a story, you know that the prefix *re* tells you to do something *again*. If a task is *im*possible, the prefix *im* tells you the task is *not* possible. Notice that a prefix is always followed by a *root*. The prefix will give the root a new meaning.

Here is a list of prefixes. Study them carefully.

Prefix	Meaning	Example
bi	two	bicycle
co	together	copilot
dis	not	disapprove
micro	small	microcomputer
mini	small	miniskirt
non	not, without	nonstop
over	above, too much	overcook
re	again	reunite
tri	three	triangle
uni	one	unicycle

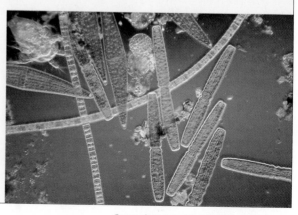

Green algae magnified through a microscope

Activity A

Copy the chart below, and fill in the missing parts. The first one is done for you.

	Prefix	Root	New Word	Meaning
1.	re	trace	retrace	trace again
2.	_____	load	_____	to load too much
3.	_____	_____	microwave	small electric wave
4.	non	returnable	_____	_____
5.	mini	van	_____	_____
6.	_____	lateral	_____	two-sided
7.	_____	satisfied	dissatisfied	_____
8.	tri	color	_____	_____
9.	co	_____	cowinner	_____
10.	_____	_____	unisyllabic	with one syllable

Activity B

Complete each sentence with the correct word by adding a prefix from the list to the word at the left.

grown   1. The field was _____ with bushes and weeds.

set   2. Because of the electrical failure, we had to _____ the clocks.

bike   3. If I had a _____, I could ride to school every day.

sense   4. Humorous poems are often called _____ poems.

cycle   5. I remember riding a _____ when I was very small.

operate   6. If this project is to succeed, everyone must _____.

corn   7. There was a picture of a _____ in the mythology book.

scope   8. In science class, I spent fifteen minutes looking through a _____ at different kinds of leaves.

agreed   9. "Strike three," yelled the umpire, but the batter _____.

weekly   10. Jamie receives the magazine every two weeks. It must be a _____ subscription.

Chapter 2

Refining Your Writing Skills

Lesson 1 Expanding Sentences

You can expand a sentence by adding adjectives, adverbs, and phrases that help to give the reader a clearer picture.

Adding Adjectives and Adverbs

Sometimes you may decide that a paragraph you have written is dull and uninteresting because it fails to give the reader a clear *picture*. Sentences in such a paragraph can come to life, if you add colorful and expressive adjectives and adverbs.

If you write *The lanterns swayed*, for example, your sentence is not very specific. You could add adjectives and an adverb to make the sentence read, *The colorful Chinese lanterns swayed rhythmically*. Now the reader gets a clearer picture!

Study this example. Note the words that are added to the second sentence.

> The tightrope walker balanced herself.
> The daring, graceful tightrope walker balanced herself effortlessly.

The writer has added

> the adjectives *daring* and *graceful*
> the adverb *effortlessly*

Lighting a lantern helps you see more clearly. Can the words you use when you write help you to see your ideas more clearly? How?

Activity

These ten sentences could use improvement. Whenever you see this symbol, ∧ (called a caret), put in one or more adjectives or adverbs.

1. The ∧ rain fell ∧.
2. The ∧ hikers ∧ walked through the ∧ forest.
3. The ∧ pirates ∧ boarded the ∧ ship.
4. ∧ bees swarmed ∧ over the rose garden.
5. The puck flew ∧ past the ∧ goalie.
6. The ∧ campfire blazed ∧.
7. The artist did a(n) ∧ painting.
8. I bought a(n) ∧ frozen yogurt.
9. Two ∧ shadows ∧ emerged from the ∧ spaceship.
10. The ∧ frog leaped ∧ from the log.

Adding Prepositional Phrases

You have seen how adjectives and adverbs can make your sentences come to life. Prepositional phrases are another helpful tool that you can use.

Look at this sentence again.

> The colorful Chinese lanterns swayed rhythmically.

You could also add a prepositional phrase to make the sentence read

> The colorful Chinese lanterns swayed rhythmically *in the light breeze.*

With the addition of a prepositional phrase, the picture becomes even clearer.

Study the example below. Note the phrases that are added to the second sentence.

The graceful, daring tightrope walker balanced herself effortlessly.

The graceful, daring tightrope walker in a red leotard balanced herself effortlessly on the wire above the crowd.

The writer has added

the phrase *in a red leotard* after a noun
the phrases *on the wire* and *above the crowd* after the verb

Activity A

The sentences below are not very specific. Add a prepositional phrase or phrases to each sentence to give a clearer picture.

1. The Frisbee landed.
2. Doug dribbled the ball.
3. The river overflowed.
4. The drums boomed.
5. The snow drifted.
6. Cactus grew.
7. The scuba diver floated.
8. Crowds of people stood.
9. The lion crouched.
10. The rocket rose.

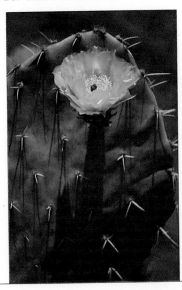

Activity B

Expand the following sentences. Add colorful adjectives, adverbs, and phrases. Try doing this activity in two steps: first add adjectives and adverbs, and then go back and add prepositional phrases where you think they are needed.

1. David was a keyboard player.
2. He wanted to start a rock group.
3. He knew that John and Eddie were guitar players.
4. They agreed to join the group.
5. The next member was Josh, a drummer.
6. David heard a singer named Maggie.
7. He asked Maggie to join, and she agreed.
8. The group got together and practiced.

Write Away!

Make this dull paragraph come alive by adding interesting adjectives, adverbs, and prepositional phrases. If you need to, you may also change other words in the paragraph.

The canoe moved along the Amazon River. The three explorers and their guide gazed at the rain forest. The forest looked like a green wall. Monkeys and other animals made noises. Above, birds flew. Fish and crocodiles swam nearby. The explorers saw snakes on the shore. The explorers wanted to reach their destination.

Lesson 2 Combining Independent Clauses

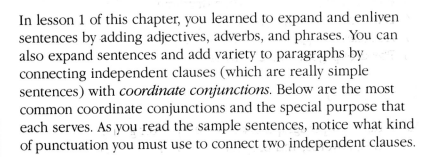

You can add variety and length to a paragraph by combining independent clauses.

In lesson 1 of this chapter, you learned to expand and enliven sentences by adding adjectives, adverbs, and phrases. You can also expand sentences and add variety to paragraphs by connecting independent clauses (which are really simple sentences) with *coordinate conjunctions*. Below are the most common coordinate conjunctions and the special purpose that each serves. As you read the sample sentences, notice what kind of punctuation you must use to connect two independent clauses.

Coordinate Conjunction	Special Purpose
and	*And* connects two ideas that are similar or that happen together. *Bernard and Darnell went to the movie theater, and they saw an exciting western.*
but, yet	*But* and *yet* connect clauses that have opposite or contrasting ideas. *Bernard had a lot of homework, but he went to the movie anyway.*
or	*Or* suggests that there is a choice. *Darnell could stay home to watch his favorite TV program, or he could go to see the movie.*

Activity A

Choose the best coordinate conjunction to combine the following pairs of sentences. Explain each of your choices.

1. Liza likes to play the saxophone.
   The orchestra leader wants her to try the clarinet.
2. I rode over to the bike repair shop.
   It was closed.
3. Enrique reads many detective stories.
   Sometimes he even writes a mystery of his own.
4. Ballets tell a story.
   The dancers do not speak any words.
5. After high school, you can go to college.
   You can find a full-time job.
6. The test seemed very easy.
   I got a low grade.
7. Tony is an excellent shortstop.
   He is a good hitter.
8. Delia wants to be a nurse.
   Sheila wants to be one, too.
9. Sugar can give you energy quickly.
   It can also cause your teeth to decay.
10. Marti must practice each day.
    She won't make the field hockey team.

Activity B

Here is a paragraph of short sentences for you to revise. Combine at least two pairs of sentences by using coordinate conjunctions. Expand as many sentences as you can with adjectives, adverbs, and phrases. If you need to, you may change other words in the paragraph.

One of the most famous cowboys was a black man. His real name was Nat Love. People called him Deadwood Dick. Love was born a slave in Tennessee in 1854. He was freed when he was fifteen years old. Then Love had a choice. He could work on his father's farm. He could go west and become a cowboy. Love decided to become a cowboy. He worked on cattle drives for twenty years. His riding ability was exceptional. His roping was unmatched. He even won a contest among cowboys in Deadwood, South Dakota. There he got his nickname. As Love grew older, he wanted to tell his story. He wrote his autobiography. He called it *The Adventures of Nat Love, Better Known in Cattle Country as Deadwood Dick.*

Write Away!

Write three sentences for each coordinate conjunction: *and*, *but* or *yet*, and *or*. Then, to prove that you have connected independent clauses, take the coordinate conjunction out of each sentence and see if you have two simple sentences.

Lesson 3 Revising Rambling and Run-on Sentences

Sentences that contain too many ideas to be clearly understood must be divided.

Rambling Sentences

In the previous two lessons, you have learned to lengthen sentences in two ways: by adding adjectives, adverbs, and phrases, as well as by connecting independent clauses. However, do not let "longer is better" become your motto for writing. A well-written paragraph usually has sentences of varying lengths. Some of the sentences in a paragraph may become *too* long and complicated. Often the reader cannot tell where one idea ends and another begins. To improve a rambling sentence, divide it into two or more sentences. Notice how the following rambling sentence can be broken down to form a few clearer sentences.

Rambling Sentence

Rebecca was watching her favorite television program, which is a show about a group of young scientists, and today's story was especially interesting because it was about scientists who discovered a "caveman" who had never had contact with modern society and who was found walking across the Golden Gate Bridge, and he was as confused about how he got there as the scientists were about finding him.

Improved Sentences

Rebecca was watching her favorite television program, a show about a group of young scientists. Today's story was especially interesting. It was about scientists who discovered a "caveman" who had never had contact with modern society. The "caveman" was found walking across the Golden Gate Bridge. He was as confused about how he got there as the scientists were about finding him.

Activity A

Improve these rambling sentences. You may add or change words to make your improved sentences read smoothly.

1. In 1985, a massive earthquake jolted Mexico City, killing thousands of people and destroying millions of dollars worth of property, and groups across the United States immediately began sending medical aid and money to the battered city because they hoped to save lives and help the homeless.

2. This was my best summer ever because my family spent the entire month of August in Wisconsin where we rented a cabin that was on a lake and we could swim, row our boat, windsurf, dive off a raft, or just lie in the sun on the sandy shore.

3. William Penn was a Quaker and he believed in the people's right to practice their religion freely and so he founded a city in Pennsylvania and he called this city Philadelphia, which means "brotherly love."

4. The forests of the world are one of its most valuable resources but they are disappearing and we should do what we can to protect them because it would take many years to replace them when they are gone.

5. The telegraph was invented by Samuel F. B. Morse and the first message sent across the wires read, "What hath God wrought!" and it was flashed from Baltimore to Washington.

6. My neighborhood is near the airport and when planes fly directly overhead, the noise is deafening and we can hardly hear each other speak, so last week a group of neighbors went to visit the mayor to see if she could arrange to have the takeoff and landing patterns changed.

7. The pampas are grassy plains covering a large area in Argentina in South America, and the humid eastern pampas do bear some crops but the dry western ones support only livestock, and the pampas are well known as the home of the gaucho, the Argentine cowboy.

8. Two teenage Frisbee "experts" toss their disk every summer day in a vacant lot on Foster Avenue and I enjoy watching their long, arching throws and their almost impossible one-finger or behind-the-back catches and many other people are likewise entertained.

9. Copper is a strong, tough metal and it carries heat and electricity well and it has many important uses and among them is its use in wires of all kinds, including telephone, telegraph, and power lines.

10. Jennifer likes to read and she usually reads historical fiction but last week she read the science fiction novel *The Martian Chronicles* by Ray Bradbury and she enjoyed it very much and so she has decided to read more science fiction.

Activity B

Here is a paragraph for you to revise. Shorten the rambling sentences so the reader can understand the paragraph more easily.

Florence Nightingale was a British nurse who became famous for her work during the Crimean War in which Britain and France fought Russia, and she was the leader of a small group of nurses who had to care for hundreds of wounded soldiers but there were not enough medical supplies or hospital cots. Florence worked hard to organize the army hospital and get it cleaned up, and she demanded medical supplies from British leaders and every night walked the hospital halls to check on the patients. She even visited the battlefield where she caught a serious illness called Crimean Fever but she did not let her illness stop her work and said, "I can stand out this war with any man." Florence Nightingale's tireless, unselfish efforts saved many lives and set an example of organization, cleanliness, and hard work that are the basis of the nursing profession today, and all modern nurses should be thankful to her.

Write Away!

The following paragraph has a number of dull, lifeless words. Liven up the paragraph by substituting either a picture word or a more precise word for each word in italics. Use a dictionary or thesaurus if you need help.

As I *walked* through the park Saturday afternoon, I *saw* a *big* Indian totem pole. The pole itself was painted brown, but the faces *made* on it were *bright* reds and yellows. They were faces of people and of *odd* animals, both *funny* and *scary* at the same time. What an interesting thing to see in the middle of a *big* city!

Lesson 5 Using Similes and Metaphors

Similes and metaphors are comparisons of unlike things. Both can help you write more expressively.

You have learned how to enliven your sentences with colorful picture words. Another way to make writing vivid is with comparisons. Read these comparisons.

> The spiderweb, wet with dew, was like a piece of fine lace. The hang gliders were enormous colorful birds against the sky.

Notice how each comparison creates a clearer image. The first example is a *simile*, a comparison that uses the words *like* or *as*. Since lace is delicate and exquisite, the sentence gives a picture of a spiderweb as a delicate, airy work of art.

The second example does not use the words *like* or *as*. It states directly the hang gliders *were* birds. Such a comparison is called a *metaphor*. In this metaphor, the comparison with birds gives the reader a picture of a sky filled with brilliant flying objects. Vivid similes and metaphors help writers *paint pictures* in their sentences.

Sometimes a simile or a metaphor is overused. For example, have you ever heard the expression "as cold as ice" or "as happy as a lark"? Such overused similes and metaphors are clichés. In using similes and metaphors, be creative and avoid clichés.

Below is a list of comparisons describing white clouds, a stream, and fireworks. Can you tell which are similes and which are metaphors?

White Clouds

like scoops of vanilla ice cream
white elephants, whales, hippopotamuses in the sky
floating like parachutes

A Stream

a silver serpent
bubbling like soda pop
a shiny ribbon unrolling through the forest

Fireworks

bouquets of light
as bright as a million lightning bugs
popping popcorn in the sky

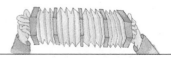

Activity A

Read these ten sentences and tell whether the comparison is written as a simile or a metaphor. Then name the two objects that are being compared and explain how they are different and what they have in common.

1. The giant redwoods are the skyscrapers of the forest.
2. The opposing fullback was as wide as a garage door.
3. To the astronaut, the earth was a huge blue-green ball.
4. The sun was a player in a game of hide-and-seek.
5. The corridors of the building are like a maze.
6. Dina's arrival brightened the room like a light bulb.
7. The last day of school crawled as slowly as a turtle.
8. When the skunk came out from behind the tree, Teddy ran like an Olympic gold medal sprinter.
9. The entire class was chattering like a bunch of monkeys.
10. Aunt Lou's face is an accordion of wrinkles.

Activity B

Complete the following sentences on a sheet of paper. If the phrase uses *like* or *as*, create a simile. If it does not, create a metaphor. Remember to use things that are unlike in your comparisons.

1. During rush hour, the cars move like _____.
2. When it is full, the moon is _____.
3. The water lilies cover the pond like _____.
4. The room on the cold winter morning was _____.
5. The creatures who emerged from the spaceship seemed like _____.
6. The hose lying on the grass was _____
7. The sound of the squeaking door is like _____.
8. As Julie looked down from the mountain, the city was _____.
9. After José ran a mile, he felt like _____.

Write Away!

Practice writing some of your own similes and metaphors. The paragraph below has none. Revise it by adding *at least* two similes and one metaphor. You may change or add sentences if you want.

Beth loves to ride her bicycle on the path by Lake Michigan. It is always an interesting adventure, full of wonderful sights. The lake is so wide that Beth cannot see across it. She likes the clear, sunny days when the water is bright blue. On windy days, the lake is choppy, and water splashes on the concrete path. Then Beth gets soaked, and her bike hisses as she rides over the wet concrete. Whenever she rides, she notices everything around her—joggers, skaters, swimmers, trees, bushes, and even the city skyline. When Beth is on the bicycle path, she feels happy and free.

Revising Your Writing

The skills that you have studied in this chapter will be very useful when you revise any piece of writing. Revising is an important part of the writing process. It involves rereading to correct and improve your writing.

Consider these general questions as you revise your work:
—Does my writing make sense?
—Will a reader be able to understand what I am saying?
—Do all the sentences develop the specific idea?

Also review the skills you have learned in this chapter as you revise.
—Do I need to lengthen sentences by adding information or combining ideas?
—Do I need to shorten rambling sentences or correct run-on sentences?
—Have I used precise, vivid words?

Finally, proofread your work. Check capitalization, punctuation, and spelling.

To indicate changes as you reread your work, you may want to use these proofreading symbols:

∧	add	The giant panda _may_ become extinct.
ℒ	omit	The giant panda may, ~~perhaps~~ become extinct.
≡	capitalize	the giant panda may become extinct.
/	lowercase	The giant Panda may become extinct.
∿	reverse	The giant panda may become extinct.
¶	begin a new paragraph	¶ The giant panda may become extinct.

After you proofread your work, you may want to recopy it in order to hand in a neat, correct paper.

48

Study how the symbols used in the following paragraph show changes and corrections.

Penguins are ~~bizarre~~ *unusual* creatures. They are able to stand out in blizzards of below-freezing tempratures for weeks they do not even have to eat a meal during that time. Their feathers provide them with insulation Their fat provides them with food. Penguins cannot run nor fly They are able to walk clumsily on land. In water, however, these seabirds use their wings as ~~as~~ paddels to propel themselves. They swim *like Olympic champions* ~~very well~~ as they *hunt* ~~look~~ for fish.

Writing Corner 2

Poetry into Prose

A poem and a paragraph can present the same ideas, but in very different ways. Both are fun to write, but each requires a different style of writing. Carefully read the poem below.

Fourth of July Night

Pin wheels whirling round
Spit sparks upon the ground,
And rockets shoot up high
And blossom in the sky—
Blue and yellow, green and red
Flowers falling on my head,
And I don't ever have to go
To bed, to bed, to bed!

Dorothy Aldis

Now read this paragraph.

Celebrating Independence!

The Fourth of July is one of the best celebrations of the year. The picnics and games in the afternoon are great fun, but the fireworks at night are the highlight of the day. When the time comes for this spectacular display, I grab a front-row seat. I love to watch the pinwheels swirling and the rockets shooting high above me. Their sudden cracking sound turns them into colorful flowers blossoming in the sky. The excitement goes on late into the night, and on this special occasion, everyone gets to stay up way past bedtime.

Which piece of writing uses fewer words but contains very vivid images? Which piece uses rhyme? Which piece uses mainly words that describe? You would be right if you said the *poem*.

Chapter 3

Kinds of Writing

Lesson 1 Using Transition Words

Transition words help to make smooth connections between sentences and paragraphs.

A good writer knows how to take the reader through a series of connected ideas or events skillfully. The reader never has to wonder how two ideas or two sentences fit together. A good paragraph flows smoothly, and it has no gaps. One of the best tools for creating a smooth paragraph is the use of transition words, which show the relationship between two sentences or ideas.

Many transition words create a time relationship. When you write a paragraph or story, you often put events and ideas according to the *time sequence* in which they occur. Here are some connecting words that indicate time. They can help make your paragraphs read more smoothly.

afterward	later
at first	meanwhile
at last	next
at the same time	now
earlier	second
finally	soon
first	then
last	third

Bridges help shorten the distance between people and places. How would bridges bring people of other races and cultures together?

Read the sentences below, for example. On the left are five unconnected sentences. On the right, transition words have been added at the beginning of sentences 2, 3, and 5. The transition words are *First, Then,* and *Soon.* Adding transition words makes the paragraph flow more smoothly.

1. Paul couldn't decide what he wanted to be for Halloween.
2. He told us that he would be Dracula and wear his mother's old black cape.
3. He changed his mind and said he would be a pirate and wear one of his sister's earrings.
4. On Halloween, we noticed someone dressed as a ghost, completely covered in a sheet.
5. We recognized that it was Paul by his old orange sneakers.

Paul couldn't decide what he wanted to be for Halloween. *First,* he told us that he would be Dracula and wear his mother's old black cape. *Then* he changed his mind and said he would be a pirate and wear one of his sister's earrings. On Halloween, we noticed someone dressed as a ghost, completely covered in a sheet. *Soon* we recognized that it was Paul by his old orange sneakers.

Activity A

Here are some events that could make up a narrative paragraph. On a sheet of paper, write the events in the correct order.

1. "Calm down; we'll work this out," said Jason's father.
2. Jason's parents decided to take the family to New Orleans for a month during the summer vacation.
3. "That's not fair—my friends and I are planning a bike trip then!" Jason exclaimed.
4. Jason's father suggested that Jason call his friends to see if they could make their trip at a later date.
5. "Let's all think of solutions," said Jason's mother.
6. He offered to help the boys choose a place to ride and take them there.
7. "And next time," said Jason's mother, "we'll include you when we make our plans."
8. They told Jason about it one evening at supper.
9. "Wow," said Jason, "that's a pretty good offer! I'm sure my friends will change their plans."
10. Jason and his parents talked over the problem for the next half hour.

Activity B

Here are some more events that are out of order. Put them in order in paragraph form, and add at least four transition words. Then review the paragraph to make sure it reads smoothly.

1. Everyone in the family was pleased to see such a delicious meal awaiting them at home.
2. With two overflowing pails in the basket of her bike, she took the ferry back to shore.
3. Last summer Bobby Jeanne and her family were spending the month of August at a seaside cottage in Maine.
4. Clever Bobby Jeanne had $11.25 to show for her skill at cooking on a budget.
5. For seventy-five cents, she bought a ticket to an island called Islesboro.
6. Bobby Jeanne had an idea, and she quickly rode her bike to the ferry landing.
7. "We'll be back from the beach at 6:30," she added as they left.
8. Once she was home, she steamed the clams and mussels, made some butter sauce, and chopped up vegetables for a salad.
9. One afternoon Bobby Jeanne's mother said to her, "Dinner is up to you tonight."
10. She rode to a little beach on the island where she knew she could collect plenty of clams and mussels.
11. She gave Bobby Jeanne $12.00 and said, "Whatever is left over, you can keep."
12. She dug for shellfish—clams and mussels.

Write Away!

Now write your own narrative paragraph. First, brainstorm for an idea. You could write about an unusual or interesting experience you have had. Then list the events as they happened. Finally, write them out as one paragraph. Make sure you use transition words to keep the paragraph flowing smoothly. Reread your paragraph and continue to revise it until you are satisfied with your work.

Revision: Time to Take Another Look

As you reread your narrative paragraph, ask yourself the following questions:

—Are all the events in correct time order?

—Did I use appropriate connecting words?

—Did I use strong verbs in my paragraph? (Don't count *is* or *was*. Avoid overusing these verbs.)

—Do I have some simple and some compound sentences? Try to have both long and short sentences.

—Did I write an interesting beginning sentence?

—Does the ending sentence draw my story to a close?

—Will a reader be able to understand my paragraph easily?

If you need to work on anything from the above list, *do it now*. *Delete* or *add* words. *Rearrange* ideas if necessary. After your revision, rewrite the paragraph and go on to proofreading.

Proofreading: Time to Look at Capitalization, Punctuation, and Spelling

⋏	Add
ℒ	Omit
≡	Capitalize
╱	Lowercase
∾	Reverse
¶	New paragraph

—Did I begin each sentence with a capital letter?

—Did I indent the first word of the paragraph?

—Did I use the correct mark of punctuation at the end of each sentence?

—Do some transition words need a comma following them?

Start at the last word of the paragraph and read backwards to check for spelling errors. If necessary, rewrite the paragraph in your best handwriting.

Lesson 3 Using Your Senses in Writing

Writing can come alive when you use your senses—seeing, hearing, touching, smelling, and tasting.

To become a skilled writer, you must create *pictures* in the minds of your readers. You need to *show* them what you mean, not just *tell* them. One way to help create a picture is to describe things in terms of the senses: seeing, hearing, smelling, tasting, and feeling.

Read these two sentences and notice the difference between them. Which sentence just tells and which one shows? What do you see, hear, smell, taste, or feel? What words appeal directly to the senses?

The campfire blazed.   The huge, crackling campfire blazed a bright red in the dark forest clearing.

Study the sentences below. Notice how each appeals to a different sense.

Sight

The snow-white horses wore shining silver harnesses and were hitched to a brightly painted circus carriage.

Activity A

A good way to plan a persuasive paragraph is to state the opinion and then list a series of "becauses"—supporting arguments. For each topic below, give four details that favor the idea and four that oppose it. Model your answers on the example.

Example:

I. Recess should be longer
  A. *because* we would have more of a break from our studies
  B. *because* it would give us more time to relax or exercise
  C. *because* it would help us come back to our schoolwork feeling more refreshed
  D. *because* it would make the school day more enjoyable
II. Recess should not be longer
  A. *because* a longer recess might make it harder for us to get back to concentrating on schoolwork
  B. *because* we have enough time after school to relax and exercise
  C. *because* there is hardly enough time in the school day to get in all the subjects
  D. *because* school is a place for learning, not for relaxing or running around

1. Everyone should study a foreign language in grammar school.
2. Children under twelve should be able to enter all museums, movie theaters, and sports events free of charge.
3. A law should be passed that all bicyclists must wear helmets.
4. Schools should arrange more field trips for students.

Activity B

Choose one of the topics in activity A and write a persuasive paragraph. Model your paragraph on the one in the lesson.

Write Away!

Write a persuasive paragraph on one of the topics listed below.
1. There is a neighborhood festival near your house that lasts until ten o'clock at night. Persuade your parents to let you stay out later than usual.
2. Persuade other students that you should be the class president.
3. Persuade your teacher that radio headsets should be allowed in class.
4. You have heard both rock music and jazz. Write a paragraph explaining why one is better than the other.

Revision: Time to Take Another Look

As you reread your persuasive paragraph, ask yourself the following questions:

—Does the first sentence state my opinion?
—Did I use enough reasons to support my opinion?
—Is my last reason the strongest and best?
—Did I use exact words and not repeat ideas?
—Did I use strong verbs instead of *is* and *was*?
—Does the ending sentence restate my opinion?
—Will a reader be able to understand my paragraph easily?

If you need to work on anything from the above list, *do it now*. *Delete* and *add* words. *Rearrange* ideas if necessary. After your revision, rewrite the paragraph and go on to proofreading.

Proofreading: Time to Look at Capitalization, Punctuation, and Spelling

⋏	Add
ℒ	Omit
≡	Capitalize
/	Lowercase
∾	Reverse
⁋	New paragraph

—Did I begin each sentence with a capital letter?
—Did I indent the first word of the paragraph?
—Did I use the correct mark of punctuation at the end of each sentence?

Start at the last word of the paragraph and read backwards to check for spelling errors. If necessary, rewrite the paragraph in your best handwriting.

Writing Corner 3

Art into Writing

When you watch a sports event on television or a film recorded on a videocassette, have you ever seen action "frozen" in time? Artists who paint need skillful techniques to freeze action in their paintings. Study the actions frozen in these two paintings.

★ Choose one of the following two assignments to complete.
  A. Imagine that you are a person *in* one of the paintings. Describe the event that is taking place. Express your feelings about your part in what is happening.

Chapter 4

Learning More about Writing

Lesson 1 Taking Notes and Preparing an Outline

Taking notes and making an outline help you organize your ideas before you begin to write.

Taking notes and outlining are especially helpful when you are writing a factual composition, or *report*. Suppose you choose "earthquakes" as the topic of your report. You first need to read some books and articles about your topic. You also need to think of at least three questions you would like answered about the topic. Write each question at the top of a separate index card.

For a report on earthquakes, here are three possible questions:

1. What causes earthquakes?
2. Where do earthquakes occur?
3. What damage can they cause?

As you find answers to your questions, jot the answers down on the appropriate card. At the bottom of each card, write the *source* of your information. *A source is a book or article you may have read in order to gather information about your topic.*

Would words capture the beauty of this scene just as well as a photograph?
What words would you use to describe it?

Scenes from the San Francisco earthquake in 1906

Your index cards might look like this:

What causes earthquakes?

Earthquakes are sudden shocks to the surface of the earth. They occur when great pressure is put on rock. The rock begins to bend and fold. The pressure becomes so great that the rock splits and the earth moves. These splits are called faults.

All about Earthquakes, p. 11

Where do earthquakes occur?

Many earthquakes occur along fault lines. The lines usually are in areas where new mountains or trenches have formed, rather than on older, flat parts of the earth. Most earthquakes occur under the sea. Many occur along the circum-Pacific belt, along the edge of the Pacific Ocean.

Young Adult Encyclopedia, vol. 3, p. 75

What damage can they cause?

Buildings collapse, tidal waves form, and fires often break out. Thousands of people can lose their lives.

Earthquakes, p. 123

REACTION: The novel *Johnny Tremain* held my interest from beginning to end. Reading about the exciting adventures of those early days in Boston, I saw a picture of the struggle for American liberty through the eyes of a clever, courageous, and patriotic boy of fourteen.

Activity A

Review the model book report and answer these questions.
  1. Who is the author of *Johnny Tremain*?
  2. Who is Johnny Tremain?
  3. What is the problem, or conflict, in *Johnny Tremain*?
  4. How is the problem resolved?
  5. Why does the writer of the book report like *Johnny Tremain*?
  6. Would you like to read *Johnny Tremain*? Why, or why not?

Activity B

Think of a book or short story that you particularly enjoyed and answer these questions about it.
  1. What is the title?
  2. Who is the author?
  3. What kind of book or story is it?
  4. Who are the important characters?
  5. What is the problem or conflict?
  6. What does the main character do to solve the problem?
  7. What is the conclusion?
  8. Why did you like this book or story?

Write Away!

The information you provided for activity B gives you the basic outline for a report on the book or story. Complete a report on that book or story in book report form. Remember to make the *summary* and *reaction* colorful and interesting. Draw a picture of one scene from the story and include it in your report.

Writing Corner 4

How and Why Tales

Have you ever wondered *how* things in nature came about? For example, *why* do animals have certain characteristics? A long time ago, people did not have science to explain nature. They made up reasons of their own for what happened. Usually they put these reasons in the form of a story or tale. They may have told a tale about

how the rainbow got its colors   why kangaroos hop
how the turtle got its shell   why the sun is hot

These have come to be called *how and why tales*. These kinds of tales often begin with phrases such as

When the world was very young...
Once, many thousands of years ago...

Characters are introduced, and a plot develops. Within the plot, a difficulty or complication often arises. The main character may have to overcome an obstacle, make a decision, or confront danger. Dialogue is often added to help make the characters seem real. On the next page is a tale about "How the Giraffe Became the Tallest Animal in the Forest."

Long ago, Giraffe was a very small creature. He was so small that he couldn't even see himself. One day he mentioned his complaint to Elephant. Elephant told him about a pool deep in the forest. This pool was so clear that Giraffe would surely be able to see himself. Giraffe was excited and Elephant promised to lead the way. When they arrived, Giraffe dashed to the edge of the pool, but being so short, he could not stretch over the water to see himself. Every time he tried, he fell into the pool.

"This will never do!" cried Giraffe.

"I have an idea," said Elephant. "If I hold your legs, you can stretch over the water and that way you can see yourself."

So Elephant held Giraffe's legs, and Giraffe stretched his head and neck over the water. He liked seeing himself so much that he stretched again and stretched again.

"Oh, I am beautiful!" exclaimed Giraffe, and he kept stretching and stretching until he stretched his neck right across the pool. Then when he could see himself no longer, Elephant pulled Giraffe straight up with his strong trunk. Now Giraffe stood taller than any other animal in the forest. To this day, no animal is as tall as the giraffe.

The ending of a *how and why tale* should answer the question the title raises. In this tale, Giraffe stretched so much to see himself that his neck became very long and he ended up being the tallest animal in the forest.

★ Brainstorm for other *how and why* titles to add to the list given. Then choose one and write an explanation with dialogue of *how* or *why* something happened. Be as imaginative and creative as you can. Illustrate your work if you like when you are finished. Then read your tale to the class.

Homophones

Homophones are words that sound alike but that have different spellings and meanings.

Many writers are confused by words that sound alike but that have different spellings and meanings. These words are called homophones.

Into the pitch black *night*, the *knight* rode on his white charger.

In this sentence, *night* and *knight* are homophones.

Be careful to use the correct spelling of words that are homophones. Always check the dictionary if you are unsure of a spelling.

Activity A

Give the definitions for each pair of homophones below. Use a dictionary if necessary.
1. bough—bow
2. coarse—course
3. knot—not
4. patience—patients
5. peace—piece
6. root—route
7. stationary—stationery
8. some—sum
9. threw—through
10. weather—whether

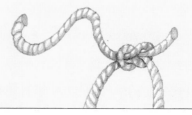

Activity B

Complete each sentence with the correct homophone. Use the list in activity A. Each word on the list should be used once.

1. A multicolored bird sat on the _____ of the tree and sang.
2. Vegetables, such as turnips, that grow underground are called _____ vegetables.
3. The submarine was far off _____.
4. Radar is an instrument used in _____ forecasting.
5. _____ seabirds travel more than 20,000 miles in their migrations.
6. Tricia fielded the ground ball and _____ it to first base.
7. The nomads wear loose garments made out of a _____ material that they weave themselves.
8. Gabriel could _____ decide _____ to study arithmetic or play volleyball.
9. After one week on the exhausting paper _____, Janine added up the _____ of her earnings.
10. Making a tiny model plane requires _____.
11. We drove _____ a long tunnel on our way into New York.
12. Afraid his arm was broken, Alex sat in the emergency room among the other _____.
13. Violet uses _____ with purple violets on it.
14. The sailor fastened the rowboat to the pier with an expertly tied _____.
15. The magician took a _____ and disappeared from the stage amid smoke and applause.
16. The important telephone number was on a tiny _____ of paper.
17. Now, desks in schools are movable; in the past, they were often _____.
18. The dove is a symbol of _____.

Chapter 5

Writing Letters

Lesson 1 The Parts of a Social Letter

A social letter is made up of a heading, salutation, body, complimentary close, and signature.

Do you have a close friend who lives in another city? A favorite relative who lives hundreds or even thousands of miles away? Unfortunately, the people you like best do not always live near you. Even though you cannot see them often, you can keep in touch with friends and relatives by writing *letters*.

What are some of the things you can share in a letter? When you are with a friend, you probably tell stories and jokes, and you talk about new experiences and future plans. You can share the same things when you write a friendly letter. Letters can be enjoyable to write and to receive.

You probably have already written some, or even many, social letters. Let's review the *parts* of a social letter, so that you will use the correct form. A social letter contains five parts: (1) the heading, (2) the salutation, (3) the body of the letter, (4) the complimentary close, and (5) the signature.

In this picture, many pieces of writing are being saved. How valuable is a letter to you? Why?

Read the following letter, and take careful note of each part.

2690 Rouen Street
Denver, Colorado 80220
December 3, 19_

Dear Roberta,

I enjoyed getting your letter last week. It really made me homesick for all my old friends in Houston. I am getting to like Denver, though. I especially like the Colorado Heritage Center. It has items from the early cliff dwellers who once lived in this area.

Another thing I like about Denver is the snow. I've never seen so much snow! I'm taking skiing lessons, and my mom is going to buy me a complete ski outfit for Christmas (I hope!). So far, this city seems as if it will be great to live in.

Write soon and let me know what's going on with all my Houston friends.

Body

Complimentary close Your good friend,
Signature Jenny

Here are some rules for each of the parts of a social letter.

1. Heading

The heading of a letter contains the address of the writer and the date. It is usually written on three lines. The address is written on the first line; the city, state, and zip code on the second line; and the date on the third line. The heading is written slightly to the right of the center of the paper, about an inch from the top of the sheet. If the letter is extremely short, the heading may be lowered. Ordinarily each line is written directly under the one above it. This is called *block form*.

Brief letters, or *social notes*, sometimes use only the date in the heading. Invitations, thank-you notes, and notes of acceptance or regret are examples of social notes.

2. Salutation

The salutation is the greeting at the beginning of a letter. It is only one line long and begins at the left-hand margin. The salutation varies, depending on the person to whom the letter is written. The first word and the person's name are always capitalized, and there is always a comma at the end of the salutation in a social letter.

These are examples of salutations:

> Dear Denise,
>
> Dear Uncle Mac,
>
> My dear Aunt,

3. Body

The body of the letter is the most important part because it contains the message. In this part, you carry on a conversation with the person to whom you are writing. In the next lesson, you will learn more about writing the body of some special kinds of social letters.

4. Complimentary Close

The complimentary close lets the reader know that the letter is ending. The first word begins with a capital letter and should line up with (be exactly under) the first word of the heading. The complimentary close is always followed by a comma. Make sure that the complimentary close is appropriate for the person to whom you are writing.

These are examples of complimentary closes:

Your friend,

Your classmate,

Your daughter,

5. Signature

The signature is the name of the person who is writing the letter. When you are writing to relatives and close friends, use your first name only. If the person to whom you are writing does not know you very well, use your full name. The name always begins with a capital letter, and there is no punctuation mark after the name. *Write* your signature neatly under the first word of the complimentary close.

Activity A

Arrange each of the following addresses and dates in the proper form for the heading of a letter. Use the current year for the date in your headings.

1. April 27, 19__, Anchorage, Alaska 99510, 123 Yukon Avenue
2. Chicago, Illinois 60613, June 29, 19__, 3843 North Greenview Avenue
3. 438 North Street, June 10, 19__, Norfolk, Virginia 23500
4. August 1, 19__, Pennsbury Hospital, Jonesboro, Arkansas 72401

Activity B

Write the salutation for a letter written to each person listed below.

1. Your mother
2. A very close friend
3. Your cousin Teresa
4. Mrs. Gurek, a teacher in your school
5. Your Aunt Sally
6. A classmate
7. Mr. Santelli
8. Your brother

Activity C

Write the complimentary close for a letter written to each person listed below.

1. A classmate
2. Your uncle
3. Your brother
4. The captain of your soccer team
5. Your teacher
6. A friend
7. Your parents
8. Your cousin Alan

Write Away!

Think of three people you know who live too far away for you to visit very often. On a sheet of paper, write a heading, a salutation, and a complimentary close for a letter to each of them.

Lesson 2 Writing Social Letters

Types of social letters include the friendly letter, the invitation, and the thank-you letter.

The social letter is a form of writing that helps you keep in touch with people you know. The more you improve your writing skills, the more entertaining and informative your social letters will be.

Three types of social letters are the *friendly letter*, the *invitation*, and the *thank-you letter*. Remember the following points as you write each type of letter: (1) Talk about one topic only in each paragraph and finish that topic before introducing a new one. (2) Always write complete sentences. (3) Indent the first sentence of each paragraph about one inch.

In *friendly letters,* friends exchange news about each other (just as the writer of the letter in lesson 1 did). Read the friendly letter on the next page, in which a boy tells of his new hobby. Does the letter writer follow the rules of a good paragraph in describing his hobby? Does he write complete sentences? Is each paragraph indented?

Model: A Friendly Letter

105 Powder Boulevard
Dixon, Illinois 60329
December 17, 19__

Dear Jim,

    It was really great to hear from you. Your fitness class sounds like lots of fun. I'm glad to hear that you saved up enough money to buy a drum set. It seems as if you're keeping very busy.

    I've been quite occupied myself. You know that I was never the type to have hobbies, but in the past few months I've become a stamp collector. It started when my Uncle Ted sent me postcards as he traveled throughout Europe. I never realized before how many different stamps there were in the world. Now I look forward to the mail delivery and to each new collection that I have been able to order. Friends from all over have promised to watch carefully for any unusual stamps. Would you like to help me too?

    Say hello to your family, Jim. I'm glad you all like your new home.

Your friend,
Jason

An *invitation* should be as natural as a friendly letter. It should also state very clearly the kind of event, the day, the time, and the place. An invitation should be written so that the person who receives it will want to accept. Read this model invitation. Does it provide all the needed information? Does it make you want to attend the party?

Model: An Invitation

1666 Wall Street
Chattanooga, Tennessee 37400
December 5, 19—

Dear Anne,

Are the first blasts of winter's cold getting you down? Does the early darkness make you feel like hibernating until April? If that's how you feel (or even if it isn't), please join us in cheering up the season with a tree-trimming party and dinner on December 17. My family would love to have you come to our house at two o'clock.

Your friend,
Becky

A *thank-you letter* shows your appreciation for a favor you have received. In your letter, you should try to make the person feel good about what he or she did. Read the following and decide if it is an effective thank-you letter.

Model: A Thank-you Letter

99 Hamp Street
Denver, Colorado 80220
January 5, 19___

Dear Aunt Gail,

    Thanks so much for giving me your old baseball card collection. It has many players that will make me the envy of all my friends who are collectors. Now I have cards of Roberto Clemente and Willie Mays!

    Thank you again. We are all looking forward to your visit at Easter.

Your delighted niece,
Jayne

Activity A

Choose one of the following topics and write a paragraph that you might include in a letter to your cousin in another city. Include a heading, salutation, complimentary close, and signature.

1. A good book you have read
2. A sport you have been playing
3. A visit to a museum
4. Your favorite television program
5. A day when everything went wrong
6. A movie you liked
7. Your favorite new record
8. (Choose your own)

Activity B

From the topics listed below, write one letter of invitation and one thank-you letter. Include a heading, salutation, complimentary close, and signature.

Invitations

1. An invitation to a Halloween party
2. An invitation to your grandparents to attend a school play in which you will appear
3. An invitation to an evening of VCR movies at your house

Thank-you Letters

1. A thank-you note to your aunt and uncle after you spent a week of your summer vacation on their farm
2. A thank-you note to your best friend for visiting you while you were in the hospital
3. A thank-you note to a friend for a birthday gift

Write Away!

Write a friendly letter to someone you would like to know: a book character, a movie or sports star, or a person from history. Tell this person why you are interested in him or her, ask questions, and comment on the things this person has done.

Revision: Time to Take Another Look

As you reread a social letter, ask yourself the following questions:

—Are there three lines in the heading?
    street address
    city, state, zip code
    month, day, year
—Do all the words in the heading fit without being squeezed?
—Does the salutation begin at the left-hand margin?
—Does each paragraph contain only one topic?
—Are the complimentary close and signature in line with the heading?
—Does the letter make sense?

If you need to work on anything from the above list, *do it now*. *Delete* or *add* words and *rearrange* ideas if necessary. After your revision, rewrite the social letter and go on to proofreading.

Proofreading: Time to Look at Capitalization, Punctuation, and Spelling

λ	Add
$\wp$	Omit
$=$	Capitalize
$/$	Lowercase
$\cap$	Reverse
$\P$	New paragraph

Heading: Did I use a comma between city and state, day of the month, and year? Are all proper nouns capitalized?
Salutation: Is the first letter of each important word capitalized? (*Dear* is not capitalized unless it is the first word.) Did I put a comma at the end?
Body: Did I indent each paragraph? Is all the punctuation correct?
Complimentary close: Is the first word capitalized? Do the other words begin with a small letter? Is there a comma at the end?
Signature: Did I write my name clearly and legibly?

Start at the last word of the letter and check for spelling errors. If necessary, rewrite the letter in your best handwriting.

Lesson 3 The Parts of a Business Letter

A business letter is made up of a heading, inside address, salutation, body, complimentary close, and signature.

Sometimes you need to write to a business firm or an organization to request information, to order a product, or to complain about an unsatisfactory product. Such *business letters* have the same five parts as a social letter, as well as a part called the *inside address*. Read the following business letter and note the differences between business and social letters.

Heading
1111 Tenth Street
Moline, Illinois 61265
February 10, 19__

Carlson Book Shop
1425 Fifth Avenue
Moline, Illinois 61265

Dear Sir or Madam : Salutation

    Please send me one package of five hundred stamps titled "World Collection" (#302 in your summer Body catalog). I am enclosing a money order for eight dollars ($8.00), which includes postage.

Complimentary close Very truly yours,
Signature Barbara Cox
Barbara Cox

Here are some rules for each of the parts of a business letter.

1. Heading

The form for the heading of a business letter is the same as for the heading of a social letter. It contains the writer's street address, city, state, and zip code, and the month, day, and year. The heading is written slightly to the right of the center of the paper, about an inch from the top.

2. Inside Address

The inside address should begin on the left-hand margin, below the heading. It consists of the full name and address of the business or organization to which the letter is being sent. The inside address follows the same form and punctuation as the heading except for one difference. If the letter is being written to a specific person, that person's name and title are included on the first line of the inside address. The name of the business or organization then appears on the second line. Make sure that the inside address is the same as the address on the envelope.

3. Salutation

The salutation of a business letter is followed by a colon (:) and is made up of a formal phrase such as the following:

Dear Ms. Spaulding:
Dear Sir or Madam:

The salutation is directly below the inside address.

4. Body

The body of a business letter follows the same form as that of a social letter. It is short and courteous, and contains only necessary information.

5. Complimentary Close

The complimentary close of a business letter is more formal than that of a social letter. Such phrases as the following are used:

Yours truly,   *Sincerely yours,*

Very truly yours,   *Respectfully yours,*

It is directly in line with the heading.

6. Signature

The signature of a business letter is also more formal. Directly below the complimentary close, write your full name. Below that, you should type or neatly print your name. This form is necessary for the signature of a business letter so that your name is readable.

Business letters are often typed since typed letters are easier to read. However, it is acceptable for you to send handwritten business letters.

Activity A

Arrange each of the following addresses in the proper order for an inside address. Write a salutation to go along with each inside address.

1. 229 West Forty-third Street, *New York Times*, New York, New York 10000
2. Agriculture Department, Ames, Iowa 50010, University of Iowa, Professor Leslie Brock
3. Marshall Field and Company, Chicago, Illinois 60602, 111 North State Street
4. 3441 North Ashland Avenue, Managing Editor, Chicago, Illinois 60657, Loyola University Press
5. New York, New York 10000, Program Director, National Broadcasting Company, 645 Third Avenue

Activity B

Copy this business letter on a sheet of paper and fill in the
missing parts.

Marshall School
4358 Utica Avenue
Cheyenne, Wyoming 82001

_____

Business Manager

_____

2120 Market Street
Cheyenne, Wyoming 82001

_____

   A recent article in your newspaper indicated that you
offer guided tours in which you show grade-school
groups how the *Cheyenne News* is written and printed.
The sixth-grade class that I teach would be quite
interested in taking such a tour sometime in April.

_____

_____ We need to make our plans by March 15.

_____

_____

Elizabeth Lopez
Teacher, Room 301

Write Away!

Write a heading, inside address, salutation, complimentary close,
and signature for a business letter to each of the following.
   1. A local grocery store
   2. A nearby department store
   3. The mayor
   4. The place of business of a family member
   5. A business that you would like to visit

Lesson 4 Writing a Business Letter

A business letter should be short, courteous, and to the point.

A business letter is more formal than a social letter. A social letter helps people keep in touch and exchange various bits of news about each other. The purpose of a business letter is much more specific. The most common kinds of business letters do one of the following:

1. order a product
2. make a request
3. complain about a product or service
4. request that the writer be considered for a job

Since its goal is so specific, a business letter should be short and to the point. The letter writer must remember to be just as courteous in a business letter as in a social letter.

Letters Ordering a Product

One of the most common kinds of business letter is a letter in which the writer is ordering a product. It is important for the writer to give complete and precise information about what is being ordered. In addition, the writer should mention the method of payment.

Revision: Time to Take Another Look

As you reread a business letter, ask yourself:
—Is the heading in the proper form?
—Is the inside address in the proper form? (Name of person, if known; name of company; street address; city, state, zip code)
—Is the salutation appropriate for the letter?
—Is the body of the letter brief, to the point, and courteous? Have I given all the necessary information?
—Is the complimentary close appropriate?

If you need to work on anything from the above list, *do it now*. *Delete* or *add* words and *rearrange* sentences as necessary. After you have revised the business letter, go on to proofreading.

Proofreading: Time to Look at Capitalization, Punctuation, and Spelling

⅄	Add
℔	Omit
≡	Capitalize
/	Lowercase
∿	Reverse
¶	New paragraph

Heading and Inside Address: Did I use a comma between city and state, day of the month, and year? Are all proper nouns capitalized? Is each of the parts in the proper place?
Salutation: Is the first letter of each important word capitalized? Is there a colon at the end? Does it begin at the left-hand margin?
Body: Did I indent the first line of the paragraph? Does every sentence end with correct punctuation?
Complimentary Close: Is the close in line with the heading? Is the first word capitalized? Does each of the other words begin with a small letter? Is there a comma at the end?
Signature: Is the signature in line with the heading? Did I write my first and last names neatly? Did I type or print my name under the written signature?

Start at the last word of the letter and check for spelling errors. If necessary, rewrite the letter in your best handwriting.

Lesson 5 Addressing the Envelope

The front of an envelope has the name and address of the person to whom the letter is being sent. It also has the return address of the sender.

You have probably addressed many envelopes. Let's review the rules to make sure that you have been addressing your envelopes correctly. Look at the following example.

Margaret Parker
Box 159
Arlington, VA 22200

Dr. Maria Sanchez
506 Long Street
Portland, OR 97200

Note that the envelope contains the full name and address of the person to whom the letter is being sent, including a title such as Dr., Mr., Miss, Mrs., or Ms. The form and the punctuation should follow the style of the inside address of a business letter. The person's name should begin just above the center of the envelope and slightly to the left. The street address goes below the name, and the third line gives the city, state, and zip code. Each line in the address is exactly under the line above it. This is called *block form*.

Write Away!

Find a form to fill out. It can be from a magazine, newspaper, local store, community center, post office, or anywhere else. Complete the form and share it with the class.

Writing Corner 5

Writing Answers

Many homework assignments and tests require that you answer questions in *clear* sentences and in *short* paragraphs. To do this, you need to

> *understand* exactly what the question is asking
> *focus* your answer on that point
> *select* the information that fits the question

Study the questions and answers that follow. Which of the two answers *focuses* better on what the question is asking?

Where is Washington, D.C.?

A. Washington, D.C., lies between Maryland and Virginia. Many people who work in Washington live in those two states.
B. Washington, D.C., is in the southeastern United States. It lies between Maryland and Virginia.

You are right if you noticed these points:

> Answer A includes the correct information, but the second sentence loses the focus on the question *where*.

> Answer B keeps the focus on *where* throughout, and it locates Washington first by region and then by state.

Describe the main characteristics of Washington, D.C.

A. Washington, D.C., is a beautiful city. It attracts visitors from all over the world. It has many fine buildings. In the spring, cherry blossoms are in bloom, adding to the beauty of the city. It is an interesting and educational city to visit. There are many museums to visit. More important, it is the capital of our nation. American citizens everywhere can take pride in the beauty of this city.

B. Washington, D.C., the capital of the United States, is noted for its fine buildings, its museums, and its natural beauty. The city has many government buildings—most impressive of all is the gleaming white Capitol with its imposing dome. There are many historical monuments, including the Lincoln Memorial with its colossal statue of the president. The Smithsonian Institution is the largest museum in the country, and its Air and Space Museum is the most visited. The city is also famous for its green areas and spring cherry blossoms.

You are right if you noticed these points:

> Answer A *discusses* many of Washington's characteristics rather than *describing* them.
>
> Answer B *describes* Washington's characteristics by giving specific *details*. It is a better answer.

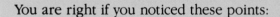

★ Choose one of the activities below, and answer the questions. Use books and travel brochures to help you answer. Try to focus on answering the question clearly and directly.

A. 1. Where is Disneyland?
   2. Name some of the features of Disneyland that attract visitors.
   3. Describe the fun of a visit to Disneyland.
B. 1. Who was Walt Disney?
   2. List the name of some of Walt Disney's productions.
   3. Select one of the characters Walt Disney created. Describe the character. Tell what the character looks like and how it acts.

Homographs

Homographs are words that are spelled the same but that have different meanings and are often pronounced differently.

Homographs can be confusing because they are words that are spelled alike. You can only identify a homograph by the way it is used. For example:

> From the rocky cliff, Manolo *dove* into the ocean.
> (*Past tense of* dive, *pronounced* dōv)

> As the sun broke through the clouds, a *dove* rested on the white picket fence in Jennie's yard.
> (*A kind of bird, pronounced* dəv)

Notice that the pronunciation of *dove* changes. There is a change in the *vowel sound*. The change in the vowel sound signals a difference in meaning. Look at the next two sentences:

> Akim takes pictures of any *object* that he finds interesting.
> (*A thing that can be seen or touched, pronounced* ŏb'jĭkt)

> Does anyone *object* to spending the dues on a dark room?
> (*Oppose, pronounced* əb jĕkt')

Here the pronunciation of the word changes because there is a definite change, or shift, in the *accent*. The shift in the accent signals a difference in meaning.

Activity A

Read the list of homographs below and pronounce each word. Tell whether each pair of homographs has a different pronunciation because of a vowel change or a shift in accent. Then give the meaning of each word. Use a dictionary if necessary.

1. a. bow (bō)   b. bow (baù)
2. a. lead (lēd)   b. lead (lĕd)
3. a. live (līv)   b. live (lĭv)
4. a. present (prĕz′ nt)   b. present (prĭ zĕnt′)
5. a. record (rĭ kôrd′)   b. record (rĕk′ ərd)

Activity B

Complete each sentence with the correct homograph from the list in activity A. Indicate whether the homograph you use is labeled *a* or *b* on the list.

1. I would like to _____ the new president of our class, Patty Layton.
2. The storm tossed the ship against a jagged rock, opening a massive hole in the _____.
3. During the 1800s, Galena, Illinois, was a center for the mining of _____.
4. Excitedly, Tisa tore the wrapping off the unexpected _____.
5. Charlie looked silly in that polka dot _____ tie.
6. Do any people _____ in Antarctica?
7. Jason's towering home run put his team in the _____.
8. Mary Lou will _____ today's important events in her diary.
9. Laura got tired of studying, so she put on a _____ and began to dance.
10. The cat's toy looked so real that for a moment I thought it was a _____ mouse.

Chapter 6

Speaking and Listening Skills

Lesson 1 Tools for Speaking Clearly and Correctly

Skilled speakers can use the tools of pitch, stress, and enunciation to speak more effectively and make their words come alive.

You have already learned a variety of ways to improve your writing. Although writing is an essential form of communication, it is not the only one—it is not even the most common. Days may pass when you do not write anything. Can you imagine a waking hour, however, when you do not express your thoughts and feelings through speech? Speech is such a common activity that you probably take it for granted. It includes a wide range of activities, such as casual conversation, reading aloud, introducing people to each other, debating, and making formal reports. The next few lessons will help you improve your skills of speaking and—just as important—listening.

Speaking requires many of the same skills as writing. A good speaker presents ideas in an organized and logical manner and makes these ideas more vivid by using language that "paints a picture." Speakers have another important tool—the voice. When you speak, you use the qualities of voice to make your words clearer and more vivid.

A tapestry is carefully designed and planned before it is woven. What kind of planning is needed to be an effective speaker?

Pitch

Pitch is the highness or the lowness of the speaker's voice. Variations in pitch can bring a spoken message alive. The speaker's voice becomes higher or lower in order to give the correct meaning to words.

Think about the following situation and listen to the pitch of your voice. Imagine that you have a role in a school play. The opening song is your cue that the play is about to begin. You hear the first notes of the song and say, "It's starting." You are stating a simple fact. The pitch of your voice is even. Now say the same sentence as a question, "It's starting?" The pitch of your voice is higher at the end. The meaning of the sentence is different. Through pitch, the listener understands that you are asking a question. Now say "It's starting!" with enthusiasm. The pitch of your voice starts high and then lowers. It shows your excitement.

Activity

Read the following sentences in at least two different ways by varying the pitch. Then tell what kind of feeling you are expressing with each change in pitch.
1. It snowed last night.
2. This pizza's delicious.
3. Stop it.
4. Let someone else do it.
5. This music is too loud.

Stress

Stress is the emphasis or degree of force you put on a word. The meaning of a sentence can change depending on what words are stressed. Read the following sentences aloud and listen to how different stress changes the meaning of the sentence. Put the emphasis on the italicized word.

Will *you* walk ten miles tomorrow? (This sentence emphasizes the person.)
Will you *walk* ten miles tomorrow? (This sentence emphasizes the action.)
Will you walk ten miles *tomorrow*? (This sentence emphasizes the time.)

Activity

Read the following sentences in at least two different ways by varying the stress. Tell what meaning you are expressing with each change in stress.

1. Anna and Carlos went to the zoo.
2. Did you like that old movie?
3. Paula won first prize.
4. We planted those tomatoes yesterday.
5. Will you practice with me now?

Enunciation

Enunciation, or exact pronunciation, conveys the spoken message clearly. When you *enunciate*, you say vowels and consonants clearly and fully. Your listener can easily understand what you are saying.

Activity A

Now try some *tuning-up* exercises to practice proper breathing and enunciation.

1. Inhale through your nose and hold your breath for ten counts. Then exhale with the sound of *ah*. This opens your throat and helps to relax the muscles so that you may breathe more easily as you speak.
2. Practice the long and short sounds of *a*.

māy	măt
māte	măn
sāy	păn

3. Practice these consonant sounds. Concentrate on enunciating each consonant clearly.

   D   The double dip delighted Donna.
   T   Tinkering Tom took ten toadstools.
   S   The sight of the sea surprised the sailor.
   Sh   Shall she shake the shawl?
   Z   Zebras zoom through Zanzibar.
   Zh   Azure sky measures pleasure.
   J   Jeff and Jason jumped for joy.
   Ch   The chattering chimps chuckled cheerily.
   Th   Theodore thought his thumb had thawed.

It Couldn't Be Done

LIGHT VOICES	Somebody said \ that it couldn't be done, // But he with a chuckle replied //
DEEP VOICES	That "maybe it couldn't," \ but he would be one \ Who wouldn't say so \ till he'd tried. //
LIGHT VOICES	So he buckled right in \ with the trace of a grin \ On his face. // If he worried \ he hid it. //
UNISON	He started to sing \ as he tackled the thing \ That couldn't be done, // and he did it. //
LIGHT VOICES SOLO	Somebody scoffed: \ "Oh, you'll never do that; \ At least no one ever has done it"; //
DEEP VOICES	But he took off his coat \ and he took off his hat, // And the first thing we knew \ he'd begun it. //
LIGHT VOICES	With a lift of his chin \ and a bit of a grin, // Without any doubting or quiddit, //
UNISON	He started to sing \ as he tackled the thing \ That couldn't be done, // and he did it. //
DEEP VOICES	There are thousands to tell you \ it cannot be done, // There are thousands \ to prophesy failure; //
LIGHT VOICES	There are thousands to point out to you, \ one by one, // The dangers that wait to assail you. //
DEEP VOICES	But just buckle in \ with a bit of a grin, // Just take off your coat \ and go to it; //
UNISON	Just start to sing \ as you tackle the thing \ That "cannot be done," // and you'll do it. //

Edgar A. Guest

Velvet Shoes

UNISON

Let us walk in the white snow \
  In a soundless space; //
With footsteps quiet \ and slow, \
  At a tranquil pace,\
  Under veils \ of white lace. //

LIGHT VOICES

I shall go shod in silk, \
  And you in wool, //
White as a white cow's milk, \
  More beautiful
  Than the breast \ of a gull. //

DEEP VOICES

We shall walk \ through the still town \
  In a windless peace; //
We shall step upon white down. /
  Upon silver fleece, \
  Upon softer \ than these. //

UNISON

We shall walk in velvet shoes: /
  Wherever we go //
Silence \ will fall like dews \
  On white silence below. //
  We shall walk \ in the snow. //

Elinor Wylie

**Model: A Telephone Message Received by Scott's Mother
While Scott Was at the Doctor's Office**

Message from Mike to Scott

—History quiz tomorrow, chapter on Roman Republic and
Empire
—Math homework for tomorrow—Chapter 12, exercises 1–7
—Charity drive begins tomorrow. Bring your contribution.
—Trip to the Science Museum next Thursday, June 3. Be sure to
pick up a permission slip.
—Practice for softball playoffs tomorrow at 3:00. Bring your
"Roger Maris" bat.
—Hope you're feeling better. See you tomorrow.

Model: Classroom Notes

—Abraham Lincoln elected President in 1860.
—Many Southerners did not like Lincoln because of his stand
against slavery.
—Soon after election, eleven states withdrew from Union and
formed Confederate States of America.
—(and so on)

Activity A

Imagine that you have just answered the phone. The caller has
asked for your mother, but she is not at home. Your teacher
will pretend to be the caller and give you the message. Listen
carefully and jot down notes. Then write out the message as
accurately as you can.

Activity B

Make up a realistic-sounding telephone message that includes
names, dates, and times. Read the message to another student,
and have that student take notes. After the notes have been
rewritten as a reminder, or *memo*, check to see that the
information is clear and accurate. Then reverse roles. You
take notes as your partner gives a message.

Writing Corner 6

Interviewing

Interviewing people is an interesting way for you to collect information for a report. In an interview, you would talk with someone and ask questions related to the report you were preparing. Study how Martin used an interview to prepare a report for his class.

Martin's class was working on a project called "Living History." The class realized that there were older people in their families and neighborhoods who were living history references. Each class member would *interview* one of these interesting people, write a report about the interview, and share it with the class.

Martin had heard his neighbor, Mrs. Haywood, talk about her childhood memories of the years when the United States was involved in World War II. He decided to interview Mrs. Haywood. These are the steps he followed.

Before the Interview

1. Martin called Mrs. Haywood *well in advance*. He explained the project and asked her for a short interview.
2. After she agreed, Martin asked her to suggest a *time* and *place* that would be convenient for her. He also asked her to *suggest* a few *ideas* she might like to talk about.
3. From her suggestions, and from an article he had read about United States civilians during World War II, Martin *prepared several thoughtful questions*. He wrote each question on the top of a separate card before the interview.

> What are your clearest memories about World War II?
> Do you recall anything about your experiences with food rationing, war bonds, or conserving scrap metal?
> Did your house have a small flag in the window with a star on it? Tell what you remember about this custom or any other special customs.

During the Interview

As Mrs. Haywood responded to the questions, Martin wrote a few words on each card. Most of the time, however, Martin did *not* write. He *listened* very carefully. If something wasn't clear, he asked about it. Then he listened again to Mrs. Haywood's response. At the end of the interview, Martin thanked her politely.

After the Interview

1. Right after the interview, Martin wrote the details he could remember from Mrs. Haywood's answers on the cards with the questions. He used these cards to write a report for the class.
2. He divided his report into paragraphs according to topic. For example, he wrote everything Mrs. Haywood remembered about food rationing in one paragraph.
3. Martin left out ideas that were repeated and selected the most interesting parts.
4. He wrote a paragraph at the beginning of his report about why he decided to interview Mrs. Haywood. At the end of the report, he said how he felt about what he had learned.

★ Interview a person who could answer the same questions that Martin prepared. Write your own report on this topic.
OR
Prepare questions for a person you know who could give you and your class interesting information about a different topic. Report on your interview.

Here are some topic ideas: how to run faster, how to care for houseplants, special activities in your community in which sixth-graders can participate.

Misused Words

Certain words that sound alike or that are similar in sound or spelling are often misused.

Pairs of similar words may cause confusion. One may be incorrectly used instead of the other. Some pairs are homophones, such as *passed* and *past*. Other pairs are words that are quite close in sound and in spelling, such as *were* and *where*. When you write, be careful to spell similar-sounding words correctly.

Activity A

The words in each set are often misused. Give the definition for the part of speech listed. Use the dictionary to complete the activity.

	Part of Speech	Definition
1. accept	verb	_____
except	preposition	_____
2. its	adjective	_____
it's	contraction	_____
3. loose	adjective	_____
lose	verb	_____
4. passed	verb	_____
past	preposition/adverb	_____
5. quiet	adjective	_____
quite	adverb	_____
6. than	conjunction	_____
then	adverb	_____
7. right	adjective	_____
write	verb	_____
8. were	verb	_____
where	adverb	_____

Activity B

Complete each sentence with the correct word from the list of misused words in activity A.

1. A famous quotation of the frontiersman Davy Crockett was "Be sure you're _____ and _____ go ahead."
2. Name one animal that is larger _____ an elephant.
3. _____ chilly outside today.
4. _____ _____ you when the electricity went out?
5. Mr. Pariser looked with horror at his new car and _____ dented fender.
6. When the bus was ready to leave, everyone was accounted for—_____ Amy.
7. The operator asked, "Will you _____ a collect call?"
8. In 1863, Jules Verne began to _____ his fascinating science fiction stories.
9. Walking through the snow on Christmas Eve, Miguel noticed how _____ the neighborhood was.
10. The seaplane _____ over the shore and landed smoothly on the lake.
11. Did anyone here _____ a black and white ski mitten?
12. The two sprinters streaked _____ the finish line at the same time.
13. The doorknob on the old house was _____, and it squeaked when I turned it.
14. Thomas Rockwell's book *How to Eat Fried Worms* is _____ popular with children.
15. Babies actually have more bones _____ adults.

Grammar, Correct Usage, Mechanics

Exercise 2

Write a proper noun for each common noun.

Example: common noun, *state*
          proper noun, *Wisconsin*

river	ocean	hero	explorer
island	street	museum	teacher
continent	building	holiday	author

Exercise 3

Write a common noun for each proper noun.

Example: proper noun, *Poland*
          common noun, *country*

Kentucky	Dodgers	Paris	*Santa Maria*
Edison	Alps	Labor Day	Mediterranean
Mexico	Picasso	Amazon	Amy

Collective Nouns

> **A collective noun names a group of persons, animals, or things considered as a unit.**

Our *class* is large.

This sentence names all the students in a grade as one group. They make up the group known as our *class. Class* is, therefore, a collective noun. It is the name of a group of persons *considered as one.*

Here are some groups of persons or things that may be named by collective nouns.

GROUPS OF PERSONS OR THINGS	COLLECTIVE NOUNS
worshipers in church	congregation
ships of a navy	fleet
athletes who play together	team

Exercise 4

Find the collective nouns in these sentences.

1. Our committee uses a computer to plan the year's basketball schedules.
2. Today I saw a flock of geese flying south.
3. The storm took the crew of the sailboat by surprise.
4. The troop of scouts learned how to fold a tent.
5. The team of horses belonging to George Washington had a daily tooth cleaning.
6. The secretary of a club writes the minutes.
7. A bear on roller skates juggled eggs for the crowd.
8. Tom's family wanted an apartment near the city park.
9. The audience heard squeals instead of music when a mouse ran through the orchestra.
10. A colony of bees has workers, drones, and a queen.

Exercise 5

Make two columns on a paper. In the first, list all the collective nouns in these sentences. In the second, list the group of persons or things named by each collective noun.

Example: The fleet sailed at dawn.

COLLECTIVE NOUN	GROUP OF PERSONS OR THINGS
fleet	ships

1. The shepherd took special care of his flock.
2. Our organization is raising money to help save the whales.
3. Ray directed the cowhands who were trying to stop the stampeding herd.
4. Is the band rehearsing this afternoon?
5. As the audience applauded, the cast bowed.

Abstract Nouns

> An abstract noun expresses a quality or condition. It names something that cannot be seen or touched.

A marathon runner needs *strength* and *confidence* to finish a race.

Notice the abstract nouns in this sentence. They are *strength* and *confidence*. They name *qualities* a person can have.

Collective and *abstract* nouns are usually included among common nouns.

Exercise 6

Find the abstract nouns in these sentences.
1. Kim showed her flying ability as she landed the plane in a rocky field.
2. We admired the beauty of the handmade quilt.
3. If goldfish are left in darkness, they may turn white.
4. Can anyone ever have complete freedom?
5. Perseverance helped Shawn win the pie-eating contest.
6. It was Lloyd's idea to put the lobster in his mother's bathtub.
7. A cockroach will run to safety and clean itself if it touches a human being.
8. Joe spent most of his childhood on an Indian reservation.
9. George loses his patience when the bus is late.
10. Mrs. Cowell's knowledge of giraffes amazed the zookeepers.
11. A fear of water kept the puppy away from the flooded river.
12. The aviator Amelia Earhart possessed great courage.
13. The principal kept her promise—a free lunch for all.
14. Seth was in the garden when he noticed a strange smell.
15. Greta's ambition is to be the best soccer player in the city.

Exercise 7

Use these abstract nouns in sentences of your own.

charity	cleanliness	cheerfulness
sickness	enthusiasm	confidence
patriotism	pride	vitality
strength	happiness	pleasure
truth	humility	bravery

Exercise 8

Many abstract nouns may be formed from other words by adding the suffixes *-hood, -ion, -ity, -ment, -ness, -ship,* or *-ty.* Make abstract nouns from these words by adding the proper suffix. Then use each of the nouns in a sentence.

loyal	friend	swift
good	truthful	companion
enjoy	bright	protect
kind	knight	rapid
honest	celebrate	entertain
leader	major	detect

Exercise 9

Tell whether each noun is *abstract* or *collective*. Then use each one in a sentence of your own.

committee	hope	crew
carelessness	ambition	fleet
convoy	honesty	band
group	wisdom	gratitude

Concrete Nouns

> **A concrete noun names a thing we can see or touch.**
> **Most of the nouns we use are concrete nouns.**

Here are examples of concrete nouns.

bridge	violet
pilot	seal
Japan	Mount Everest

Exercise 10

Find the concrete nouns in these sentences.

1. Did you see the mischievous raccoon?
2. The dictionary was so big the librarian could barely lift it.
3. Huge waves washed the rocky cliffs.
4. Larry stood on the icy sidewalk with a shovel.
5. The Hawaiian Islands are actually the tops of volcanoes.
6. A strange dog dashed through our yard.
7. Early hunters in the Philippine Islands used the yo-yo as a weapon.
8. Who baked these delicious cookies?
9. The young boy needed a map to find the subway.
10. The students could see Mars clearly through the telescope.
11. The plumber took the pipe apart and found a ring inside.
12. A book of poems was selected.
13. Don't you wonder what is hidden in that old wooden trunk?
14. Some termites in Africa build mounds thirty feet tall!
15. Do you like jam on your bread?

A termite mound in Africa

205

Words Used as Nouns and Verbs

A noun is a name word. A verb expresses action or being. Many words can be used as either nouns or verbs.

We decided not to go to the *dance*. (*Noun*)
I *dance* to all kinds of music. (*Verb*)

Exercise 11

Tell whether each italicized word is a noun or a verb.

1. We left our blankets in the *shade* of the beach umbrella.
2. Elm trees *shade* Marina's prizewinning tulip beds.
3. Did Mark Twain really *pilot* a riverboat?
4. The *pilot* double-checked the map of small airports.
5. The Giorgio brothers still *work* in their Italian restaurant.
6. That *work* on the farm was harder than I expected.
7. We're planning a solar *experiment* for the first of May.
8. I *experiment* with color before I do a final design.
9. The top *step* was coated with ice.
10. Do not *step* on the mousetrap.
11. *Cover* the aquarium before you vacuum!
12. Kate drew a kangaroo on the *cover* of my notebook.
13. The *cut* required three stitches!
14. Paul Bunyan could *cut* a tree in half with one easy swing!
15. After pinning the pattern to the material, I *cut* the pieces for the dress.

Practice Power

Last night you met a very unusual person in a dream. Write a short paragraph about this interesting character. Include proper, collective, and abstract nouns.

Lesson 2 Qualities of Nouns

A noun has number, gender, and case. These are the *qualities* of a noun.

In this lesson, you will study *number* and *gender*. In the next lessons, you will learn about *case*.

Number

Number shows whether a noun refers to one person or thing (singular number) or more than one (plural number).

That *rose* is the most beautiful of all the *roses* in our garden.

Rose is singular; *roses* is plural. This change in the form of a noun to show whether the noun refers to one or more than one is called number.

Rules for Forming the Plural

Here are ten rules for forming the plural of nouns. If you want to use the plural of a noun that does not seem to be included in the rules, use the dictionary. You will find that a choice of plural forms is given for some words. In such cases, more than one form would be correct: for example, volcanos, volcanoes.

1. Most nouns form the plural by adding *s* to the singular.

SINGULAR	PLURAL	SINGULAR	PLURAL
home	homes	book	books
nurse	nurses	song	songs

2. Nouns ending in *s, x, z, ch,* and *sh* form the plural by adding *es* to the singular.

SINGULAR	PLURAL	SINGULAR	PLURAL
gas	gases	torch	torches
fox	foxes	sash	sashes
topaz	topazes	wish	wishes
dress	dresses	box	boxes

3. Nouns ending in *y*:

   a. Nouns ending in *y* preceded by a consonant form the plural by changing the *y* to *i* and adding *es.*

SINGULAR	PLURAL	SINGULAR	PLURAL
country	countries	baby	babies
melody	melodies	city	cities
duty	duties	fly	flies
colony	colonies	cry	cries

   b. Nouns ending in *y* preceded by a vowel form the plural by adding *s* to the singular.

SINGULAR	PLURAL	SINGULAR	PLURAL
day	days	pulley	pulleys
turkey	turkeys	play	plays
valley	valleys	chimney	chimneys
key	keys	attorney	attorneys

4. Nouns ending in *f* or *fe*:

   a. Most nouns ending in *f* or *fe* form the plural by adding *s* to the singular:

SINGULAR	PLURAL	SINGULAR	PLURAL
roof	roofs	safe	safes

   b. Some nouns ending in *f* or *fe* form the plural by changing the *f* or *fe* to *ves*:

SINGULAR	PLURAL	SINGULAR	PLURAL
scarf	scarves	loaf	loaves
half	halves	shelf	shelves
knife	knives	wolf	wolves
life	lives	thief	thieves

Use a dictionary if you are not sure of a spelling.

5. Nouns ending in *o*:
   a. All nouns ending in *o* preceded by a vowel form the plural by adding *s* to the singular.

SINGULAR	PLURAL	SINGULAR	PLURAL
radio	radios	bamboo	bamboos
cameo	cameos	studio	studios
trio	trios	portfolio	portfolios

   b. Nouns ending in *o* preceded by a consonant generally form the plural by adding *es* to the singular.

SINGULAR	PLURAL	SINGULAR	PLURAL
tomato	tomatoes	hero	heroes
potato	potatoes	echo	echoes
mosquito	mosquitoes	torpedo	torpedoes

   c. Some nouns ending in *o* preceded by a consonant form the plural by adding *s* to the singular.

SINGULAR	PLURAL	SINGULAR	PLURAL
piano	pianos	alto	altos
solo	solos	silo	silos

6. A few nouns form the plural by a change within the singular.

SINGULAR	PLURAL	SINGULAR	PLURAL
man	men	woman	women
tooth	teeth	goose	geese
mouse	mice	foot	feet

7. A few nouns form the plural by adding *en* or *ren*.

SINGULAR	PLURAL	SINGULAR	PLURAL
ox	oxen	child	children

8. A few nouns have the same form in the plural as in the singular.

SINGULAR	PLURAL	SINGULAR	PLURAL
deer	deer	corps	corps
trout	trout	salmon	salmon
sheep	sheep	Chinese	Chinese

9. Compound nouns usually form the plural by adding *s* to the principal word.

SINGULAR	PLURAL
brother-in-law	brothers-in-law
editor in chief	editors in chief
drive-in	drive-ins

10. Letters form the plural by adding *s* or *'s*. Lowercase letters and capital letters that would be confusing if *s* alone were added form the plural by adding *'s*.

SINGULAR	PLURAL
TV	TVs
a	*a*'s
I	*I*'s

The plural of numbers is formed by adding *s*.

SINGULAR	PLURAL
1980	1980s
3	3s

Exercise 1

Write the plural of the following words. Then go back to the rules that begin on page 207 to check your answers. Write the number of the rule that applies.

Example: fife   fifes   **4a**

dish	journey	candy
grape	piano	deer
cherry	loss	birdhouse
radio	dairy	wish
door	ox	sister-in-law
church	leaf	alley
sky	ostrich	gulf
alto	hero	goose
vessel	studio	family
daisy	fairy	child
monkey	i	Japanese
roof	1970	ax

Here are some characteristics of appositives:
1. The appositive may be omitted from the sentence and a complete thought remains.
2. The appositive follows another noun.
3. The appositive has the same meaning or refers to the same person or thing as the noun it explains.
4. The appositive is frequently set off by commas.

Exercise 8

Copy these sentences. Draw two lines under each appositive and one line under the word it explains.
1. Clair, the lifeguard, rescued a toddler from the pool.
2. Leif Ericson, a bold Viking, visited North America.
3. Jai alai, a Spanish game, uses small wicker baskets.
4. Harry Houdini, a magician, would free himself from a locked box underwater.
5. The Cape Fear Cyclists, a new club, will have training rides every Sunday.
6. Wilma Rudolph, a famous American runner, won three gold medals in a single Olympics.
7. The pyramids, royal tombs, were built thousands of years ago in Egypt.
8. Mrs. Clarkton, the postal carrier, doesn't like loose dogs.
9. Pennsylvania, the Keystone State, produces much coal.
10. Theta Carson, a beekeeper, sells honey during the summer.
11. Washington, D.C., the nation's capital, was named for George Washington.
12. Mr. Wood, an ornithologist, photographs rare birds.
13. Steven, my brother, drew a purple dinosaur on the wall.
14. The flounder, a saltwater fish, can change its skin color to look like a checkerboard.
15. Benjamin Parkway, a busy street, will be closed for repairs.

Exercise 9

Copy these sentences. Put commas where they are needed to set off the appositives.

1. The South Pole the coldest place on earth has snow all year round.
2. The Eiffel Tower a popular tourist attraction is in Paris.
3. My second cousin Barry raises peacocks.
4. Chris Stevens a textile worker lost his job when the factory closed.
5. Gray Dove Chief Lone Star's daughter built her own tepee.
6. Mrs. Vance the newspaper's proofreader checks for errors.
7. Harriet Tubman a former slave helped many slaves escape to freedom before the Civil War.
8. Jason a young inventor is trying to think of a new use for paper clips.
9. Saturn the second largest planet takes almost thirty years to orbit the sun.
10. *A Wrinkle in Time* a book by Madeleine L'Engle tells of a girl traveling into another time dimension.

Exercise 10

Rewrite each sentence and put an appositive after the subject. Remember to use commas to set off the appositives. Choose from the appositives below.

Example: Roy asked his track coach to accept the trophy.
　　　　　Roy, the winner, asked his track coach to accept the trophy.

1. Tortoises have been known to live up to one hundred and fifty-two years.
2. Jack found an opossum asleep in the vegetable bin.
3. Pegasus is seen in the night sky of the Northern Hemisphere.
4. Arnold Lovitt draws cartoons for a children's magazine.
5. Grizelda cast a spell on the vain prince.

　　　our cook　　　the witch of Clearwell　　　the constellation
　　　the longest-living animals　　　an artist

Exercise 11 Review

Tell why the italicized nouns in these sentences are in the nominative case. The choices are *subject, subjective complement, noun in direct address,* or *appositive in the nominative case.*

1. Saint Bernard *dogs* are very strong *animals.*
2. *Bruce,* have you seen our candle-making project?
3. *Nadia,* my *grandmother,* wept when she visited the town where she was born.
4. Have you learned your part for the play, *Eileen?*
5. The very earliest *books* were *slabs* of stone.
6. *Nancy,* your *brother* was on the telephone all morning.
7. *Rome,* the *Eternal City,* is located on the Tiber River.
8. *Birds* have many different feeding habits.
9. The *currency* in Russia is the *ruble.*
10. *Thomas,* our *classmate,* carves wooden duck decoys.
11. *Leaves* floated lazily from the lower branches of the tree.
12. *Beverly Cleary* is a *writer* of children's books.
13. I promise you, *Olga,* that I'll return your book tomorrow.
14. *Hawks* are *birds* with excellent eyesight.
15. *Sasquatch,* a legendary *creature,* is also called Bigfoot.

Practice Power

A. To show your ability to use nouns in the nominative case, write two sentences using a noun as the subjective complement, two using a noun in direct address, and two using an appositive in the nominative case.

B. We often use appositives to add information to a sentence. This information helps explain a difficult or unusual idea. Add an appositive where indicated in each of the following sentences. Tell whether the appositive explains the subject or the subjective complement. Use a dictionary or an encyclopedia for the information you need.
   1. Henry is a serious philatelist∧.
   2. Claustrophobia∧is a common sensation to have in an elevator.
   3. Our destination was the hacienda∧.
   4. The water ouzel∧can run underwater.
   5. Asteroids∧are photographed by satellites.

Lesson 4 Possessive Case

A noun that expresses possession or ownership is in the possessive case.

Bill's voice announced the winners.

The voice that announced the winners belonged to or was possessed by Bill. The word *Bill's*, therefore, is in the possessive case. The sign of the possessive case is the apostrophe (') and *s*.

Exercise 1

Find the nouns in the possessive case in these sentences. Then tell what is being owned or possessed.

1. We need Fran's notes for help on this math problem.
2. A ptarmigan's feathers change from white in the winter to brown in the summer.
3. The knight's armor gleamed in the sunlight.
4. Ellen's new red sneakers lay in the middle of the road.
5. The racers' cars were not damaged.
6. Shel Silverstein's humorous poems are popular with children and adults.
7. A person's eye blinks about ten million times a year!
8. Five of John's companions went with him to the dentist.
9. Our neighbors' cottages are covered with ivy.
10. Lizabel gave me the family's special recipe for perfect fudge.
11. On the calf's flank was the brand of the Rocking R Ranch.
12. Using Matt's compass, we managed to find our way back to the clearing.
13. The barks from the Harrisons' beagles warned us that someone was nearby.
14. Rising water slowly covered Annie McPhearson's cornfields.
15. Fred read all night to finish Ted's book.

Rules for Forming the Possessive Case of Nouns

1. The singular possessive is formed by adding *'s* to the singular form of the noun.

> The *robin's* egg is blue.
> Listen to the *comedian's* joke.

2. The plural possessive of plural nouns ending in *s* is formed by adding the apostrophe only.

> The *robins'* eggs are blue.
> Listen to the *comedians'* jokes.

If the plural form of the noun does not end in *s*, add *'s*.

> Ginny found the *children's tickets.*
> Did you see the display of *women's* gloves?

3. Proper names ending in *s* usually form the possessive case by adding *'s*.

> *James's* bicycle has just been repaired.
> *Dickens's* novels are widely read.

4. In compound nouns the *'s* is added to the end of the word.

POSSESSIVE SINGULAR	POSSESSIVE PLURAL
My *brother-in-law's* car is new.	My *brothers-in-law's* cars are new.

Exercise 2

Write the singular possessive and the plural possessive forms for these nouns.

baby	trout	princess	child
sparrow	nurse	snake	witness
wife	artist	robot	dancer
coach	pharaoh	uncle	hedgehog
astronaut	reindeer	carpenter	owlet
classmate	woman	mouse	stepsister

Exercise 3

Write each group of words in another way to show possession.

Example: trick of the magician
the magician's trick

1. poems of Longfellow
2. wheelchair of Bobby
3. red nose of the clown
4. diary of the detective
5. hats of the cowboys
6. slipper of Cinderella
7. courage of the firefighters
8. daffodils of Mr. Beetle
9. colors of the chameleon
10. command of the sergeant
11. joy of the children
12. assignment of the reporter
13. pet shop of Uncle Louis
14. hiding place of the pirates
15. crown of the princess

Practice Power

Think of unusual or interesting presents for five people or groups of people you know. As you think of the people, use both singular and plural nouns. Plural nouns could be *parents, classmates, sisters*. Write two sentences about each gift.

Example: My neighbors' gift from me would be a pet alligator.
My neighbors' alligator could be walked on a leash.

Lesson 5 Objective Case

Direct Object

> **A noun used as the direct object of a verb is in the objective case.**

The championship team met the *governor*.
The school bought several *computers*.

The direct object of a verb may be determined by placing *whom* or *what* after the verb. The team met *whom*? The team met the *governor*. The school bought *what*? The school bought *computers*. The nouns *governor* and *computers* are, therefore, direct objects.

A noun used as a direct object is in the objective case.

Exercise 1

Find the direct object in each sentence.
1. In the parade, Theresa twirled a baton.
2. At the Chinese restaurant, we ate spicy soup.
3. Whitcomb Judson invented the zipper in 1893.
4. Kerry has moved the parsley from the windowsill.
5. I carry Mr. O'Connor's groceries upstairs to his room.
6. The Pueblos built their homes on the sides of cliffs.
7. Sergei slowly turned his flashlight toward the noise.
8. Did you see the double rainbow this morning?
9. A large dog patiently guarded the door.
10. Becky will weave these long strips into a basket.
11. A construction worker pushed an enormous wheelbarrow.
12. The male emperor penguin holds the female's egg on his feet!
13. Paul Revere once made a tiny collar out of silver for a customer's pet squirrel.
14. Lady Knotsworth sets a place at the table for the hound!
15. Columbus made four voyages to the Americas.

Exercise 2

Copy each sentence. Underline the verb and add a direct object.

1. Divers gather unusual _____ from the ocean floor.
2. Mr. Soon's art class made _____ for Fire Safety Week.
3. Kyle baked a(n) _____ for the first time.
4. The crowd anxiously watched the _____ in the darkening sky.
5. Nora lost her favorite _____ on her way to school.
6. Our class might visit a(n) _____ tomorrow.
7. A group of motorboats carry _____ to the island every month.
8. Earl read a(n) _____ to his blind friend.
9. I covered the _____ with a large, colorful quilt.
10. Evita wrote a(n) _____ about the dangers of smoking.
11. Roger dropped the squirming _____ into a huge bucket of water.
12. Sometimes you can find a(n) _____ in your own backyard.
13. Beth mails _____ to her pen pal in Denmark.
14. I cut the _____ in half with the rusty scissors.
15. Cary made a(n) _____ out of paper.

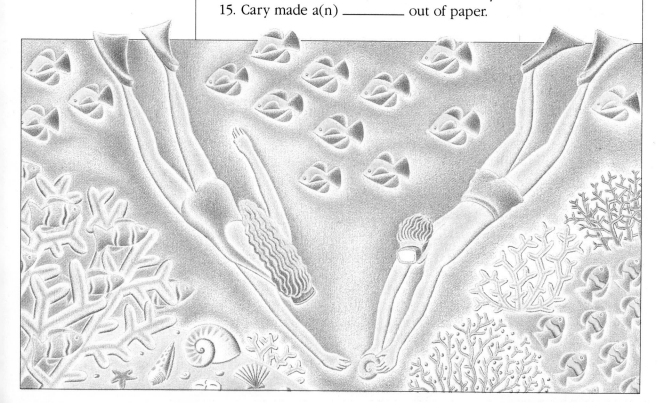

Object of a Preposition

> **A noun used as the object of a preposition is in the objective case.**

Dr. Santilli lives and works in *Detroit*.
On *Thursday*, there will be a lunar eclipse.
During the *night*, rain washed away the snow.

In the first sentence, the noun *Detroit* is the object of the preposition *in*. In the second sentence, the noun *Thursday* is the object of the preposition *on*. In the third sentence, the noun *night* is the object of the preposition *during*. The nouns *Detroit*, *Thursday*, and *night* are in the objective case.

A noun used as the object of a preposition is in the objective case.

Exercise 3

Find the nouns that are objects of prepositions and name the prepositions.
1. The first Olympic Games were held in Greece.
2. The Venus's-flytrap catches insects in its spiked leaves.
3. We found the baseball mitt underneath the porch.
4. We watched the rat escape into the junkyard.
5. John's kite bobbed above our heads.
6. A clay flowerpot crashed on the sidewalk.
7. The longest day of the year is in June.
8. We get oxygen from the air.
9. Prairie dogs often dig tunnels ten feet under the surface of the ground.
10. The division problems on the blackboard had mysteriously disappeared.
11. Rodney's face lighted with surprise.
12. Wes called to the engineer of the locomotive.
13. Janet Guthrie drove in the Indianapolis 500.
14. Dazzling fireworks exploded over the lake.
15. Along the coastline, citizens prepared for Hurricane Kate.

Exercise 4

Complete each sentence with a preposition followed by an object.

1. Mrs. Wright took a trip _____.
2. _____, Sadie received a present.
3. Have you ever seen a collection _____?
4. The Arabian colts were _____.
5. Lennie found a large snake _____.
6. Some pigeons wobbled _____.
7. Most first-graders like books _____.
8. Not looking, Miguel ran _____.
9. Nonnie sang an Irish song _____.
10. _____, a herd of antelopes grazed.

Write sentences using each of the following.

11. over the rainbow
12. beside the flamingos
13. between the buildings
14. onto a horse
15. up the stairs

Indirect Object

> **A noun used as the indirect object of a verb is in the objective case.**

Some sentences contain two objects—the direct object or receiver of the action and another object that tells *to whom* or *for whom* the action is done. The object to whom or for whom something is done is called the *indirect object*.

> The librarian gave an *award*. (*Direct object*)
> The librarian gave *Amos* an award. (*Indirect object*)

The direct object of the verb *gave* is *award*. *Amos*, the indirect object, tells *to whom* the award was given.

The indirect object is ordinarily placed between the verb and the direct object. The preposition *to* or *for* can usually be placed before the indirect object without changing the meaning of the sentence.

> The librarian gave (to) Amos an award.

The following verbs may take indirect objects: *assign, bring, buy, deny, do, forbid, forgive, get, give, grant, hand, lend, offer, owe, pardon, pay, promise, read, refuse, remit, sell, send, show, sing, teach, tell, wish, write.*

Exercise 5

The direct objects in these sentences are italicized. Find the indirect objects. Put the word *to* or *for* in front of the indirect object to check your answer.

Example: Edna offered (to) her friend a *popsicle*.
　　　　　Indirect object: friend

1. Leon sends my sister handmade *cards*.
2. The peasant woman sells tourists llama-hair *blankets*.
3. Frances wrote her father *directions* to the camp.
4. Mr. Key assigned the French class a three-page *report*.
5. I still owe my sister a *dollar* for Mother's present.
6. The mail carrier handed the clerk a large, oddly shaped *package*.
7. Show Maggie your new *calculator*.
8. You should give Jean some *advice* on the care of canaries.
9. Early bikes gave their riders a bumpy *trip*.
10. Ellen, tell the students the *story* of your kayak trip on the Haw River.
11. Mason handed the teacher the extra *copies* of the test.
12. Sandra gave her mother a microwave *cookbook*.
13. I'll read the class a *haiku* about snowflakes.
14. Jason lent his brother his *skates*.
15. Our father denied Marty *permission* to swim.

Exercise 6

Copy each sentence. Add an indirect object and underline the direct object.

1. Andrew writes _____ letters in code.
2. Give _____ the grasshopper before it escapes!
3. Donnie will buy _____ a newspaper at the corner.
4. A seismologist gave _____ an explanation of the Richter scale.
5. Who taught _____ that card trick?
6. Dorothy sent _____ an invitation to her birthday party.
7. Ms. McIver tells _____ unbelievable stories about the Loch Ness Monster!
8. I am happy to lend _____ my telescope.
9. First, read _____ the directions on the box.
10. In 1985, one Girl Scout sold _____ eleven thousand boxes of cookies!

Appositive in the Objective Case

> A noun in apposition is in the same case as the noun it explains.

We cannot see oxygen, a colorless *gas*.
The players have confidence in Maria Ciardi, their *center*.

When you studied the nominative case you learned that an appositive explains a noun. The appositive is in the same case as the noun that it explains.

Appositives that explain nouns in the objective case are in the objective case. In the examples above, *gas* explains *oxygen*, the direct object. Therefore, *gas* is in the objective case. *Center* explains Maria Ciardi, the object of a preposition. Therefore, *center* is in the objective case.

An appositive is usually set off by commas.

Exercise 7

The appositives in these sentences are italicized. Name the word that each appositive explains. Give the case of the appositive and the reason it is in that case.

1. The adventurers crossed the Sahara, the largest *desert* in the world, in vehicles powered by the wind.
2. Bonnie did the Highland Fling, a lively Scottish *dance.*
3. The boy jumped onto the junk, a small wooden *sailboat.*
4. The visitors fed the noisy ducks, brightly colored *mallards.*
5. The stethoscope was invented in 1819 by René Laënnec, a French *doctor.*
6. A warm summer breeze drifted into the cottage, the families' vacation *house.*
7. The scientist spoke to Eliza, a talking *robot.*
8. I just met my new boxing coach, *Glenn Reilly.*
9. Yesterday we put our pottery bowls into the kiln, a special *oven.*
10. Miss Barrett eagerly opened the box, a *gift* from her sister in England.
11. A local lawyer saved Old Baldy, a hundred-year-old *lighthouse.*
12. We often buy flowers from Mr. Golgi, the street *vendor.*
13. King Arthur valued Excalibur, his magical *sword.*
14. A herd of deer appears every winter on Mr. Fenton's property, a Christmas tree *farm* near the state line.
15. Lynn played the part of Billie, the mysterious *stranger.*

Exploring the Poem...

Have you ever seen a peacock? A peacock's tail has a very interesting and colorful design. Do you know what unusual marks appear on its tail?

In this poem, what do you think the peacock's "fantasy of color" means? What is its "rainbow fan"? Do you get a clear picture of the peacock's tail from these images? Where on the peacock can you find "feathered eyes"?

This kind of poem is called a *cinquain* (pronounced "sĭng kān´"). *Cinquain* comes from the French word *cinq*, which means "five." The poem has five lines.

A pattern is a specific form to follow. It is a model that you can use to make another just like it. For example, look at each line of this poem. Count the number of words in each line and discover the pattern. You can see that the first line has five words, the second line has four words, the third line has three words, and so on. The pattern is 5-4-3-2-1. The five lines make up one complete sentence.

A cinquain contains just one idea. Think of some ideas for your own cinquain. You will want to be specific because you only have *one* sentence to describe your subject. Instead of "sports" you will want to think of just one sport. Try writing a colorful, descriptive sentence about your idea. Then work with the words. Put them into cinquain form. Add or take out words until your poem fits the pattern.

Practice putting this sentence into a cinquain before you write your own.

A roller coaster ride takes you up and down over hills and valleys until your stomach drops!

Chapter 2

Pronouns

Brown Fat and the Magic Potion

by Margery Facklam

from *Do Not Disturb: The Mysteries of Animal Hibernation and Sleep*

When Charles Blagden was a scientist at the Royal Society of London about two hundred years ago, he asked two friends to help him with an experiment. Dr. Blagden took the two men, a dog, and a raw steak into a comfortable 70-degree room, which was gradually heated to 260 degrees Fahrenheit.

Forty-five minutes later, when they dragged themselves out of that hot room, neither the men nor the dog felt very good. All were thirsty and exhausted. The men were dripping with sweat and the dog was panting hard. The steak, however, was cooked.

It was a dangerous experiment, but it did show that living mammals adjust to temperature changes with some kind of built-in system. This inner system works like a thermostat, the gadget that senses when room temperature changes and switches a furnace or air conditioner on or off. The living thermostat is centered in a part of the brain called the **hypothalamus** (*hi-po-thal-a-mus*). It also controls, along with temperature, hunger, thirst, and blood pressure. And it is the hypothalamus that controls hibernation and sleep.

Hibernation is a way for animals to save energy and survive through the winter when food is hard to find. (*Hiberna* is a Latin word that means "winter.") **Estivation** is a way for animals to survive the long, hot, dry spells of summer. (The Latin word *aestivare* means "to reside through the summer.") Some animals do both. The Columbian ground squirrel disappears into its

Grizzly bear by Michio Hoshino

underground burrow late in July and sometimes isn't seen again until March. It estivates and hibernates for two hundred days.

There are different levels of hibernation. The animals known as the "real" hibernators sleep so deeply that they are almost impossible to wake up. When they become **dormant,** their body temperature drops to near freezing. But even so, every few weeks the woodchucks, ground squirrels, and other "real" hibernators get up to nibble on food and use their underground toilet rooms.

Bears are the largest animals to hibernate. Unlike the "real" hibernators, they can be awakened easily. One scientist, who went into a den to see a dormant black bear, found out just how easily. The bear growled and started toward him. "I just punched that bear in the nose," said the scientist, "and I got out fast." A hibernating bear can wake up fast because it has only to move around a bit to warm its body up a few degrees to normal.

The in-between hibernators really take only long winter naps. Skunks, raccoons, and a few others lower their body temperature a couple of degrees and breathe more slowly, but they wake up to forage for food between winter storms.

And then there are the "daily dormants," those tiny animals such as hummingbirds and pygmy mice who can survive only if they turn down their thermostats into a kind of mini-hibernation every day.

In one experiment to find out how hibernation works, a biologist took a small amount of blood from hibernating ground squirrels. He froze the blood. In spring, he defrosted it and injected it into a different group of ground squirrels who had been running around full of energy. Not long after, the energetic ground squirrels curled up and began to hibernate.

Scientists have found in the blood of hibernating animals a substance they call HIT, which stands for Hibernation Inducement Trigger. Although they do not know exactly what this "magic potion" is, they have learned that this trigger goes into action when one of three things happens: when the days become shorter and there is less light; when there are big changes in temperature (either extreme cold or heat); or when food is scarce.

In order to survive weeks or months without food, most hibernating animals go on an eating binge in late summer and

early fall. The fat they build up supplies energy and keeps them warm while they sleep. But along with this regular white fat, hibernating mammals have patches of special brown fat across their shoulders and back. The brown fat works like a fast-food restaurant. It delivers quick energy whenever it is needed.

A hibernating animal must warm up before it can wake up, and its brain has to warm up first in order to send messages to the rest of the body to get moving. In its handy location across the shoulders and back, the patches of brown fat are close to the hibernating animal's brain, heart, and lungs. These important organs, like the engine of a car, must get the first spurt of fuel, which is delivered by the blood vessels in the brown fat.

When a dormant ground squirrel wakes up, its head and front legs move first. Its hind legs are still "asleep" and numb because they may be fifteen degrees colder than the head and front legs warmed by the brown fat.

During hibernation warm-blooded animals turn down their thermostats until they become almost cold-blooded, and cold-blooded animals get so cold that they are barely alive. Hibernation is an amazing way for some animals to survive.

Illustration by Pamela Johnson
from *Do Not Disturb*

The Writer's Craft

1. What information did you find new or interesting in this excerpt?
2. Scientist Charles Blagden described the hypothalamus as a "living thermostat." Recall the purpose of a thermostat. Why do you think Blagden made this comparison?
3. Margery Facklam explained the hibernating animal's waking process. Have you ever experienced anything like it?
4. Reread the first two paragraphs to see how the author used pronouns to avoid the constant repetition of some nouns. What pronouns did she use for *Charles Blagden* and *Blagden, men,* and *dog*?

Illustration by Pamela Johnson
from *Do Not Disturb*

Lesson 1   Personal Pronouns

A pronoun takes the place of a noun.

Read the following paragraph.

> [1]Bears are the largest animals to hibernate. [2]Unlike the "real" hibernators, bears awaken easily. [3]One scientist, who went into a den to see a dormant black bear, found out just how easily. [4]The bear growled and started toward the scientist. [5]"I just punched that bear in the nose," said the scientist, "and I got out fast." [6]A hibernating bear can wake up fast because a bear has only to move around a bit to warm its body up to normal.

The nouns *bear* and *bears* are used seven times in the above paragraph. The noun *scientist* is used three times. Now read this paragraph to see how Margery Facklam made use of *pronouns*.

> [1]Bears are the largest animals to hibernate. [2]Unlike the "real" hibernators, they awaken easily. [3]One scientist, who went into a den to see a dormant black bear, found out just how easily. [4]The bear growled and started toward him. [5]"I just punched that bear in the nose," said the scientist, "and I got out fast." [6]A hibernating bear can wake up fast because it has only to move around a bit to warm its body up to normal.

In this paragraph pronouns replace many of the nouns. The pronouns *they* and *it* take the place of the nouns *bears* and *bear*. *Him* replaces *scientist*.

The word to which a pronoun refers is its *antecedent*.

Margery Facklam wrote the book but did not illustrate *it*.

In the sentence above, the antecedent of *it* is the noun *book*.

Since pronouns take the place of nouns, they have the same qualities as nouns: gender, number, and case. You will study more about the qualities of pronouns in this chapter.

Person

> **A personal pronoun shows by its form**
> **the speaker (first person)**
> **the person spoken to (second person)**
> **and the person or thing spoken about (third person)**

I saw a woodchuck gathering nuts.
Pam said *you* knew about brown fat.
They were very thirsty.

Pronouns that indicate the speaker are not the same as pronouns that indicate the person spoken to or the person spoken about. Since the forms of pronouns change in this way, personal pronouns are said to show *person*.

The personal pronouns of the first person (speaker) are *I, me, we, us.*

The personal pronoun of the second person (person spoken to) is *you*.

The personal pronouns of the third person (person or thing spoken about) are *he, she, it, him, her, they, them.*

Exercise 1

Find the personal pronouns in these sentences. Give the person of each: *first, second,* or *third.*

1. During hibernation they look dead but wake up for food.
2. Did you know that they have storerooms underground?
3. Ground squirrels also have them.
4. Yesterday I saw a chipmunk carrying food to its burrow.
5. Can you show me where it went?
6. In winter you rarely see a northern chipmunk.
7. Do we know of any other hibernators that live in this area?
8. Raccoons hibernate too, but they awaken to get warm.
9. Look! The mother raccoon has three babies with her.
10. He told me that animals dream.

Complete each sentence with personal pronouns. Give the person of each.

11. Have _____ read any other books by Margery Facklam?
12. Yes, _____ have read *Frozen Snakes and Dinosaur Bones.*
13. _____ worked at the Buffalo Museum of Science.
14. _____ also worked at the Aquarium of Niagara Falls.
15. Did _____ know that clown fish wear pajamas?

Number

> A singular pronoun takes the place of a singular noun.
>
> A plural pronoun takes the place of a plural noun.

The singular personal pronouns are *I, me, you, he, she, it, him, her.* These pronouns refer to one person or thing.

The plural personal pronouns are *we, us, you, they, them.* These pronouns refer to more than one person or thing.

Exercise 2

Find the personal pronouns in these sentences and tell whether each is *singular* or *plural.*

1. Don't blame me if the power goes off!
2. He sent us a burlap bag full of oysters.
3. They yelled at him from across the crowded sidewalk.
4. The race began when he set off the cannon.
5. We will hang bunches of mistletoe from the rafters.
6. She fell asleep in the grass as bagpipes droned in the distance.
7. They strung together the turquoise beads for her.
8. Maria, you have been chosen by them to head the cleanup committee.
9. I plan to take it to obedience school.
10. They left a message on the electronic bulletin board for us.

Gender

A pronoun that refers to males is masculine gender.

A pronoun that refers to females is feminine gender.

A pronoun that refers to an object is neuter gender.

Only pronouns in the third person singular change form to show gender. The masculine pronouns are *he* and *him*. The feminine pronouns are *she* and *her*. The neuter pronoun is *it*. In the plural, the pronouns *they* and *them* are used for all three genders.

Exercise 3

Give a pronoun that will take the place of each of the following nouns. For some nouns, more than one pronoun can replace the noun.

Rick	brothers	travelers
campfire	Maggie	gossip
carpenter	stereo	mother
aunt	men	necklace
arcade	nephew	joke
hairbrushes	pasta	keyboard
refrigerator	giraffe	actor
pilots	apartment	clerk
screams	newspaper	clown

Compound Personal Pronouns

Compound personal pronouns end in *self* or *selves*.

Forms of the Compound Personal Pronouns

	SINGULAR	PLURAL
FIRST PERSON	myself	ourselves
SECOND PERSON	yourself	yourselves
THIRD PERSON	himself, herself, itself	themselves

Andrea *herself* met us at the airport.
Muhammad Ali called *himself* "The Greatest."
Cats groom *themselves* diligently.

Exercise 4

Find the compound personal pronouns in these sentences.

1. You should give yourselves extra time for this math quiz.
2. We made the antismoking posters ourselves.
3. Freddie will have to do the dishes by himself.
4. Mickey Mouse himself greeted us at Disney World.
5. Sally wrote the award-winning play herself.
6. Did you hurt yourself in the sledding accident?
7. I myself will play the drum and trumpet at the same time.
8. Please relax and make yourselves comfortable.
9. The cat itself opened the cabinet door!
10. Sea urchins move themselves by using the spines on their bodies.

Complete each sentence with the correct compound personal pronoun.

11. Mr. Mackie _____ saw the Loch Ness monster.
12. The children _____ pulled the heavy crate up from the basement.
13. Couldn't you keep _____ from opening the present before your birthday?
14. Nancy _____ kept the fire burning through the night.
15. We decided to dig up the treasure _____.

Practice Power

Choose any ten nouns from exercise 3 in this lesson. Write sentences using both the noun and the pronoun in two related sentences.

Example: The *pasta* was difficult to eat. *It* kept wiggling off my fork.

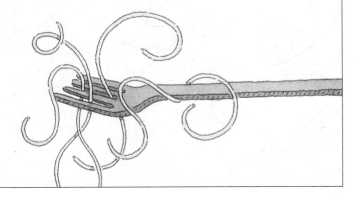

Lesson 2 The Case of Personal Pronouns

Nominative Case

Subject of a Verb

> A pronoun used as the subject of a verb must be in the nominative case.

Grace and (I, me) joined the spring cleanup committee.

Here is the correct form: Grace and *I* joined the spring cleanup committee.

The pronoun *I* is in the nominative case because it is the subject of the verb *joined* together with the noun *Grace*.

The nominative case personal pronouns are

	SINGULAR	PLURAL
FIRST PERSON	I	we
SECOND PERSON	you	you
THIRD PERSON	he, she, it	they

252

Exercise 1

Choose the correct form of the personal pronoun for each sentence.

1. The McLeans and (we, us) went white-water rafting on the Snake River.
2. Justin and (me, I) tried on the worker's hard hat.
3. Chip and (he, him) are watching the sailboat race.
4. Tommy and (her, she) climbed up on the Indian elephant.
5. The boys and (us, we) tried panning for gold.
6. (They, Them) will try to ride their bikes up the high hill.
7. My sister and (I, me) are good friends.
8. Tyler and (him, he) learned to play square ball.
9. Lauren and (she, her) pitched a tent in our backyard.
10. Did (them, they) catch the bus to the mall?

Complete each sentence with the correct form of a personal pronoun. Be sure to vary your choice of pronouns.

11. Marian and _____ will be here early.
12. You and _____ need to cut Mr. Collie's grass.
13. Did Elizabeth and _____ go to the table tennis match?
14. He and _____ will feed the puppies for you.
15. Jean and _____ want to see your four-foot-tall cactus.
16. The twins and _____ washed Ms. Kelso's Saint Bernard.
17. Carl and _____ raced home today.
18. Tonya and _____ will wait until two o'clock.
19. Will Julio and _____ watch the television special tonight?
20. Myron and _____ bought a program at the circus.

Subjective Complement

> **A pronoun used as a subjective complement is in the nominative case.**

The acrobat on top of the pyramid is (she, her).

Here is the correct form: The acrobat on top of the pyramid is *she*.

She is in the nominative case because it is the subjective complement. *She* follows the linking verb *is* and refers to the same person as the subject, *acrobat*.

Exercise 2

Choose the correct form of the personal pronoun for each sentence. Notice that the subject and the subjective complement can often be switched.

Example: The winner was *he*.
        He was the winner.

1. The farmhand who swept the barn floor was (she, her).
2. That is (him, he) without the sunglasses.
3. Is that (he, him) at the kitchen door?
4. The slow car washers were (they, them).
5. Was it (her, she) on the phone?
6. The first ones to get tickets were (us, we)!
7. The person in the lion mask is (she, her).
8. The champion skaters were (they, them).
9. Was it (him, he) in the cab?
10. Those boys on the baseball field are (they, them).

Complete each sentence with the correct form of a personal pronoun. Be sure to vary your choice of pronouns.

11. The man in the sweat suit must be _____.
12. Was that _____ in the wrinkled photograph?
13. The most impressive hula dancers were _____.
14. Which one of you made this mess? It was _____!
15. That was _____ with the stack of books.

Exercise 3

Choose the correct form of the personal pronoun for each sentence. Tell whether the personal pronoun is the *subject* or the *subjective complement*.

1. My friend and (me, I) built a robot for our science project.
2. Aren't those pilots on the runway (they, them)?
3. Ennis and (him, he) bought a long-haired guinea pig.
4. Is that (she, her) in front of the fire station?
5. Margie and (me, I) made the whole wheat bread.
6. That was (we, us) on the news last night.
7. Was it (he, him)? No, it was (me, I)!
8. Either Fay or (I, me) will rinse the alfalfa sprouts.
9. Has (her, she) sent her story to the newspaper?
10. (Them, They) gave us the wrong directions to the miniature golf course.
11. Eddie and (he, him) created a comic book.
12. It is (him, he) banging at the door.
13. This is (her, she) speaking.
14. That is (they, them) on the Ferris wheel.
15. Helen and (him, he) will grill hamburgers tonight.

Objective Case

Object of a Verb

A pronoun used as the direct object of a verb is in the objective case.

Dorothy invited (I, me) to the rock concert.

Here is the correct form: Dorothy invited *me* to the rock concert.

Me is the direct object of the verb *invited*.

The objective case pronouns are

	SINGULAR	PLURAL
FIRST PERSON	me	us
SECOND PERSON	you	you
THIRD PERSON	him, her, it	them

Exercise 4

Choose the correct form of the personal pronoun for each sentence.

1. Maxie will have to call (he, him) about our lunch order.
2. They sent Armand and (me, I) to the citywide math contest.
3. The white laboratory mice fear (them, they).
4. I know (she, her) from somewhere, I'm sure!
5. A carpenter helped (we, us) with the doghouse blueprints.
6. Jenna admires Pat and (him, he) for their knowledge of antique toys.
7. The smell of smoke in the room alarmed (we, us)!
8. Did the talent scout choose (her, she)?
9. Flora blamed Meryl and (I, me) for that mix-up!
10. Jonathan wants (they, them) on his soccer team.

Complete each sentence with the correct form of a personal pronoun. Be sure to vary your choice of pronouns.

11. The class election results surprised the principal and

_____.

12. Did the snake handler impress _____?
13. Of all of the science fiction writers, I like _____ best.
14. The baby lions amused Ramona and _____ with their attempts at ferociousness.
15. The roller coaster car slowly carried Sally and _____ to the top.

Object of a Preposition

> **A pronoun used as the object of a preposition is in the objective case.**

Directions for feeding the hamsters came with (they, them).

Here is the correct form: Directions for feeding the hamsters came with *them*.

The pronoun *them* is the object of the preposition *with*.

Exercise 5

Choose the correct form of the personal pronoun for each sentence.
1. Can she show the shortcut to (we, us)?
2. That is a secret between my mom and (I, me).
3. Did you leave the leftovers in the microwave for (they, them)?
4. The new pitcher threw a fast ball to (she, her).
5. On the stairs, I could hear heavy footsteps above (me, I).
6. A slow-footed donkey trailed behind Frank and (him, he).
7. Is this bunch of mail from Alicia and (her, she)?
8. The house was painted last summer by (they, them).
9. I hope the skywriter will speak to Ted and (we, us).
10. Please save the leftover plum pudding for Marsha and (I, me).

Complete each sentence with the correct form of a personal pronoun. Be sure to vary your choice of pronouns.
11. The restless crocodile gnashed its teeth at _____.
12. Cheryl offered to toast pumpkin seeds for Brigid and _____.
13. The ice-cream vendor stopped near _____.
14. The hall monitor grabbed the jump rope from Curtis and _____.
15. We'll learn to play the lute with _____.

Exercise 6

Choose the correct form of the personal pronoun for each sentence. Tell whether the personal pronoun is the *direct object* or the *object of a preposition*.

1. The librarian asked the children to sit beside (she, her).
2. Dominique rolled the baby carriage toward (them, they).
3. Tony's grandfather will help (I, me) with repairing the rocking chair.
4. Won't you take (we, us) to the horror movie?
5. That cornhusk doll was made by (him, he).
6. Coach Simmons hurled the basketball down the court to (she, her).
7. Did you see Roland and (they, them) up on the roof?
8. Kyle practiced his bird calls for (us, we).
9. We found (they, them) in the garden beside the scarecrow.
10. Don't touch that diary! It belongs to (me, I)!

Complete each sentence with the correct form of a personal pronoun. Be sure to vary your choice of pronouns. Tell whether the pronoun is the *direct object* or the *object of a preposition*.

11. Emilie brought _____ to Mr. Fred's Fudge Factory.
12. Joan knit a heavy sweater for _____ last winter.
13. I quilted a simple pattern on the pillow top for _____.
14. Mom sent _____ to the store for cayenne pepper.
15. A tall man sat in front of _____ just as the movie began.

Exercise 7 Review

Find the word to which each italicized pronoun refers (antecedent). Then give the case of the pronoun.

1. Rhoda's favorite books have many illustrations in *them*.
2. The ballerina who lost a shoe was *she*.
3. Did Jason take all twenty pints of blueberries with *him*?
4. Buddie, how did *you* fix the bicycle gears?
5. The owner of this unusual drawing is *he*.
6. The boys dragged the bag of newspapers behind *them*.
7. Tessie unfolded the map and studied *it*.
8. The two sisters playing marbles are *they*.
9. Ruby's canary landed on top of *her*.
10. The fish with white spots is *it*.

Exercise 8   Review

Find the personal pronoun in each sentence. Then give the case of each pronoun and tell how it is used: *subject*, *subjective complement*, *direct object*, or *object of a preposition*.

1. He ate every chocolate chip in the cookie dough.
2. They read the newspaper from front page to back.
3. That child without a scarf is she.
4. The blue envelope was addressed to her.
5. We deserve the tug-of-war prize!
6. The lion tamer warned them to stay away from the animals.
7. Marilyn did not recognize him in a coat and tie.
8. The Frisbee spun straight toward me!
9. I looked around the firelit igloo.
10. Paula rowed the boat through the marsh for us.

Exercise 9   Review

Choose the correct form of the personal pronoun to complete each of these sentences. Give the reason for your choice.

1. Fanny and (her, she) are paper carriers.
2. The pilot spoke to Karen and (him, he).
3. The tent will shelter my brother and (I, me).
4. Allan and (I, me) offered to work backstage for the play.
5. Ted and (she, her) will work together to solve the clues for the crossword puzzle.
6. I bought the book on genealogy for (they, them).
7. Richard and (they, them) forgot their gym clothes.
8. Alice and (he, him) saw a bear across the lake.
9. The woman asked (us, we) about the way to the beach.
10. The person flipping the pancakes was (she, her).

Complete each sentence with the correct form of a personal pronoun. Be sure to vary your choice of pronouns.

11. Una and _____ spent two hours watching the workers put up the building.
12. The acrobats' stunts really amazed _____.
13. Was it _____ who left the burned popcorn in the sink?
14. Ryan and _____ are about to leave for the game.
15. Grace, give the paintbrush to _____.

Practice Power

Complete each sentence with a personal pronoun. The person, number, and gender to use for each pronoun are given in parentheses. Be sure to use the correct case.

Example: Greta blew the balloon so much that __it__ burst. (*third, singular, neuter*)

1. Where are ____?
   (*third, plural, masculine/feminine*)
2. The librarian told ____ about the new riddle books.
   (*first, plural, masculine/feminine*)
3. ____ was large, dark, and loud.
   (*third, singular, neuter*)
4. ____ saw lovebirds in the open-air market.
   (*third, singular, masculine*)
5. Garrison brought a copy of the contest rules for ____.
   (*third, singular, feminine*)
6. ____ explained that the koala is really not a bear.
   (*third, plural, masculine/feminine*)
7. ____ baked a batch of soft pretzels for the yard sale.
   (*first, singular, masculine/feminine*)
8. The robot mouse rolled into ____.
   (*third, singular, masculine*)
9. The baby-sitter called ____ about ten o'clock.
   (*third, plural, masculine/feminine*)
10. ____ plans to grow petunias in the window box.
    (*third, singular, feminine*)

Lesson 3 Possessive Pronouns and Contractions

Possessive Pronouns

> Possessive pronouns are used to show *possession* or *ownership* by the speaker, the person spoken to, or the person or thing spoken about.

The yellow tennis balls are *mine*, and the white ones are *yours*.

The possessive pronouns are

	SINGULAR	PLURAL
FIRST PERSON	mine	ours
SECOND PERSON	yours	yours
THIRD PERSON	his, hers, its	theirs

Exercise 1

Find the possessive pronouns in these sentences.
1. Stephen found an aardvark. Has Michiko lost hers?
2. I put mine in the closet last week.
3. His is playing the piano.
4. We got ours from a traveling circus.
5. Yours is hiding underneath the bed.
6. I just saw theirs in the refrigerator.
7. Hers just called on the phone.
8. This one can't be mine!
9. David has his on a leash.
10. Those must be its!
11. Mine will not eat split pea soup.
12. The Rutherfords took theirs to Alaska.
13. The one climbing out of the washer must be yours.
14. Hers is purple with orange stripes.
15. Ours was wearing Joannie's new backpack.

Exercise 2

Complete each sentence with an appropriate possessive pronoun. Be sure to vary your choice of pronouns.

1. This is _____, but not _____.
2. The flying saucer is _____.
3. _____ has already been to outer space.
4. Keep a lookout for _____.
5. All this strange equipment must be _____.
6. If _____ is fixed, then please fix _____.
7. Collect _____ and store the rest in the barn.
8. Let's make a new one and pretend it's _____.
9. It has to be better than _____.
10. Everyone will be impressed by _____.

Contractions Containing Pronouns

> The personal pronouns are used with verbs to form contractions. The apostrophe (') is used to show where a letter or letters have been left out.

Study the spelling and meaning of these contractions.

CONTRACTION	MEANING	CONTRACTION	MEANING
I'll	I will	it's	it is
they're	they are	they'll	they will
I've	I have	they've	they have
we're	we are	you'll	you will
I'm	I am	he'll	he will
you're	you are	she'll	she will

Exercise 3

Find the contraction in each sentence and tell what pronoun and verb have been used to form it.

1. I'll stir this bubbling pot of spaghetti sauce.
2. You're going to walk into a huge sticky spider web!
3. It's time for the leaves to start changing colors.
4. Boyd said that he'll finish the soap carving tomorrow.
5. We're learning origami, Japanese paper folding.
6. They'll be happier if they can run through the sprinkler.
7. I'm looking for a suspenseful mystery story.
8. You'll be late if you watch one more television program.
9. Edna, you're holding the marshmallows too close to the fire!
10. They're on their way to a surprise party.

Exercise 4

Complete each sentence with an appropriate contraction.

1. _____ planning a trip to Timbuktu!
2. Did you know that _____ be in a three-legged bag race?
3. _____ try to answer your questions.
4. The builders report that _____ found a hole in the roof.
5. _____ already put two coats of paint on the motorcycle.
6. I believe that _____ the first person to discover this.
7. _____ going to be guests of the governor!
8. _____ happy to see the crocuses bloom.
9. The weather reporter promised that _____ not going to rain.
10. Carron Haddad hopes that _____ buy a subscription to the newspaper.

264

Correct Use of Possessives and Contractions

Possessives are often confused with contractions because they sound alike. Possessives express ownership or possession. They *do not use* apostrophes.

Its leg is hurt. (*Possessive*)

A contraction is one word made from two words. The apostrophe is used in a contraction to show where a letter or letters have been left out.

It's time for school. (*Contraction*—It is)

Study these possessives and contractions and learn the difference between them.

POSSESSIVES	CONTRACTIONS
its collar	it's (it is) sleeping
your friend	you're (you are) late
their house	they're (they are) not here

Exercise 5

Tell whether each italicized word is a *possessive* or a *contraction*.
1. *Their* basketballs are in the equipment room.
2. *It's* the biggest bullfrog that is the loudest croaker!
3. A sunflower will turn *its* head to follow the sun.
4. What would you trade for *your* latest baseball card?
5. Children used to do *their* handwriting with quill pens.
6. Helena, *you're* not going to believe this!
7. *Your* sister is digging earthworms for her fishing trip.
8. *They're* going to learn a new song in music class today.
9. *It's* a huge bowl of steaming chili.
10. André says that *it's* too stormy to fly a kite.

Exercise 6

Choose the correct word for each sentence.
1. (You're, Your) painting must be dry before you frame it.
2. Pandas try to limit (their, they're) diet to bamboo shoots.
3. (You're, Your) wearing my new sneakers again.
4. (They're, Their) ready to start the backgammon game.
5. An oil-covered bird cannot clean (its, it's) own feathers.
6. (You're, Your) next in line, Elijah.
7. Some people believe they can remove (they're, their) freckles with lemon juice.
8. (Its, It's) a good time to try that new brownie recipe.
9. The men left (their, they're) work boots at the front door.
10. How is (you're, your) headache?
11. (They're, Their) the biggest apples I've ever seen!
12. Large acorns fell from (it's, its) gnarled branches.
13. I would like to know if (your, you're) finished with the Monopoly game.
14. The turtles climbed out of (their, they're) box.
15. We heard that (its, it's) going to snow all day!

Practice Power

You and your friend(s) are dressed alike for Halloween, but there are some differences in your costumes and makeup. Write five sentences comparing *theirs* (*his* or *hers*) with *yours*. Make sure you use possessive pronouns.

Lesson 4 Interrogative Pronouns

An interrogative pronoun is used in asking a question.

The interrogative pronouns are *who, whom, which, what,* and *whose.* Study the following examples.

Who is used in speaking of persons.

> *Who* opened the door?

Who is the subject of *opened.*

Whom is used in speaking of persons.

> *Whom* did they elect?

Whom is the direct object of *elect.*

Which is used in speaking of persons or things.

> *Which* is your favorite writer?
> *Which* of the ingredients did you forget?

In the first sentence, *which* is the subject of *is.* In the second sentence, *which* is the object of *did forget.*

What is used in speaking of things and in asking for information.

> *What* will you do?

What is the object of *will do.*

Whose is used in speaking of persons.

> *Whose* is the pink-striped umbrella?

Whose shows possession.

Exercise 1

Find the interrogative pronouns in these sentences. Tell whether they refer to persons or to things.

1. Which of the Wright brothers was the older?
2. What does a yak eat?
3. For whom was the Taj Mahal built?
4. Which would you choose to put in a time capsule—a photograph or a diary?
5. Who brought an early version of the hamburger to America?
6. What would a podiatrist check?
7. Which of these writers created Frankenstein?
8. What should a first-aid kit contain?
9. Whose were the words "All the world's a stage"?
10. What does the Richter scale measure?

Exercise 2

Complete each sentence with an interrogative pronoun, *who, which,* or *what.* Use *who* for persons, *which* for persons or things, and *what* for things or general information.

1. _____ invented the safety match?
2. _____ is the duty of a forest ranger?
3. _____ of the deserts is largest?
4. _____ are the three primary colors?
5. _____ wrote *Alice in Wonderland*?
6. _____ was Duke Ellington's full name?
7. _____ of the mountains has the highest peak, Mount McKinley or Mount Everest?
8. _____ of the jewels is the most valuable?
9. _____ is Anne Frank?
10. For _____ is the Red Sea named?
11. _____ is a synonym for *zephyr*?
12. _____ did Jack Sprat not eat?
13. _____ of the Indian chiefs wrote an alphabet for his people?
14. _____ would you measure with a craniometer?
15. _____ is the name of our galaxy?

You Are the Author

Work with a partner or in a small group on ONE project.
1. Create cartoon ads for hibernation/estivation rental space.
2. Research the different levels of hibernation. Write a paragraph on each level and include examples of animals. Illustrate your report if you wish.

Chapter Challenge

Read this paragraph carefully and answer the questions.

¹Helen Keller was less than two years old when she was afflicted by a serious disease. ²It left her blind and deaf. ³For the next five years, she wasn't able to speak. ⁴She was a frightened and bewildered child who couldn't understand the strange silence around her. ⁵Helen's life began to change when Anne Sullivan, from the Perkins Institute for the Blind, became her teacher. ⁶Helen learned to understand the names of objects spelled into her hand. ⁷A whole new world opened up for her. ⁸She proved that every struggle could end in victory. ⁹Few have had to overcome the enormous obstacles she faced. ¹⁰Helen herself enjoyed a brilliant career helping the deaf and the blind.

1. Find the personal pronouns in sentences 1 and 2.
2. Give the case of each of the pronouns in sentences 1 and 2.
3. What is the antecedent of the pronoun *It* in sentence 2?
4. What pronoun is the subject of sentence 3?
5. How is the pronoun *She* in sentence 4 used?
6. In which case is the pronoun *her* in sentence 4? Why?
7. In which case is the pronoun in sentence 7? Why?
8. Name the person, number, and gender of the pronoun in sentence 8.
9. Name the compound personal pronoun in the paragraph.
10. Name the indefinite or distributive pronoun in the paragraph.

Helen Keller and Anne Sullivan

Creative Space 2

City

In the morning the city
Spreads its wings
Making a song
In stone that sings.

In the evening the city
Goes to bed
Hanging lights
About its head.

Langston Hughes

Exploring the Poem...

We usually think of a city as a big, busy place with many people, cars, and buildings. In this poem, the poet Langston Hughes has a fresh, new vision of the city.

The poet uses a metaphor to help you "see" the city differently. *A metaphor is a comparison of two unlike objects or things.*

In the first stanza, to what does the poet compare the city in the morning? (The word *wings* is a clue.) What are some city noises you might hear?

Name the sets of words that rhyme in the poem. How would you describe the way the poem rhymes (for example, each pair of lines, every other line)?

★ You can build a poem around a clear metaphor. First try to think of two things that are *unlike* in the way they look, but *alike* in what they do. Here are some ideas:

> The *airplane* was an *arrow* shooting across the sky...
> The *moon* is a floating *ship* in the night...
> The *ice* was a polished *mirror*...
> *Lucy*, a spinning *top*, twirled across the stage...

Now work with your own metaphor and write one stanza of a poem. You can add rhyme if you want to. Here are two example poems.

The moon floats	In winter the ice
Like a ship	Is a polished mirror
Across the dark sky	And the silver sound of skates
On its night trip.	Is all you can hear.

Chapter 3

Adjectives

A Style of Her Own

by Elisabeth P. Myers

from *Mary Cassatt: A Portrait*

She went first to Seville, in southwest Spain. It had been, she knew, the seat of a flourishing school of painting in the seventeenth century. Raimondi had told her that Murillo was especially well represented in the gallery there.

Mary had seen some of Murillo's religious paintings in the Paris **Louvre,** but she had never before seen his forceful pictures of humble street life. The minute she looked at them, she knew why Raimondi had been sure she would be enchanted. The little **urchins**—dirty, ragged, but still full of childish exuberance—seemed ready to dance right off the canvas. Here, surely, was proof of what she had come to believe firmly. Realism in pictures, as in life, was more to be admired than artificiality!

Mary loved Seville. She thought it even more colorful than Parma, and certainly more exciting. For one thing, it was the capital of bullfighting in Spain. At this season, that meant a weekly program of pageantry for the town. First, on the day of the bullfight, there would be the running of the black bulls through the streets to the arena. Then would come the stately march of the grandly dressed **toreadors.** The crowds would cheer, and *señoritas,* watching from balconies, would flirt with their fans. Some would throw flowers and candies.

Another thing that made Seville exciting for Mary was the colorful presence of the Andalusian gypsies. She never knew when she would come upon a group of them, dancing with a swirl of bright skirts and shaking tambourines.

Young Mother Sewing by Mary Cassatt

Mary longed to record everything she saw on paper or canvas. Since that was not possible, she had a hard time settling down to paint anything. Her first attempts were too ambitious. They included too much activity, too many people.

"Overdone, like burned toast," she said, looking at their muddy color, their heavy lines.

For inspiration, she went back to study Murillo's street scenes. They were successful, she decided on reflection, because they were uncomplicated. The eye did not have to jump around to "get the picture."

Holding fast to the ideal of simplicity, Mary painted a picture she titled *During Carnival*. It showed three people on a balcony: two girls throwing candies to an unseen person below; a handsome young man, partly shadowed, behind them.

"It's good," Mary whispered when it was finished. "The first really good thing I've done!"

She decided to pack it up and send it without delay to the Salon jury in Paris. Perhaps, if it was as good as she thought it was, the jury would accept it for the exhibit of 1872.

She was enough afraid that the picture would not be accepted, however, that she did not sign it with her full name. She used her middle name—Stevenson—with her given name instead. She had the odd feeling that it would not hurt quite so much if Mary Stevenson, not Mary Cassatt, were rejected.

When *During Carnival* was accepted, Mary regretted her timidity. She mourned because fellow artists, viewing entry No. 1433, would not know it was the work of their friend Mary Cassatt. She had done herself and them a disservice, for they would have rejoiced with her.

Annoyance with herself made Mary unfairly annoyed with Seville, as well. She felt nothing anymore, she said, even when she looked at the Murillos. It was therefore time to seek inspiration elsewhere.

Madrid was the "elsewhere" she chose. The Prado Museum there contained one of the outstanding art collections of the world.

At the Prado, Mary discovered the Flemish painter Peter Paul Rubens. His work excited her so greatly that she marveled that she had ever thought herself a disciple of Correggio.

She tried to analyze why she felt as she did about Rubens's paintings. They were full of color. They were flooded with light.

They were full of movement. The secret, though, it seemed, was that they were joyous.

"Rubens must have loved life so much," Mary decided, "that he had to express it on huge canvases."

Nothing would satisfy her but going where she could really study Rubens. That meant going to Belgium. Rubens had lived a good share of his life in Antwerp and had done his greatest work there.

During Carnival: On the Balcony
by Mary Cassatt

Mary settled down in Antwerp, and there in 1873 her mother came to visit her. Mrs. Cassatt obligingly sat for her portrait at this time. It shows certain Rubens influences in the way the flesh of her face is highlighted and in the expression of her eyes.

Much more important as examples of this period in Mary Cassatt's career are two bullfighter pictures. Both show the Rubens influence in the use of broad brush strokes, bright color, and light. One, showing a *señorita* offering a glass of some liquid to a ***torero***, was accepted for the Salon of 1873. Good as it was, the other—the bullfighter alone—is perhaps better. Mary herself thought so.

"The one could be any bullfighter," she said. "The other is one particular bullfighter—a recognizable character. That's the important difference."

The Writer's Craft

1. Elisabeth Myers explains that Cassatt admired realism in paintings. Look at a dozen or so examples of artwork in this book. Choose a piece of art or a photograph that appeals to you and tell why you like it.
2. In this excerpt we read about the beginning stage of Cassatt's career when she was trying to arrive at her own style. Her style was eclectic in that she selected and chose what she considered best from various artists. What do you think is the difference between copying from someone and being influenced by someone?
3. What adjectives does the author use in describing Murillo's work? Look at Cassatt's painting facing the opening page in this chapter. Use three adjectives to describe it.
4. Once Mary, dissatisfied with her paintings, called them "overdone" and compared them to "burned toast." The adjectives here convey an image. Find another passage in which adjectives create a clear mental picture.

Recalling What You Know

1. Rewrite *the child of France* to include a proper adjective.
2. A limiting adjective points out an object or indicates number. Use a limiting adjective in this sentence—*Mary's painting won _____ place.*
3. Possessive adjectives indicate ownership. Change the possessive adjective in this sentence—*My brushes are dirty*—to show ownership by (a) your brother (b) your class.

Lesson 1 Descriptive Adjectives

An adjective describes or limits a noun or a pronoun.

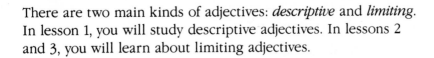

There are two main kinds of adjectives: *descriptive* and *limiting*. In lesson 1, you will study descriptive adjectives. In lessons 2 and 3, you will learn about limiting adjectives.

> **A descriptive adjective describes a noun or a pronoun.**

Read these sentences.

> The artist sketched the horse.
> The skillful artist sketched the sleek chestnut horse.

In the second sentence, notice that the word *skillful* describes the noun *artist*. The words *sleek* and *chestnut* describe the noun *horse*. These words are descriptive adjectives. A descriptive adjective modifies a noun or a pronoun. It usually tells *what kind* about the noun or pronoun it modifies.

There are two classes of descriptive adjectives: *proper adjectives* and *common adjectives*.

> **A proper adjective is formed from a proper noun.**
> **A common adjective is any adjective not formed from a proper noun.**

PROPER ADJECTIVES	COMMON ADJECTIVES
American artist	*popular* artist
French paintings	*colorful* paintings
European exhibition	*international* exhibition

Exercise 1

Find the descriptive adjectives in these sentences. Tell whether they are *common* or *proper*.

1. Although Mary Cassatt lived in a European country, she always considered herself an American artist.
2. Mary admired the realistic paintings of Murillo.
3. The colorful presence of the Andalusian gypsies greatly excited her.
4. The gypsy women dressed in bright skirts.
5. Mary was inspired by Murillo's uncomplicated scenes.
6. *During Carnival* was her first entry to the Parisian judges.
7. Later, Mary was impressed by the joyous paintings of the Flemish artist Rubens.
8. His use of bright colors was a strong influence on her bullfighter paintings.
9. Mary attended a show of the French Impressionists.
10. With Degas and Monet, she joined the new movement.

Complete each sentence with a common or proper adjective according to what is indicated in parentheses.

11. My favorites are *(proper)* painters.
12. That *(common)* painting of the *(common)* fire is huge.
13. Ben painted *(proper)* horses at the state fair.
14. The artist is planning to sketch the *(proper)* ship in the *(common)* sunset.
15. I'd like to paint with *(common)* colors.

Exercise 2

Form adjectives from each of these proper nouns. Use a dictionary to check your spelling.

Example: proper noun, *China*; proper adjective, *Chinese*

Spain	Italy	Alaska
Arabia	France	Ireland
Greece	Europe	Peru
Japan	America	Egypt
Africa	Denmark	Switzerland

Exercise 3

Form adjectives from each of these common nouns. Use a dictionary if you need help.

Example: common noun, *winter*; common adjective, *wintry*

wind	gold	truth
wood	mischief	hero
silk	luck	mountain
athlete	storm	skill
courage	cloud	courtesy

Exercise 4

Write one synonym for each of these adjectives.

comical	clever
faithful	amiable
ignorant	sincere
dangerous	famous
expensive	ancient
angry	clumsy
confident	beautiful
peaceful	odd
huge	lively

Greek ruins

Exercise 5

Write one antonym for each of these adjectives.

ugly	clean	beneficial
enormous	early	tame
awkward	distant	plentiful
strong	incorrect	dark
sweet	idle	brave
proud	silent	flimsy
dull	rich	high
swift	coarse	friendly
kind	careless	shallow

Position of Adjectives

> **The usual position of the adjective is *before* the noun.**

The *agile* acrobats amazed the audience.

In this sentence, *agile* comes right before *acrobats*, the noun it describes.

> **Some adjectives follow and complete a linking verb. Such adjectives are called subjective complements.**

The pretzels are *chewy*.
That gorilla looks *intelligent*.

The first sentence describes *chewy* pretzels, and the second sentence describes an *intelligent* gorilla. In both of these sentences, the adjective does not come before the noun. Instead, it follows a linking verb. The most common linking verb is *be*. An adjective that completes a linking verb modifies the subject. It is called a subjective complement.

Exercise 6

Find the adjective used as the subjective complement in each sentence and tell which noun it modifies.

1. The chairs for dollhouses are tiny.
2. This jar of peanut butter was full yesterday.
3. The plan for a bake sale might be workable.
4. This velveteen seems smooth.
5. Suddenly the wind was silent.
6. A trip into the haunted house could be dangerous.
7. Frances Hodgson Burnett's novels remain popular with children and adults.
8. The lemonade tasted bitter.
9. The noses of the presidents on Mount Rushmore are really gigantic!
10. The basket of laundry is heavy.

Complete each sentence with an adjective used as a subjective complement.

11. Buck's saddlebags are _____.
12. This morning the chimes from the cathedral were

_____.

13. Those mugs are _____.
14. Mr. Graham's antique sleigh looks _____.
15. The mountains ahead of us appear _____.

Exercise 7

Tell whether each italicized adjective comes before a noun or is a subjective complement.

1. Can you name the *smallest* ocean?
2. The *natural* beauty of Switzerland is described in this book.
3. Becky is planning a *big* party for her cat.
4. The results of Arno Sierra's experiment were *remarkable*.
5. These streets are *narrow* and *steep*.
6. She heard a *weird* sound.
7. We gazed upon *endless* miles of *dusty* desert.
8. Abebe Bikila was *barefoot* when he won the Olympic marathon in 1960.
9. The *ordinary* incident was described in an *exaggerated* manner by Rodney.
10. The Taj Mahal in India is an *exquisite* building made of *white* marble.
11. Sean will travel through *Italian* vineyards.
12. The Assyrians were *firm* rulers.
13. Mr. and Mrs. Seton have been *generous* neighbors.
14. *Twenty* guards have already surrounded the *open* vault.
15. The *large* praying mantis on the vine was *motionless*.

A hilltop in Italy

Words Used as Nouns and Adjectives

> The use of a word in the sentence determines its part of speech. Some words can be used as nouns or adjectives.

It frequently happens that the same word may be used as different parts of speech. Notice the use of the word *light* in the following sentences:

> Ron extinguished the *light*. (*Noun*)
> I couldn't find the *light* switch in the dark. (*Adjective*)

A noun is a name word. An adjective describes or limits a noun.

Exercise 8

Tell whether each word in italics is a noun or an adjective.
1. Her fingers flew over the *ivory* keys on the piano.
2. Elephant and walrus tusks are made of *ivory*.
3. Marbles are sometimes made by melting scraps of *glass*.
4. The old books are protected in a *glass* case.
5. Early trains were often called "*iron* horses."
6. The *iron* left a brown spot on my shirt.
7. The swimming pool should reopen in *May*.
8. Because of the harsh winter, I don't think there will be many *May* blossoms.
9. In some parts of France, there are *cave* homes.
10. By the entrance to the magical *cave* was a small dragon.
11. I can't write my report if I don't have any *paper*.
12. Some potato chips are packaged in *paper* cans.
13. This *country* road will lead you through fields of cantaloupes.
14. Can you name the smallest *country* in the world?
15. My uncle has a *country* house where he spends the summer.

Practice Power

A. Rewrite the following paragraph and add descriptive adjectives. Try to add at least five descriptive adjectives.

The sun shines through the water near the shore. Here the floor of the sea is a garden. Stones and shells and coral rest on the bottom. Schools of fish flitter past. Seaweed moves with the waves. In places, a can or an object shows the presence of people on the beach nearby.

B. Write five descriptive sentences about the picture on this page. Some of these sentences should use descriptive adjectives before the noun, and some should use descriptive adjectives following the verb.

Lesson 2 Limiting Adjectives

A limiting adjective either points out an object or indicates number.

The band marched down the street. (*Points out an object*)
There are *twenty* jellybeans in the jar. (*Indicates number*)
This gift arrived from South America. (*Points out an object*)

You will learn about the most important kinds of limiting adjectives in this lesson and in lesson 3.

Articles

The articles are *the, a,* and *an.*
The is the definite article. *A* and *an* are indefinite.

The rodeo last week drew thousands of people. (*Definite*: refers to a *specific* rodeo)
A rodeo is exciting. (*Indefinite*: refers to *any* rodeo)

The following rules apply to articles:
1. The definite article *the* may be used with either singular or plural nouns: *the* ship, *the* brushes.
2. The indefinite articles *a* and *an* may be used only with singular nouns: *a* clock, *an* ostrich.
3. The article *an* is used before a vowel sound: *an* apple.
4. The article *a* is used before a consonant sound: *a* feather.

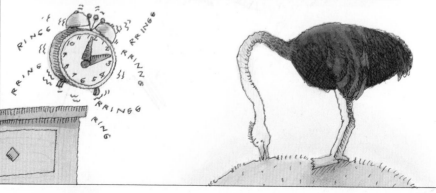

Exercise 1

Use an indefinite article before each of these nouns.

festival	hammer	relative	engineer
eggshell	curb	opening	football
pueblo	actor	villager	Icelander
umbrella	apron	antler	oboe
hour	eagle	kingdom	bonfire

Exercise 2

Complete these sentences by adding definite or indefinite articles.

1. _____ apple _____ day keeps _____ doctor away.
2. _____ unusual sight greeted us when we opened the door.
3. With bursts of speed up to thirty miles _____ hour, dragonflies are _____ fastest flying insects!
4. _____ Mississippi River is _____ longest river in North America.
5. _____ dog walked slowly along _____ railroad tracks.
6. _____ designs inside _____ kaleidoscope are formed from _____ reflections of plastic chips in small mirrors.
7. _____ crocodile slipped into _____ shallow water.
8. I felt _____ huge, hairy arm wrap around my shoulders!
9. We did not have _____ answer to _____ riddle.
10. _____ skinny dog followed Ms. Lopez into _____ butcher shop.

Numeral Adjectives

> **A numeral adjective indicates exact number.**

I have *one* sandwich and *two* cookies in my lunch bag.
The *first* day of the week is Sunday.

Numeral adjectives may refer to the number of things or to the arrangement of things in numerical order. *One* and *two* tell how many. *First* gives the numerical position or rank of the day.

Exercise 3

Find the numeral adjectives in these sentences. Tell which noun each adjective modifies.

1. We celebrated my sister's fifth birthday by baking a peppermint cake.
2. After the first wolf howls, the rest of a pack often joins in.
3. We saw seven small kayaks going down the river.
4. You need the fourth edition of this thesaurus.
5. Twelve Americans have walked on the moon.
6. Four airplanes from the Blue Angels performed maneuvers.
7. All forty-one men on the ship signed the Mayflower Compact.
8. On their twentieth anniversary, our parents bought their second car.
9. Name the five contestants remaining in the spelling bee.
10. Aren't there eleven days left in this month?
11. Alfredo sat in the second row of the empty auditorium and sang aloud.
12. If the thirteenth day of a month is on Friday, some people actually believe they'll have bad luck.
13. One American flag waved in the breeze.
14. Two cars limped from the racetrack toward the pit.
15. The third little pig was smart to build its house out of brick.

Demonstrative Adjectives

> **A demonstrative adjective points out a definite person, place, or thing.**

The demonstrative adjectives are *this* and *that*. The plural of *this* is *these* and the plural of *that* is *those*. *This* and *these* refer to persons or things that are near at hand. *That* and *those* refer to persons or things that are farther away.

> *This* puzzle is impossible to solve. (*Near at hand*)
> *That* park has many bicycle trails. (*Farther away*)
> *These* machines will be very useful. (*Near at hand*)
> *Those* spectators will be late. (*Farther away*)

Each of the italicized adjectives points out a definite person, place, or thing.

A demonstrative adjective agrees in number with the noun it modifies. This is usually the noun closest to it.

Exercise 4

Put the correct demonstrative adjectives before the names of the following objects, which are *near at hand*.

_____ sandwiches	_____ kinds of problems
_____ doughnuts	_____ style of car
_____ street	_____ sort of thing
_____ dollar	_____ color of ink
_____ size of shoe	_____ styles of hair

Exercise 5

Put the correct demonstrative adjectives before the names of the following objects, which are *far away*.

_____ game	_____ pineapple
_____ magazines	_____ blueprints
_____ saxophones	_____ type of work
_____ kind of trap	_____ brands of butter
_____ sorts of pencils	_____ kinds of sports

Exercise 6

Find the demonstrative adjectives in these sentences. Tell whether each is *singular* or *plural*.

1. That stage is beautifully decorated with flowers.
2. We won the game because our shortstop fielded that last grounder.
3. This shield made of feathers belonged to an Aztec king centuries ago.
4. Amanda took these pictures of her relatives in Venice.
5. What were those strange sounds?
6. Kenneth brought this crystal radio to show the class.
7. Cotton will not grow in that hard soil.
8. The Beebes planted those kinds of vegetables last spring.
9. These colors are our school colors.
10. The scientist explained what this symbol on the chart meant.
11. That tongue twister is a tough one.
12. I didn't order this kind of soft drink.
13. These people are the hardest workers on the assembly line.
14. My mother uses this brand of flour for biscuits.
15. Are those model trains on sale?

Those and *Them*

> *Those* is used to point out something. *Those* may be an adjective or a pronoun. *Them* is always a pronoun. It can never be used as an adjective.

Don't pick *those* flowers. (*Adjective*)
She likes these, but I prefer *those*. (*Pronoun*)
Do you like *them*? (*Pronoun*)

Exercise 7

Choose the correct word to complete each sentence.
1. I watched (those, them) sky divers jump from the plane.
2. Who knows how to handle (them, those) snapping crabs?
3. We plan to invite (them, those) to a jazz concert in the park.
4. Mr. Ziegler is going to move (those, them) bales of hay with a tractor.
5. Where did you buy (them, those) hockey sticks?
6. Dietra bought a pet mongoose from (those, them) yesterday.
7. The yard was bright with the flickering of (those, them) fireflies.
8. (Them, Those) toy cars have windup spring motors.
9. Whitney presses (those, them) flowers in a book.
10. Ms. McKay met (them, those) on a streetcar in San Francisco.

Complete each sentence with the correct word, *those* or *them*.
11. _____ boiled ears of corn are dripping with butter.
12. Did you meet _____ after their concert?
13. Scuba divers removed _____ pieces of red coral from the ocean floor.
14. Henry found _____ old photographs in a shoe box.
15. Who will carry _____ bags of cement to my car?

Practice Power

Find the words that describe or limit nouns in these sentences.
1. These trees are sturdy and strong.
2. A black spaniel jumped from the car!
3. These modern highways actually follow old Indian trails.
4. Those small white boats will try to dock at the busy harbor.
5. We believe the Babylonians made wise laws.
6. Those villagers have a Dutch tulip festival in the spring.
7. That hungry squirrel thought the small toy was an acorn.
8. Three players have already fouled out.
9. Brown bears climbed over the wooden fence.
10. An oasis is a fertile spot in a desert.

Lesson 3 More Limiting Adjectives

Possessive Adjectives

> **A possessive adjective indicates ownership.**

My dress is green.   *Our* car is in the garage.
The change is in *her* pocket.   I met *your* uncle.
Its wing is broken.   *Their* house is new.

Because the italicized words in these sentences modify nouns, they are adjectives. Since they show possession, they are called *possessive adjectives*.

The possessive adjectives are

	SINGULAR	PLURAL
FIRST PERSON	my	our
SECOND PERSON	your	your
THIRD PERSON	his, her, its	their

Exercise 1

Find the possessive adjectives in these sentences. Tell what noun each adjective modifies.

1. Why is our dog under the bench?
2. Young people all over the world read her book.
3. I want May Nguyen to sample my rice with saffron.
4. Carolyn painted her boat a soft shade of gray.
5. An oystercatcher slides its beak into the shell of an oyster, and then it cuts the muscle and pulls the meat out.
6. Did your brother bring his mitt to the ballpark?
7. Graham crackers got their name from Sylvester Graham, an early nutrition expert.
8. My friends are arriving from Australia next month.
9. This is our chance to see the world!
10. Ella stretched her long trunk to reach the marshmallow.

Complete each sentence with an appropriate possessive adjective. Be sure to vary your choices.

11. _____ new coat is made of wool.
12. Helen is named after _____ aunt.
13. Little Gordon Schuster likes to wear _____ cowboy outfit.
14. Grandfather and I enjoy sitting on _____ back porch while the sun sets.
15. Mr. Wilson is _____ candidate for president of the Senior Citizens' Craft Guild.
16. _____ son became a wise and powerful emperor.
17. The sparrow hawk missed _____ prey as it swooped down.
18. The woman felt that _____ voice was a musical one.
19. Have you seen _____ new stereo?
20. We should spend more of _____ time baby-sitting for Katrina.

Interrogative Adjectives

> **An interrogative adjective is used in asking a question.**

Which, what, and *whose* are interrogative adjectives when they modify nouns and ask questions.

> *Which* backpack is yours? *What* color is it?
> *Whose* suitcase has brown straps?

Exercise 2

Find the interrogative adjectives in these sentences. Tell the noun that each modifies.
 1. What tree grows to be the tallest?
 2. Whose first novel was called *The Pickwick Papers*?
 3. Which artist did a series of water lily paintings?
 4. What sound does a kookaburra make?
 5. In what place did salsa music originate?
 6. In which city in France was Renoir born?
 7. Whose speech is known as "I Have a Dream"?
 8. Which early Impressionist often painted ballerinas?
 9. Which leaves do silkworms eat?
10. Of what fruit is guacamole made?

Complete each sentence with an interrogative adjective.
11. _____ picture was on America's first postage stamp?
12. _____ animal is called a leviathan?
13. _____ painting is called *American Gothic*?
14. _____ materials does a painter use?
15. _____ painting *Mona Lisa* hangs in the Louvre?

Practice Power

Do you like quiz questions? How many answers do you know to the questions in exercise 2? If you don't know the answer, where do you think you can find the information? Think of three quiz questions to ask your classmates. Use interrogative adjectives and in at least one of your sentences use a possessive adjective. Use the encyclopedia or other research books if you need to!

Lesson 4 Comparison of Adjectives

Comparison is the change that adjectives undergo to express different degrees of quality, quantity, or value.

Most adjectives have three degrees of comparison: the positive degree, the comparative degree, and the superlative degree.

> **The positive degree shows a quality.**

That horse is *slow*.

> **The comparative degree shows a quality in a greater or a less degree.**

Of the two, it is the *slower* horse.

> **The superlative degree shows a quality in the greatest or the least degree.**

There goes the *slowest* horse of all.

The comparative degree is used when speaking of two persons or things. The superlative degree is used when three or more persons or things are compared.

How Adjectives Are Compared

1. Most adjectives of one syllable and some adjectives of two syllables form the comparative degree by adding *er* to the positive. They form the superlative degree by adding *est* to the positive.

POSITIVE	COMPARATIVE	SUPERLATIVE
tall	taller	tallest
rich	richer	richest
dark	darker	darkest
clear	clearer	clearest
quick	quicker	quickest
bright	brighter	brightest
soft	softer	softest
narrow	narrower	narrowest

a. If the positive degree of the adjective ends in *e*, the comparative degree is formed by adding *r*. The superlative degree is formed by adding *st* to the positive form.

POSITIVE	COMPARATIVE	SUPERLATIVE
safe	safer	safest
wise	wiser	wisest
brave	braver	bravest
ripe	riper	ripest
pure	purer	purest
large	larger	largest
tame	tamer	tamest

b. If the positive degree of an adjective of one syllable ends in a single consonant preceded by a single vowel, the consonant is doubled before adding *er* and *est*.

POSITIVE	COMPARATIVE	SUPERLATIVE
slim	slimmer	slimmest
hot	hotter	hottest
sad	sadder	saddest
big	bigger	biggest

c. If the positive degree of the adjective ends in *y*, preceded by a consonant, the *y* is changed to *i* before adding *er* and *est*.

POSITIVE	COMPARATIVE	SUPERLATIVE
noisy	noisier	noisiest
lazy	lazier	laziest
funny	funnier	funniest
friendly	friendlier	friendliest
happy	happier	happiest
pretty	prettier	prettiest
wealthy	wealthier	wealthiest
easy	easier	easiest

2. Adjectives of three or more syllables, and some of two syllables, form the comparative degree and the superlative degree by adding *more* and *most* or *less* and *least* before the positive form of the adjective.

POSITIVE	COMPARATIVE	SUPERLATIVE
courteous	more courteous	most courteous
generous	more generous	most generous
difficult	less difficult	least difficult
famous	less famous	least famous

3. Some adjectives may be compared by both methods: *worthy, worthier, worthiest; worthy, more worthy, most worthy.*

4. Certain adjectives are compared irregularly.

POSITIVE	COMPARATIVE	SUPERLATIVE
little	less	least
bad	worse	worst
good	better	best
many, much	more	most
late	later, latter	latest, last
far	farther	farthest
old	older, elder	oldest, eldest
near	nearer	nearest, next

5. Some adjectives cannot be compared; for example, *dead, perpendicular, eternal, circular, four, fifth, round, golden, this, that, square, every, all, triangular, whole, several.*

Exercise 1

Give the comparative and the superlative degrees of each of these adjectives by using *er* and *est*.

young	tough
brave	thick
mild	gentle
hazy	rude
glad	wet
lucky	shady
glossy	dim
cheap	poor
dreary	juicy
handy	strange

Exercise 2

Compare each of these adjectives by using *more* and *most* or *less* and *least*.

beautiful	common	industrious	numerous
thoughtless	successful	generous	helpful
gracious	fruitful	charitable	sensitive
reliable	dependable	comfortable	interesting
brilliant	familiar	valuable	fortunate

Exercise 3

Find the adjectives that can be compared and tell the degree of comparison of each.

1. Sir Galahad was a brave knight.
2. I prefer the smaller pumpkins for jack-o'-lanterns.
3. You gave a good description of the ghost town, Pete.
4. Courageous firefighters entered the burning building.
5. Did you see the rugged mountains in the distance?
6. Tyrannosaurus Rex was the fiercest dinosaur.
7. Let's walk down the sunnier side of the street.
8. The ripest blueberries will make the best pies.
9. These rocks are more difficult to climb over than the ones we just climbed.
10. It's a common mistake in multiplication.
11. The element mercury is the most sensitive to heat.
12. A python is longer than a boa constrictor.
13. According to the latest report, we can expect snow.
14. Is Sadie's car reliable?
15. The most valuable book in the world is a copy of the Bible printed in 1455.
16. Bicycle shops are busier in the summer than in the winter.
17. Clovers with four leaves are less numerous than those that have three.
18. We found interesting designs on the Easter eggs.
19. The deepest cave extends down 48,360 feet into the earth.
20. Much fruit is grown in California.

Correct Use of the Comparative and Superlative Degrees

Use the comparative degree when two persons or things are compared. Use the superlative degree when more than two are compared.

Miles is the *better* swimmer of the two. (*Two compared*)
Miles is the *best* swimmer on the team. (*More than two compared*)

HINT: The comparative degree is used with the word *than*.

Oranges are generally *larger than* limes.

For the comparative form, do not use *er* and the word *more* (or *less*) at the same time.

INCORRECT: more noisier

For the superlative form, do not use *est* and the word *most* (or *least*) at the same time.

INCORRECT: most noisiest

Exercise 4

Choose the correct word(s) to complete each sentence.

1. Which is (older, oldest)—the telegraph or the radio?
2. Lincoln was the (taller, tallest) president.
3. It is (colder, coldest) in Antarctica than it is here.
4. Of the triplets, Kip is the (less mischievous, least mischievous).
5. Which is (thinner, thinnest), a needle or a pin?
6. Jeanette is the (better, best) driver in her family.
7. The triangle is the (simpler, simplest) instrument in an orchestra.
8. China has the (greater, greatest) population in the world.
9. The San Diego Zoo has the (larger, largest) number of animals of any zoo in the world.
10. Which subject is (less difficult, least difficult), math or science?

Riding camels in Mongolia

Exercise 5

Complete each sentence with the correct form of the adjective in parentheses. Give a reason for your answer.

1. The Amazon River is the (long) river in South America.
2. This problem is (difficult) than the other one.
3. Researchers believe that gliding opossums of Australia are the (small) of all gliding animals.
4. The saguaro is the (tall) cactus in North America.
5. This book is the (good) one that Andy has read.
6. Moles spend (much) time underground than any other place.
7. Rhode Island is (small) than Delaware.
8. Wyatt raised the (big) pumpkin of all.
9. The diamond is the (hard) of all stones and will even cut glass.
10. Was J. P. Morgan (wealthy) than John D. Rockefeller?

Write a sentence showing the correct use of these adjectives.
11. more cheerful
12. worst
13. warmest
14. better
15. most delicate

You Are the Author

Choose one.

1. The following artists painted during the same time period, and some of their works are in your textbook: Sargent (page 28), Monet (page 47), Homer (page 80), Degas (page 81), Cassatt (pages 176, 276, and 279), and Van Gogh (page 352). Choose two paintings. Write a paragraph about your responses to them. Use a variety of adjectives when you discuss the subjects, colors, and styles.
2. With partners, decide on a profession that requires people with varying talents to work together. Research specific occupations and write a short biographical sketch or job description for each person. Make full use of adjectives. (Examples: football team—quarterback, linebacker, wide receiver, kicker, center; newscast team—anchor, reporter, weatherperson, sports-caster, editor)

Chapter Challenge

Read this paragraph carefully and answer the questions.

¹The harbor is alive with ships from around the world. ²Several freighters rock on the tide, graceful liners glide up to the piers, and tugs wander in and out of the harbor. ³The tugs, which are smaller than the other vessels, look tiny compared to the black hulls of the freighters. ⁴Two pleasure boats cruise up the river. ⁵Strains of cheerful music from their orchestras float toward shore. ⁶What a busy picture of life on American waters this port shows!

1. Name an adjective used as a subjective complement in sentence 1.
2. What noun does this subjective complement modify?
3. Name a limiting adjective in sentence 1.
4. Name an adjective in the comparative degree in sentence 3. Write the two other degrees of this adjective.
5. Name the three descriptive adjectives in sentence 3.
6. Find a numeral adjective in the paragraph.
7. What noun does the numeral adjective modify?
8. Is the word *pleasure* used as a noun or an adjective in sentence 4?
9. Is *cheerful* in sentence 5 a descriptive or limiting adjective?
10. Find a proper adjective in the paragraph.
11. Name an indefinite article in sentence 6.
12. Find a demonstrative adjective in sentence 6.
13. Does the demonstrative adjective modify a singular or plural noun?
14. Write the comparative and the superlative forms of *cheerful* in sentence 5.
15. Does the paragraph contain any adjectives in the superlative degree?

Creative Space 3

Buffalo Dusk

The buffaloes are gone.
And those who saw the buffaloes are gone.
Those who saw the buffaloes by thousands and how they
   pawed the prairie sod into dust with their great hoofs,
   their great heads down pawing on in a great pageant
   of dusk,
Those who saw the buffaloes are gone.
And the buffaloes are gone.

Carl Sandburg

Exploring the Poem...

Carl Sandburg was one of the first American poets to experiment with *free verse*. Free verse does not use rhyme. The poem in Creative Space 2, "City," uses rhyme to help express the meaning of the poem. In this poem, Sandburg uses *repetition* instead of rhyme to provide clear, powerful images.

Repetition comes from the word *repeat*. What sentences are repeated in this poem? Why do you think they are repeated? In the middle section of the poem, Sandburg describes the buffalo. What words does he repeat? Does the repetition help you to see the buffalo clearly?

★ With your classmates, think about some things that have changed from the past to today. Choose an idea and put it into a sentence, like the first sentence of Sandburg's poem. Your idea can be serious, like Sandburg's, or more lighthearted.

Here are some possible first sentences.

The summer is gone.   The Model T car is gone.
The dinosaurs are   The Pilgrims are gone.
    gone.   My favorite old sneakers are
My pet mouse is gone.   gone.

Try writing your own poem. Follow the same form as Sandburg does. Here is an example.

My pet mouse is gone.
And the cat that ate my pet mouse is gone.
The cat that eyed my pet mouse for days and dreamed
    of tasty mouse desserts in its cat sleep for nights,
    and watched my mouse with its shining cat eyes
    until today,
My pet mouse is gone.
And the cat that ate my pet mouse is gone.

Chapter 4

Verbs

First Impressions

by Jamie Gilson

from *Hello, My Name Is Scrambled Eggs*

"Flight 231 from San Francisco now arriving at gate H-12," a voice on the loudspeaker announced.

A lady in a wheelchair was first off. She didn't look Vietnamese. Then came a few families and some men and women wearing ties and carrying briefcases. This really cute girl in pink jeans and a fuzzy jacket flung her arms around a sailor as soon as he stepped into the waiting room. Traffic stopped while she gave him this massive kiss. But pretty soon the first Vietnamese appeared behind them. Twenty or so followed after him, edging around the smoochers, who were very glad to see each other. Once they stopped kissing, they rubbed noses and giggled. I couldn't help but notice.

Forget handshakes, I thought. I bet those Vietnamese are wondering what they'll do when we rush up with hugs, kisses, and public nose rubs.

The woman from Travelers Aid and the translator stepped forward to greet the cluster of anxious-looking Vietnamese who were hugging shopping bags, packages tied with twine, and tote bags that said C.A.R.E. on them. When the people looked up, they saw us all standing there with signs and things, beaming. They smiled back.

This is going pretty good, I thought. I raised my arms high over my head and waved the sign. It still felt like a party. WELCOME TO PITTSFIELD NGUYEN FAMILY, I waved back and forth. Several of the group glanced at the banner and blinked a few times, but no one came running up, hands behind backs, to say, "That's us!" There were quite a few kids, but I didn't see any

Adam's House by Edward Hopper

groups like ours. What, I thought, lowering my sign, if they'd missed the plane?

The Vietnamese translator, though, hurried over. "Perhaps I can help you," he said quietly. "Your sign may not be enough. *Most* of the families just arriving are called Nguyen. Are you the only sponsors from . . . ?"

"Pittsfield. Yes!" Jeff filled him in with the details we had and showed him the papers he was carrying with him. "Are all of these people, then, from one big family?"

"Oh, no." He smiled. "It is just that more than half the people in Vietnam are named Nguyen. It's a name like Smith—only *more* common. If I visit Pittsfield, I know from your sign that I will be welcome. My name, too, is Nguyen." He bowed slightly.

We said, "How do you do," and watched him go off in search of our family.

That was the first time we'd heard it pronounced "N-gwyn." All of us—even Jeff and the committee—had only seen it printed. We'd been saying "N-*guy*-en." Jeff and I were practicing the name out loud when the translator came up with three people, none wearing fancy **samurai** costumes. There were a short man and a small, thin boy with no long pigtail but black hair cut in bangs. He looked younger than me, shorter, too—which is really something, since I'm the kid they call Shrimp. An old woman dressed in gray stood back a step from them. Her face was wrinkled with lines deeper than any I'd ever seen, even on old farm women. Her eyes were black and damp-shiny, so small they seemed like part of the furrows. She looked as though she had never smiled.

The translator said their names, but they sounded so strange to me, I couldn't have said them back. Suzanna would have been proud of me, though. I clenched my hands in my pockets. "Hi," I said, long and slow.

Jeff stood, legs apart, hands crossed behind his back, nodding his head like a handshake. The boy and his father smiled really big. They reached their arms toward us.

"Hello," they said together, hands out. I started to laugh. I couldn't help it. Jeff and I both shot our hands back at them so fast that when we finally shook, our arms crossed like an X. I kept laughing like I had hiccups. My kid and his dad were staring down at the floor as if they wished they were back in a combat zone, anywhere but there.

"Excuse me," Jeff said to the translator, and he explained what we'd learned about handshakes.

The translator nodded. "It's generally true what you say." He spoke to the man and my kid, and they grinned at each other, said something to the translator, and then they all looked at us and started to laugh. People around us were staring like I was wearing a KICK ME sign.

"Before your guests left the refugee camp in Galang," the translator explained, grinning, "they went to a meeting. Among the many things they learned was that Americans have customs new to some of them. They were told that when they met you they should shake your hands so you would like them."

So we shook hands again. And laughed. And even bowed a little. It was crazy.

The kid was still smiling. *"Harvey,"* I yelled, pointing at myself. *"Harvey Trumble,"* I repeated, trying to break the language barrier.

Then I remembered not to shout and that pointing is supposed to be gross. Or did somebody tell them we do *that* here too? Just in case they didn't, I lifted my hand to the top of my head to find some place else to put it.

"Nguyen Tuan," he said, reaching out his hand. So that was the name of my kid. We shook hands again.

High Road
by Edward Hopper

The translator stopped his explanations to Jeff to tell me, "You should call him Tuan. In Vietnam, we say our family name first. Here, of course, he'll be Tuan Nguyen."

"Tuan," I repeated, wondering how we would get along without this translator guy. Was it because they lived on the other side of the world that they did things backward?

The translator was telling Jeff that Tuan's mother was sick and had to stay behind in the camp with his baby sister. They would come later. I didn't know what to say, and so I just grabbed a heavy green tote bag from the grandmother, smiled too big, and started down the long hall to get to the lower level where the rest of the luggage was being unloaded from the plane. The hall narrowed as we skirted a tall wooden fence. The sign on it said, PARDON OUR DUST, A SHORT-TERM BOTHER, A LONG-TERM GAIN.

Shuffling around barriers, it took us awhile to reach the down escalator. Jeff was the first one on. He held out his hand to Mrs. Nguyen, who was walking just behind him. She had reached the top of the steps when suddenly she stopped and gave a weak, small cry. Her eyes wide, she said something low and fast, and backing up, grabbed at her son. Jeff was trying to run back up the steps that carried him steadily down to the floor below.

Tuan peered down the escalator and then tilted his head at me, blinking like he had just watched a cow cruise up to the moon. "Move," he said amazed. "Steps *move*."

I nodded. And though Jeff called and waved from below, and people kept stepping onto the stairs that moved down and down, the four of us at the top just watched. We didn't move with them.

The Writer's Craft

1. Jamie Gilson humorously presents the experiences of people who do not share the same culture. Discuss what real problems the author presents, beyond the humorous level.
2. Have you ever experienced a situation in which you were not sure of how to act? What did you do or feel?
3. In this sentence the verbs vividly describe actions: *Once they stopped kissing, they rubbed noses and giggled.* What are the verbs? Find other strong action verbs in the selection.
4. With a partner, list fifteen to twenty verbs or verb phrases that help you visualize the airport scene as Gilson intends.

Recalling What You Know

1. The principal parts of the verb are the *present,* the *past,* and the *past participle.* Give the principal parts of the verbs *to call* and *to break.* Are they regular or irregular? Why?
2. Change the verb in this sentence from present tense to past and future tenses: *The plane lands in San Francisco.*
3. Verbs agree with their subjects in person and number. Why is *roam* correct? *Lions (roams, <u>roam</u>) on the plain.*

Lesson 1 Working with Verbs

A verb is a word used to express action or being.

When the bell *rang* for first period, I *delivered* the kid to the office. Even though I *said* good-bye and *wished* him good luck, I *was* certain they'd be calling me out of science or language arts to help him with the tests. The morning *went* by without a messenger, though, and I *guessed* they'd given up on him or something. So I *was* really surprised when I *got* to the cafeteria at lunch and there he *was,* still smiling, sitting with Suzanna, eating a hamburger layered with pickles, mustard, and catsup.

Some of the verbs in the paragraph above are in italics. Seven of them express action—*rang, delivered, said, wished, went, guessed, got.* One—*was*—expresses being.

Without a verb, there can be no sentence.

Jeff *greeted* the Vietnamese family with a welcome sign. (*A sentence—with the verb* greeted.)
At the airport with a welcome sign (*Not a sentence—no verb.*)

Exercise 1

Make a sentence from each group of words by adding an action verb or verb of being.

1. Mr. Taylor _____ the chicken pox, so Jeff's family became the host family.
2. Jeff _____ a WELCOME TO PITTSFIELD NGUYEN FAMILY banner.
3. They all _____ at the Vietnamese families as they entered the waiting area.
4. The translator _____ the right family.
5. He _____ their name differently.
6. They _____ our hands when we met.
7. The boy's name _____ Tuan.
8. His mother and baby sister _____ still in the camp.
9. The moving stairs _____ Tuan's grandmother.
10. Jeff _____ Tuan how to eat a hot dog.
11. Tuan _____ to school with Jeff.
12. The math teacher _____ impressed with Tuan's skills.
13. Tuan quickly _____ friends with Quint and Caroline, too.
14. Jamie Gilson also _____ the author of *Do Bananas Chew Gum?*
15. She and her husband _____ outside Chicago.

Exercise 2

Some of these groups of words are sentences. Others are not because they do not have a verb. For those that are sentences, name the verb.

1. Thousands of buffalo roamed the open prairie.
2. The graceful skaters circled the ice rink.
3. Here nearly three hundred years ago.
4. Without a shadow of a doubt!
5. Adam typed forty-five words in one minute.
6. Straight black hair, blue eyes, and high cheekbones.
7. A maroon and yellow hot-air balloon drifted overhead.
8. At the first eerie sound, the tired camper crawled quickly out of her tent.
9. On the top of the huge mountain.
10. The beagle chased the squirrel under the towels on Mrs. Pettigill's clothesline.
11. The mess on the table and in the sink.
12. Larry shoved the canoe into the muddy currents.
13. We slid across the lake on the slippery ice.
14. Marian tiptoed through the vegetable garden.
15. Down the street and around the corner.
16. My uncle handed me a foreign coin as a souvenir from his trip overseas.
17. A parade of children marched off the roller coaster.
18. Because of all their creative, exciting ideas.
19. After takeoff, Mikhail relaxed.
20. The first weavers, shoemakers, and other such craft workers.

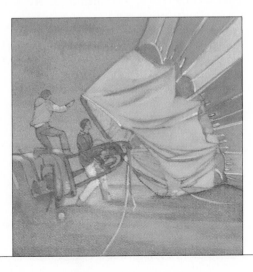

Verb Phrases

> **A verb phrase is a group of words that does the work of a single verb.**

The verb in some sentences consists of only one word. In many sentences, however, the verb is made up of two or more words, as in these examples:

The baby *was named* Leo.
The glasses *were resting* on Grandfather's stomach.
Marsha *has received* a certificate for free ice cream.

The words in italics are all verb phrases, since they do the work of single verbs.

The words that make up a verb phrase are usually written together. In some sentences, however, particularly in interrogative and negative sentences, the parts of the verb phrase may be separated.

Have you *read* about the adventures of Tom Sawyer?
When *did* you *live* in Italy and Japan?
My name *was* not *called* by the leader.

Have read, did live, and *was called* are verb phrases. The principal verbs in these sentences are *read, live*, and *called*. The other words, *have, did*, and *was*, are auxiliary verbs.

> **Any verb used with the principal verb is called an auxiliary verb.**

The common auxiliary verbs are

am	was	did	had	may	could
is	were	have	shall	can	should
are	do	has	will	might	would

Exercise 3

Find the verb phrases in these sentences. Tell which verb is the *principal verb* and which one is the *auxiliary verb*.

1. You might enjoy the pyrotechnics display.
2. A thousand weeds are growing in our garden—and only one flower!
3. Two tourists had lost their way among the winding streets.
4. Ellen will explain the dance steps.
5. Tom has tried several cleaners on this chocolate stain.
6. Have you ever watched dolphins in the ocean?
7. These topics were arranged in alphabetical order.
8. Frankly, I could eat four more hot dogs!
9. The African baobab tree can store more than twenty thousand gallons of water.
10. After that tumble, I am seeing stars.
11. How do people get those model ships into bottles?
12. Our track coach has developed special exercises for us.
13. You will always find money in a dictionary.
14. Tall Gothic cathedrals were built during the Middle Ages.
15. We shall help with the muscular dystrophy carnival.
16. Hans was secretly hoping for a postponement of his dental appointment.
17. Do you know the second verse of "Jingle Bells"?
18. Should you call a taxidermist for a rented tuxedo?
19. Coral reefs have changed the geography of the world.
20. Can you tell me the difference between a fruit and a vegetable?

Notre Dame Cathedral in Paris

Practice Power

Choose any nine auxiliary verbs from the list on page 304. Write nine sentences using these auxiliary verbs with the principal verbs listed below. Include at least two sentences that are interrogative as well as two with adverbs that divide the verb phrase.

excavate	launch	scamper
giggle	surprise	gaze
pretend	interrupt	juggle

Lesson 2 Principal Parts
of Verbs

The principal parts of the verb are the present, the past, and the past participle.

These three parts are so important that they are called the *principal parts*. If you know the principal parts, you can use any form of the verb correctly.

The *past* never takes an auxiliary or helping verb. The *past participle* is always used with an auxiliary or helping verb.

They *flipped* a coin for the last brownie. (*Past tense*)
My cousins *have lived* in Australia for three years. (*Past participle with auxiliary verb*)

Regular and Irregular Verbs

A regular verb forms its past and its past participle by adding *d* or *ed* to the present.

PRESENT	PAST	PAST PARTICIPLE
bake	baked	baked
call	called	called
like	liked	liked
offer	offered	offered
play	played	played

These verbs and many others add *d* or *ed* to the present to form the past and the past participle. They are *regular verbs*.

> **An irregular verb does not form its past and its past participle by adding _d_ or _ed_ to the present.**

PRESENT	PAST	PAST PARTICIPLE
buy	bought	bought
sit	sat	sat
wear	wore	worn
write	wrote	written

The principal parts of irregular verbs are formed in various ways, generally by a change in the word itself. That is why they are called irregular verbs. There is no general rule for forming the principal parts of such verbs. It will be necessary for you to learn the principal parts in order to use the different forms of the verbs correctly.

The past and the past participle of irregular verbs are often confused. Remember the _past_ never takes an auxiliary or helping verb. The _past participle_ is always used with an auxiliary or helping verb.

A koala bear

Australian scenery

Here are the principal parts of the more common irregular verbs. They should be carefully studied.

PRESENT	PAST	PAST PARTICIPLE
	(These stand alone.)	(These require a *helper*, such as *have*.)
am (is, be)	was	been
beat	beat	beat, beaten
begin	began	begun
bend	bent	bent
bet	bet	bet
bind	bound	bound
bite	bit	bitten
blow	blew	blown
break	broke	broken
bring	brought	brought
build	built	built
burst	burst	burst
buy	bought	bought
catch	caught	caught
choose	chose	chosen
come	came	come
do	did	done
draw	drew	drawn
drink	drank	drunk
eat	ate	eaten
fall	fell	fallen
fight	fought	fought
find	found	found
flee	fled	fled
fly	flew	flown
forget	forgot	forgotten
freeze	froze	frozen
give	gave	given
go	went	gone
grow	grew	grown
have	had	had
hear	heard	heard
hide	hid	hidden
hurt	hurt	hurt

PRESENT	PAST	PAST PARTICIPLE
keep	kept	kept
know	knew	known
lay	laid	laid
leave	left	left
lend	lent	lent
let	let	let
lie (recline)	lay	lain
lose	lost	lost
make	made	made
meet	met	met
ride	rode	ridden
ring	rang	rung
rise	rose	risen
run	ran	run
see	saw	seen
send	sent	sent
set	set	set
shake	shook	shaken
sing	sang	sung
sink	sank	sunk
sit	sat	sat
speak	spoke	spoken
spend	spent	spent
stand	stood	stood
stick	stuck	stuck
swim	swam	swum
swing	swung	swung
take	took	taken
teach	taught	taught
tear	tore	torn
tell	told	told
think	thought	thought
throw	threw	thrown
wear	wore	worn
win	won	won
write	wrote	written

Exercise 1

Complete each of the following sentences with the past tense or the past participle of the irregular verb at the left. If an auxiliary verb is given, the past participle is to be used.

see	1. Yes, I _____ him perform in a concert.
burst	2. After the party, Teddy _____ every blue balloon.
eat	3. I _____ caviar for the first and last time yesterday.
come	4. A thundercloud _____ across the valley at thirty miles an hour.
wear	5. People _____ beautifully decorated masks for the Mardi Gras festival.
send	6. The magazine _____ over a thousand valentines to subscribers.
make	7. Toby had _____ three different cakes for the baking contest.
ride	8. Have you ever _____ on the back of a yak?
freeze	9. It's so cold that the water in the birdbath has _____.
ring	10. Has the fire alarm _____ yet?
grow	11. The banana plant has _____ a foot every year.
lose	12. The tourists have _____ their map and their guidebook.
write	13. Al _____ about the customs of the early Greeks.
hide	14. Where have they _____ the colored eggs?
go	15. Who has _____ to look for Ed?
tear	16. The bird _____ the paper into strips for its nest.
throw	17. I have _____ those dirty sneakers into the washer.
shake	18. After climbing from the pond, the retriever _____ water on everybody.
fall	19. Six feet of snow had _____ while we slept.
begin	20. Commercial television _____ in 1941.
sing	21. The court jester _____ a riddle for the king.
take	22. We have _____ this rocky path as a shortcut.
find	23. Archaeologists have _____ many human fossils in Tanzania.

Let and *Leave*

> The verb *let* (*let, let, let*) means to *permit* or *allow*.
>
> The verb *leave* (*leave, left, left*) means to *abandon* or *depart*.

Let Monica play her violin. (= *permit* or *allow*)
We *left* for the parade early to get a good view. (= *departed*)

Exercise 5

Choose the correct verb form to complete each sentence.
1. Sy, (let, leave) the song end before you turn the radio off.
2. The express bus (lets, leaves) at three o'clock.
3. (Let, Leave) those pennies in the fountain!
4. Diego (let, left) his backpack behind the old shed.
5. (Leave, Let) me go with you on the nature walk!
6. He (let, left) all the dinosaur bones undisturbed.
7. Why has Deirdre (let, left) the room?
8. Ross (let, left) me help paint the St. Patrick's Day mural.
9. The plane does not (let, leave) until noon.
10. Has he (let, left) his new address with you?
11. We shall (let, leave) the children name the new park.
12. (Leave, Let) Mikey try it first!
13. I promise that I'll (let, leave) you use my mitt.
14. The puppy (let, left) a trail of cookie crumbs.
15. Don't (leave, let) anyone eat my french fries!

Teach and *Learn*

The verb *teach* (*teach, taught, taught*) means to *give* instruction.

The verb *learn* (*learn, learned, learned*) means to *receive* instruction.

I *taught* them how to yodel. (= *gave instruction*)
I've already *learned* how to yodel. (= *received instruction*)

Exercise 6

Choose the correct verb form to complete each sentence.

1. The coach (taught, learned) me how to spin a basketball on my finger.
2. Our dog, Sauerkraut, (taught, learned) to beg for German food.
3. I (teach, learn) about the world economy by reading the newspaper.
4. Abe Lincoln (taught, learned) himself by reading borrowed books.
5. Baby woodpeckers watch their parents and (teach, learn) how to find worms.
6. Linda, (teach, learn) me how to play bocce.
7. Did the scouts (teach, learn) you how to tie a half hitch?
8. Each student (teaches, learns) a first-aid procedure to a younger partner.
9. Will you (teach, learn) your lines in the play by tonight?
10. Please (teach, learn) me how to adjust the gears on my bike.

Practice Power

Write a short paragraph about wrapping a gift. You wanted to make the outside of the gift as special as the inside. Explain what you did. Use at least five irregular verbs from the list on pages 322 to 323.

Lesson 3 Transitive and Intransitive Verbs

Transitive Verbs

> A transitive verb expresses an action that passes from a doer to a receiver.

DOER	ACTION	RECEIVER
Mary	read	the book.

In this sentence, the action (*read*) passes from the doer (*Mary*) to the receiver (*book*). The verb *read* is, therefore, a transitive verb.

To determine the receiver of the action, ask the question *whom* or *what* after the verb. Mary read *what*? The word that answers the question is the receiver of the action. It is called the direct object of the verb. The direct object of the verb *read* in this sentence is *book*.

The verbs in the sentences below are transitive.

> Charlie *caught* a firefly. (*The word* firefly *is the direct object.*)
> Stella *delivers* the newspaper. (*The word* newspaper *is the direct object.*)

Exercise 1

The verb in each sentence is transitive. Identify the verb. Then name the doer and the receiver of the action.

1. With a steady hand, Mamie carefully lit the candle.
2. Simon wears a heavy cape at his magic lessons.
3. We baked the brownies just a little too long.
4. In 1891, Dr. James Naismith invented basketball.
5. The chickadees ate all the seeds in the feeder.
6. You tore a valuable piece of paper.
7. The tourists stalked the lions with their cameras.
8. The tailor made clothes for everyone but himself.
9. The Great Wall of China protected that country for centuries.
10. My dog makes spectacular catches of my Frisbee.
11. Galileo studied the moon with a telescope.
12. The winner broke the record for the school.
13. My friend wrote this letter in our secret code.
14. The class celebrated all the birthdays on one day.
15. Carolyn learned violin through the Suzuki method.

The Great Wall of China

Intransitive Verbs

An intransitive verb has no receiver of its action.

Franklin *lived* on the seventy-fifth floor.

The action of this verb, *lived*, begins and ends with the doer. There are no answers to the questions "Franklin lived *whom?*" or "Franklin lived *what?*"

An intransitive verb may be followed by a prepositional phrase or an adverb. The phrase or adverb does not receive the action.

The scouts hiked *in the wilderness*. (*Prepositional phrase*)
The ice melted *quickly*. (*Adverb*)

Exercise 2

The verb in each sentence below is intransitive because there is no *receiver* of the action. Find the verb. Then name the doer in each sentence.

1. Skiers raced recklessly down the icy slope.
2. An excited fan leaned forward.
3. Christmas Island lies in the Indian Ocean.
4. Those astronauts spoke about their next space flight.
5. Finally beside a warm fire, Gabby whistled happily.
6. A moose suddenly appeared at the edge of the lake.
7. The snowy ground glistens in the early morning sun.
8. The bells on Karin's costume jingled softly.
9. A Moroccan flag floated in the warm breeze.
10. The starlings nest in these trees every night.
11. James went to countless Little League baseball practices.
12. Houseflies walk upside down or right side up.
13. Uranus travels around the sun every eighty-four Earth years.
14. The president resides in Washington, D.C.
15. The entire group of seals plunged beneath the waves.

Verbs That Are Transitive or Intransitive

> Some verbs may be either transitive or intransitive, according to their use in the sentence.

TRANSITIVE

Orlando *counted* the pennies.
Jean *painted* stars on the ceiling.
The rock *broke* the window.

INTRANSITIVE

Orlando *counted* carefully.
Jean *painted* all day.
The glass *broke*.

Exercise 3

The verbs in these sentences can be used as transitive or intransitive verbs. Find the verb in each sentence, and tell whether it is *transitive* or *intransitive*.

1. My aunt grows prize-winning tomatoes.
2. The alfalfa sprouts grew in a glass jar on the windowsill.
3. Chewy entered a bubble-gum-blowing contest.
4. We entered quietly through the back door.
5. I actually flew in a helicopter.
6. My uncle flew an antique plane in the air show.
7. For our class project, we wrote a complicated program on the computer.
8. George always writes with a number-two pencil.
9. Carita lost the tennis match to her best friend.
10. Joe and Carlos seldom lose in Scrabble competitions.

Exercise 4

Find the verb in each sentence. Name the doer of the action. Name the receiver if there is one. Tell if each verb is *transitive* or *intransitive*.

1. The cold winds howl fiercely through the cracks in the wall.
2. Sir Spencer answered the wizard's question correctly.
3. The hot-air balloonist postponed his flight until a sunny day.
4. Cut daisies wilt quickly.
5. The fast train runs between Paris and Lyons.
6. Our dog likes chocolate, bananas, and peanut butter!
7. That factory recycles old newspapers.
8. The marching band plays during halftime.
9. Fresh sawdust completely covered the floor of the workshop.
10. Joey Weitzman hurried into the noisy henhouse.
11. We saw the old ship on display in the harbor.
12. Mitchell's cousin came from New Zealand.
13. During the day, hippopotamuses spend their time in water.
14. The excited puppy bounded after the red car.
15. Vacationers see active volcanoes in Hawaii.

Practice Power

Write sentences using these four verbs as transitive verbs:

carry, dip, explore, paint

Write sentences using these four verbs as intransitive verbs:

bounce, relax, fly, travel

Lesson 4 Linking Verbs

A linking verb links the subject with a noun, pronoun, or an adjective. The word that follows a linking verb is called a *subjective complement.*

SUBJECT	LINKING VERB	SUBJECTIVE COMPLEMENT
Those girls	are	club *members*. (*Noun*)
That boy	is	*he*. (*Pronoun*)
Ted	was	*enthusiastic*. (*Adjective*)

Each of the verbs in these sentences needs a *complement* to *complete* its meaning. The verb links this complement with the subject. The verb *are* links the complement *members* with the subject *girls*. The verb *is* links the complement *he* with the subject *boy*. The verb *was* links the complement *enthusiastic* with the subject *Ted*.

The noun, pronoun, or adjective that completes the meaning of these verbs is called a subjective complement.

The verb *be* is the most common linking verb. Its various forms are

am	is	was	being
be	are	were	been

The following verbs also can be used as linking verbs.

appear	feel	remain	sound
become	grow	seem	taste
continue	look	smell	

When these verbs are used as linking verbs, a form of the verb *be* can be substituted for the original verb.

John *looked* healthy.	John *was* healthy.
The whistles *sounded* shrill.	The whistles *were* shrill.
The day *grew* hot.	The day *was* hot.

Exercise 1

Find the linking verb in each sentence. Tell whether the italicized complement is a *noun*, a *pronoun*, or an *adjective*.

1. The beach was *sunny* all morning.
2. The girl in the chemistry class is *she*.
3. These handwoven Navaho blankets are very *warm*.
4. The duck-billed platypus is an egg-laying *mammal*.
5. Trojans were *enemies* of the ancient Greeks.
6. The trip through Mavis Hargrove's old mansion was *scary*.
7. The lumberjack in the red plaid jacket was *he*.
8. Prizes at rodeos were often *buckles* for the cowboys' belts.
9. The poppy seed bagels are still *warm*.
10. A bookmobile is a *library* on wheels.

Exercise 2

Find the linking verb and complement in each sentence. Then substitute a form of the verb *be* for the original verb.

1. The cornstalks in Kansas grow very tall.
2. This grapefruit ice cream tastes unique.
3. Marilee, the librarian, seems knowledgeable about cats.
4. The Red Sea appears reddish—but only at certain times.
5. Five blocks away, the siren still sounds clear.
6. The sky looks cloudy today.
7. Uncle Jack's fried crawfish smell appetizing.
8. We feel happy about the election results.
9. Irene Ross became our class president.
10. Somehow, Ramona remained calm throughout the Olympic competition.

Exercise 3 Review

Find the verbs in these sentences. Tell whether each is *transitive*, *intransitive*, or a *linking verb*.

1. Louis was friendly to the new boy down the street.
2. The ferocious tiger and the friendly cat are members of the same family.
3. The runaway toboggan slid down the hill.
4. Mr. Waldorf saw the Coast Guard cutter in the harbor.
5. Beavers build new dams across Lumbee Creek every year.
6. A balloon pops in a tiny fraction of a second.
7. A computer chip is actually a tiny piece of sand.
8. Wild red foxes never grow completely tame in captivity.
9. Harriet trudged to the farmhouse.
10. A brightly uniformed band leads the parade.
11. We heard the screech of a blue heron from the marsh.
12. More than twenty million people live in the Himalayas.
13. Many Spaniards danced in the streets of Pamplona.
14. An usher in a tuxedo conducted us to our seats.
15. Sir Arthur Conan Doyle, a doctor, wrote many famous detective stories.
16. The kite rose above the pine trees.
17. Louisa became an excellent gymnast.
18. The photographer waited patiently for a zebra.
19. I eagerly pulled the bundle of letters from the mailbox.
20. President Ulysses S. Grant was one of Mark Twain's friends.

Practice Power

You have just walked into the world-famous shop the Sweet Tooth. What kind of food do you think this shop sells? Describe the shop. Write sentences using some form of these six linking verbs:

taste, look, feel, smell, appear, seem

Lesson 5 Simple Tenses

The tense of a verb shows the time of the action or being.

You *walk* the dog today.
Calvin *walked* the dog yesterday.
Myra *will walk* the dog tomorrow.

Today is present time, *yesterday* is past time, and *tomorrow* is future time. Notice how the verb *walk* changes in form when used to show these various times. This quality of a verb is called *tense*. The word *tense* means "time."

> **The *present tense* shows action or being in present time.**

He *sings* in the musical today.
We *are* members of the drama club.

If the subject is a singular noun or a pronoun in the third person singular, the verb form ends in *s* in the present tense.

Josie *acts* in all the school plays.

> **The *past tense* shows action or being in past time.**

He *sang* last night.
We *were* members of the drama club last year.

> **The *future tense* shows action or being in future time.**

He *will sing* tomorrow.
They *will be* members of the drama club next year.

The auxiliary verb *shall* or *will* is used to form the future tense.

Exercise 1

Find the verb in each sentence and give its tense.

1. Big Paul Bunyan combed his curly hair with a saw!
2. Felix found his key on the dusty shelf.
3. A flea jumps two hundred times the length of its own body.
4. When will your sister return from her watercolor workshop?
5. The first surfers were the Polynesians of the South Pacific.
6. I play classical music for my plants every morning.
7. Paige will perform a solo on the grand piano.
8. Our mail carrier delivers the mail at ten o'clock every day.
9. Juan lives in a one-bedroom apartment in Dallas.
10. The pipe organ is the largest musical instrument.
11. The dancer twirled close to the edge of the stage.
12. We froze two trays of ice cubes for our lemonade stand.
13. Will you watch the last golfers tee off?
14. My cousins catch king mackerels from the pier at night.
15. Chan painted the fence with short, quick strokes.
16. Some redwood trees live more than one thousand years.
17. Will there be a holiday tomorrow?
18. The soapy water bubbled merrily over the sides of the washing machine.
19. Frankie will write a complaint to the president of the soft drink company.
20. In 1889, the reporter Nellie Bly traveled around the world in seventy-two days.

Exercise 2

Complete these sentences by supplying the tense indicated in parentheses for the verbs listed.

Talk

1. The club members _____ about their favorite books. (*Present*)
2. You _____ on the telephone for over an hour! (*Past*)
3. James _____ about nothing but his new motorcycle for a week. (*Past*)
4. The fire chief _____ to our class next week. (*Future*)
5. Mrs. Takada _____ quickly when she is excited. (*Present*)

Bring

6. My sister _____ my lunch to school when I forget it. (*Present*)
7. I _____ my bicycle inside whenever it looks like rain. (*Present*)
8. They _____ your guitar books back tomorrow. (*Future*)
9. The Spanish _____ the horse to the New World. (*Past*)
10. The museum director _____ some dinosaur bones for us to examine. (*Future*)

Burst

11. Bill grabbed the balloon and _____ it. (*Past*)
12. The dirt-covered detectives _____ through the door. (*Past*)
13. When I dropped it on the floor, the fat tomato _____ open. (*Past*)
14. The cherry trees _____ into bloom all around Washington. (*Future*)
15. My zebra finches _____ into song whenever a light is turned on. (*Present*)

Eat

16. They _____ a box of doughnuts in the bus station. (*Past*)
17. The construction workers _____ their lunch in the truck. (*Future*)
18. We _____ Italian dressing on our tossed salad. (*Present*)
19. An elephant _____ up to five hundred pounds of leaves, grass, and bark daily! (*Future*)
20. My friend has an allergic reaction if she _____ chocolate. (*Present*)

Choose

21. Magpies usually _____ thorny bushes for their nests. (*Present*)
22. The hikers _____ a spot under a sprawling oak tree for the picnic. (*Past*)
23. Oliver Smith _____ a plaid tie as his favorite. (*Past*)
24. The club _____ its slogan with a secret vote. (*Future*)
25. Lola _____ these flowers for the hall table. (*Present*)

Wear

26. The players _____ their uniforms for the first time. (*Past*)
27. Alice always _____ the ring her parents gave her. (*Present*)
28. He _____ a penguin outfit to the costume party. (*Future*)
29. The men _____ their hair short and their beards long. (*Present*)
30. I _____ an orange obi with my flowered kimono. (*Present*)

Practice Power

You probably have seen many exciting adventures in movies and on television. Pretend you are marooned on a deserted island. Write a paragraph explaining the situation you are in, how you got on the island, and what you will do to survive. Try to use verbs in the present, past, and future tenses in your paragraph.

Lesson 6 Compound Tenses

> **The *present perfect tense* shows action completed in present time.**

He already *has sung* today.
We *have studied* geometry today.

The present perfect tense is formed by the auxiliary *have* or *has* plus the past participle of the verb.

> **The *past perfect tense* shows action completed before some definite time in the past.**

He *had sung* before we arrived at the recital.
We *had studied* algebra before we studied geometry.

The past perfect tense is formed by the auxiliary *had* plus the past participle of the verb.

> **The *future perfect tense* shows action that will be completed before some specified time in the future.**

He *will have sung* the song before you return.
We *shall have studied* geometry before evening.

The future perfect tense is formed by the auxiliaries *shall have* or *will have* plus the past participle of the verb.

Exercise 1

Find the verb phrase in each sentence, and give its tense.

1. My brother has driven his car about one thousand miles.
2. The prince and the pauper had switched places.
3. By dawn, my father will have reached his secret fishing spot.
4. Have you heard any good jokes lately?
5. I have done my best with the snake-charming act.
6. Had the zookeepers decided on a name for the baby panda?
7. Josey has spilled perfume all over her dresser.
8. They will have finished their African masks by noon.
9. Where have the cowhands taken that noisy herd of longhorns?
10. The slick tires had made a strange noise on the pavement.
11. Mr. Andretti and his wife have fed the pigeons the last bread crumbs.
12. Thomas had never made apple cider before.
13. By tomorrow, they will have completed decorations for the Christmas tree.
14. The carpenter has hit his thumb with the hammer.
15. The fox had wanted the grapes.

Exercise 2

Complete each sentence by supplying the tense indicated in parentheses for the verbs listed.

Talk

1. Carl _____ about the monster movie all day.
   (*Present perfect*)
2. The bus driver already _____ to us about wearing seat belts.
   (*Past perfect*)
3. Ms. Wilson _____ to the contest committee by Saturday. (*Future perfect*)
4. Our neighbors _____ to the construction crew about the noise. (*Present perfect*)
5. The newspaper reporter _____ to many witnesses before writing the story. (*Past perfect*)

Bring

6. Lila _____ oranges from Florida for me. (*Present perfect*)
7. The substitute mail carrier _____ the mail early. (*Present perfect*)
8. Before I realized it, the dog _____ mud into the house. (*Past perfect*)
9. He _____ the film projector before you return. (*Future perfect*)
10. Carol and Jody _____ their raincoats but not their umbrellas. (*Present perfect*)

Burst

11. Last winter the pipes under the house _____ before the renters moved in. (*Past perfect*)
12. After days of rain, the sun _____ through the clouds. (*Present perfect*)
13. Mysteriously, the soda bottles _____ during the previous night. (*Past perfect*)
14. The thinnest balloons _____ before they reach the ground. (*Future perfect*)
15. _____ your bicycle tire ever _____ before? (*Past perfect*)

Eat

16. I was surprised that the acid _____ a hole in my lab coat. (*Past perfect*)
17. Helena _____ three dozen sardines in the contest! (*Present perfect*)
18. Everyone in camp _____ breakfast before sunrise. (*Future perfect*)
19. Who _____ all the peanut brittle? (*Present perfect*)
20. The campers _____ the entire box of raisins by midnight. (*Future perfect*)

Choose

21. The government _____ the rose as the national flower. (*Present perfect*)
22. The boys _____ the chicken soup with rice, but they changed their minds. (*Past perfect*)
23. Everyone _____ geography projects by Friday. (*Future perfect*)
24. _____ they _____ Sancha as the new Safety Squad leader? (*Present perfect*)
25. The worms _____ the juiciest apples in the crate. (*Past perfect*)

Wear

26. That snowman _____ the same hat every day. (*Present perfect*)
27. The coach reported that the cheerleaders _____ their new uniforms to the rally. (*Past perfect*)
28. ____ he _____ that navy suit before graduation? (*Past perfect*)
29. They _____ their graduation gowns before the actual day. (*Future perfect*)
30. I _____ holes in all of my socks. (*Present perfect*)

Exercise 3

Complete each sentence by supplying the tense indicated in parentheses for each verb.

appear 1. Stars soon _____ in the gray twilight sky. (*Past tense*)

order 2. Doctor Chin _____ him to go to a warm, sunny climate. (*Past tense*)

gain 3. By the time she joined Buffalo Bill's Wild West Show in 1885, Annie Oakley _____ fame as a sharpshooter. (*Past perfect tense*)

lay 4. Grandmother's silver thimble _____ in her sewing basket. (*Past tense*)

finish 5. The artists _____ their work with oils. (*Present perfect tense*)

study 6. The astronomer _____ the distant planets through a powerful telescope. (*Present tense*)

drift 7. The lion cubs _____ to sleep beside their mother. (*Present perfect tense*)

fall 8. Snow _____ off and on during the skiing lessons. (*Past tense*)

win 9. Our team _____ the debate on which president was the greatest. (*Past tense*)

grow 10. Thousands of buttercups _____ around the abandoned log cabin. (*Present tense*)

take 11. My brother _____ a test to check his eyesight. (*Future tense*)

hide 12. The armadillo _____ behind the trash cans on T. J.'s property for a while before we noticed it. (*Past perfect tense*)

see 13. We _____ abstract paintings in the art gallery. (*Past tense*)

bring 14. The delivery person _____ the pizza in only thirty minutes. (*Past tense*)

place 15. Under his head, she _____ a blue and white striped pillow. (*Past tense*) build   16. Wrens _____ a nest under the rusty tractor seat. (*Present perfect tense*)

close   17. The grocery store _____ at eight o'clock. (*Present tense*)

teach   18. Aristotle _____ his followers a clear method of reasoning. (*Past tense*)

tell   19. I _____ him the unbelievable news by tonight. (*Future perfect tense*)

bake   20. Vito _____ a delicious peach pie. (*Present tense*)

increase   21. Michael _____ his pitching accuracy through practice. (*Past tense*)

celebrate 22. People over the world _____ Pen Pal Day on September 23. (*Present tense*)

come   23. Shetland ponies _____ from an island off Scotland. (*Past tense*)

give   24. Gail, the zoo guide, _____ you directions to the aviary. (*Future tense*)

pack   25. Explorers _____ eighty pounds of equipment on each burro. (*Present tense*)

Practice Power

The *synopsis* of a verb is a short way to practice using a verb in all the tenses. Any nominative case pronoun can be used. Study the example below, and then try to complete two on your own —one with the verb *land* and the personal pronoun *it* and the other with the verb *run* and the personal pronoun *they*.

Synopis for the Verb *See*

PRESENT TENSE	He sees
PAST TENSE	He saw
FUTURE TENSE	He will see
PRESENT PERFECT TENSE	He has seen
PAST PERFECT TENSE	He had seen
FUTURE PERFECT TENSE	He will have seen

Lesson 7 Agreement of Subject with Verb Part I

Verbs should agree with their subjects, both in person and in number.

A verb may be in the *first person*, the *second person*, or the *third person*. The first person refers to the speaker, the second person refers to the one spoken to, and the third person refers to the one spoken about.

In addition, the verb may be *singular* or *plural* in number. Singular refers to one; plural refers to more than one.

Note the changes in the verb in the sentences below as the subject changes from singular to plural or from first person to second and third persons. *The verb always agrees with the subject in person and number*. Note that all nouns are in the third person.

	SINGULAR NUMBER	PLURAL NUMBER
FIRST PERSON	I *am* his friend.	We *are* his friends.
SECOND PERSON	You *are* his friend.	You *are* his friends.
THIRD PERSON	She *is* his friend.	They *are* his friends.
FIRST PERSON	I *have* a two-dollar bill.	We *have* a two-dollar bill.
SECOND PERSON	You *have* a two-dollar bill.	You *have* a two-dollar bill.
THIRD PERSON	He *has* a two-dollar bill.	They *have* a two-dollar bill.
FIRST PERSON	I *walk* in the park.	We *walk* in the park.
SECOND PERSON	You *walk* in the park.	You *walk* in the park.
THIRD PERSON	It *walks* in the park. The child *walks* in the park.	They *walk* in the park. The children *walk* in the park.

Exercise 1

Name the subject and verb or verb phrase in each sentence. Tell the person and number of each verb or verb phrase.

1. Conifers are the only kind of tree near the top of a mountain.
2. We usually jog all the way home.
3. Your train has left!
4. The Mediterranean Sea contains a great amount of salt.
5. You have taped my finger to the box.
6. Louie flops on the couch with a bag of barbecue-flavored potato chips after football practice.
7. The twins often burst into laughter over their secret switches.
8. I was putting blue and green candles on Mia's birthday cake.
9. These albums contain photographs of early gold miners.
10. With every crash of thunder, the dog crawls farther and farther under my bed.
11. They speak softly in the library.
12. Grandmother has always kept a box of peppermints on a high shelf.
13. The trucks have come to clean the streets.
14. Huge caves lie under the earth's surface.
15. I have already taken the prescription to the pharmacy.

Singular and Plural Subjects

A singular subject requires a singular form of the verb. A plural subject requires a plural form of the verb.

Notice the change in the form of the verb in each of the following sentences.

SINGULAR NUMBER

A picture *hangs* on the wall.
She *sleeps* well.
He *walks* to the park.
She *has* waited.

PLURAL NUMBER

Pictures *hang* on the wall.
They *sleep* well.
They *walk* to the park.
They *have* waited.

A noun or pronoun in the third person singular requires a verb that ends in *s* for the present tense.

Exercise 2

Find the subject in each sentence. Tell whether it is *singular* or *plural*. Then choose the correct verb.

1. My grandfather (sells, sell) antique furniture.
2. The logs on the truck (needs, need) a canvas cover.
3. The scouts (seems, seem) eager to leave for the mountains.
4. The starter (flags, flag) the cars to line up.
5. Noise (is, are) measured in units called decibels.
6. Seven Indian elephants (was, were) walking to the tent.
7. Those rockers (has, have) been repainted every summer.
8. The magician (show, shows) us a new trick at every performance.
9. Hail (has, have) ruined the corn crop this year.
10. The rolling hills (was, were) covered with purple and yellow wildflowers.
11. Do the avocados (looks, look) ripe enough for guacamole?
12. The sunset (has, have) beautiful shades of red and orange!
13. We (finds, find) quite a few fossils in rocky areas.
14. The most frequently sung song (is, are) "Happy Birthday to You."
15. Ms. Winston's miniature donkeys (has, have) been sold.

351

Exercise 3

Rewrite each sentence and change the italicized nouns from the plural to the singular. Then change the verb to agree with the new subject.

1. The *pictures* of sunflowers hang on the wall.
2. The *chalkboards* were full of sentences by students.
3. Have the *plates* been washed?
4. When left alone, the *puppies* climb up on the sofa.
5. Marge's front *teeth* are loose.
6. The *cookies* are cool enough to eat.
7. The *guards* direct traffic during rush hour.
8. There go the *trucks* to the fire!

Now change the italicized nouns from the singular to the plural. Then change the verb to agree with the new subject.

9. The *train* shakes the windows in our house.
10. The new *book* about outer space is on display in the library.
11. My *sister-in-law* swims a mile every day.
12. The silly *rooster* crows at sunset.
13. Does the *squirrel* bite?
14. Has the *wharf* been repaired?
15. The *messenger* brings us the daily report.

Sunflowers by Vincent van Gogh

There Is and *There Are*

There is or *there was* should be used when the subject, which follows the verb, is singular. *There are* or *there were* is used when the subject is plural.

> There (is, are) three windows in the room.

Here is the correct form: There *are* three windows in this room.

The subject *windows* is plural in number. To find the subject, omit the word *there* and rearrange the sentence: Three windows are in this room.

When a sentence begins with *there*, look for the subject after the verb.

Exercise 4

Find the subject in each sentence. Then choose the correct verb.
1. There (is, are) a thousand grams in a kilogram.
2. There (was, were) four robins eating.
3. There (is, are) many beautiful parks there.
4. There (were, was) seven wonders in the ancient world.
5. There (was, were) five kinds of flowers in this arrangement.
6. There (is, are) a group of baseball players warming up.
7. There (was, were) no key for this unusual box.
8. There (is, are) numerous groves of olive trees in Portugal.
9. There (was, were) a sudden knock at the door.
10. There (is, are) a beautiful rainbow in the sky.
11. There (was, were) several ripe peaches in the basket.
12. There (is, are) a box of saltwater taffy on the table.
13. There (is, are) thirty days in April.
14. There (was, were) ten gulls standing on the sandbar.
15. There (is, are) about one billion people in China.

Doesn't and Don't

If the subject of the sentence is in the third person, *doesn't* is the correct form in the singular. *Don't* is the correct form in the plural.

In the first and the second persons, the correct form is *don't*, whether the subject is singular or plural.

	SINGULAR NUMBER	PLURAL NUMBER
FIRST PERSON	I *don't* have a pet.	We *don't* have a pet.
SECOND PERSON	You *don't* have a pet.	You *don't* have a pet.
THIRD PERSON	He/She *doesn't* have a pet.	They *don't* have a pet.

Exercise 5

Complete each sentence with *doesn't* or *don't*.

1. Leta enjoys island life so much that she _____ want to leave Hawaii.
2. Why _____ Mr. McGregor wear his tartan kilt?
3. Leprechauns _____ really exist.
4. _____ Mrs. Rivera live northeast of the airport?
5. This _____ solve any of our problems.
6. They _____ know how to change a flat tire.
7. _____ a stalactite hang down from a cave ceiling?
8. If Kenny _____ watch out, he'll trip on the tree's roots.
9. Why _____ any of these letters have zip codes?
10. If you _____ want these photographs of old cars, let me have them.
11. Dad _____ believe in large allowances.
12. _____ you want a chance to break the piñata?
13. Apparently, I _____ know Morse code well enough.
14. This road _____ lead to the hollow oak tree.
15. Janet _____ eat red meat very often.

You as the Subject

Use the forms *you are* and *you were* whether the subject is singular or plural. Never use *is* or *was* when the subject is in the second person.

> (Was, Were) you at the game today?

Here is the correct form: *Were* you at the game today?

The subject *you* is in the second person.

Exercise 6

Choose the correct form of the verb in each sentence.
1. (Is, Are) you looking for a four-leaf clover?
2. (Was, Were) you angry about the price of a hamburger?
3. (Was, Were) you frightened when the tree fell near your house during the storm?
4. You (are, is) welcome!
5. You (wasn't, weren't) there!
6. (Were, Was) you listening to the rock musician?
7. (Is, Are) you collecting rocks?
8. Where (was, were) you during vacation?
9. You (is, are) wrong about that.
10. You (are, is) late again!

Practice Power

Pretend you are a radio announcer in an age of dragons, knights, and princesses. Describe the action as a radio announcer would. Use the nouns listed below as subjects in your sentences and use strong action verbs in the present tense. Underline the subject and verb in each sentence.

dragons	a cave	a forest	knights
a castle	a princess	fire	horses

Lesson 8 Agreement of Subject with Verb <u>Part II</u>

Compound Subjects Connected by *And*

Compound subjects connected by *and* usually require a plural verb.

> Janice and Marie (is, are) good friends.

Here is the correct form: Janice and Marie *are* good friends.

The subjects *Janice* and *Marie* are connected by *and*.

Exercise 1

Find the compound subject in each sentence. Then choose the correct verb.

1. King Arthur and Sir Galahad (was, were) friends.
2. The cat and her kitten (lie, lies) in the sun.
3. She and I (was, were) worried about the whimpering puppy.
4. Mr. Williams and his puppet (performs, perform) at the Red Globe Theater.
5. (Was, Were) your mother and father in the audience?
6. Tennis and golf (is, are) summer sports.
7. The lake and the river (was, were) covered with thin ice.
8. Hal and his staff (paints, paint) colorful designs on T-shirts.
9. Our stereo and television (are, is) both broken.
10. The parrot and the dog (sings, sing) in tune with the radio!
11. Longfellow and Whittier (were, was) early American poets.
12. The bison and the caribou (walk, walks) over eight hundred miles during migration.
13. Mathematics and history (is, are) my favorite subjects.
14. The woman and her daughter (writes, write) movie scripts.
15. Jason and I (make, makes) fancy envelopes from colorful pages out of magazines.

Special Pronouns

The distributive pronouns *each*, *either*, *neither* and the indefinite pronouns *anyone*, *no one*, *anybody*, *nobody*, *everyone*, *everybody*, *someone*, and *somebody* are always singular and require singular verbs.

Everybody (was, were) pleased with the result.

Here is the correct form: Everybody *was* pleased with the result.

The subject *everybody* is singular.

Exercise 2

Complete each sentence with the correct form of the present tense of the verb at the left.

know   1. No one _____ for certain why whales sing.

contain   2. Either of these books _____ information on Dutch holidays.

enjoy   3. I hope everybody _____ my sassafras tea.

agree   4. Neither of the students _____ with your theory.

like   5. Nobody _____ to get lost in a swamp full of snakes!

want   6. Here is a hoe if someone _____ to help with the garden.

buy   7. If our Indian corn isn't colorful, nobody _____ it.

admire   8. Everybody _____ Ada Harper's success in taming the wild raccoon.

carry   9. Neither lawyer _____ a briefcase.

know   10. Each of us _____ a shortcut to the Monroe Building.

leave   11. Someone always _____ the toothpaste uncapped.

fit   12. Neither of the jackets on sale _____ me.

ride   13. Anyone under age two _____ for free.

speak   14. Everyone _____ at once in these unorganized meetings!

believe   15. No one here _____ in mermaids.

Special Nouns

Such nouns as *deer, sheep, fish, swine, trout, salmon, cod, cattle, moose, corps,* and certain proper nouns, such as *Portuguese, Chinese, Swiss, Iroquois,* have the same form in the singular and the plural.

> This trout (is, are) twelve inches long.

Here is the correct form: This trout *is* twelve inches long. The subject *trout* is singular.

> Many trout (is, are) caught in that stream.

Here is the correct form: Many trout *are* caught in that stream. The subject *trout* is plural.

The sense of the sentence lets you know whether the subject is singular or plural.

Exercise 3

Find the subject in each sentence. Tell whether it is *singular* or *plural.* Then choose the correct verb.
1. There (is, are) several sheep grazing on the hillside.
2. This sheep (is, are) the only one that hasn't been sheared.
3. A male deer sometimes (scratch, scratches) his back with his antlers.
4. Many deer (ramble, rambles) through these woods.
5. A salmon (swim, swims) in the tank.
6. Salmon (are, is) found in the Columbia River.
7. The Swiss (has, have) four official languages: French, German, Italian, and Romansh.
8. That young Swiss (speak, speaks) four languages—and can yodel as well.
9. The Portuguese (were, was) great explorers.
10. Portuguese (is, are) a musical language.

Exercise 4   Review

Choose the correct verb form for each of the following sentences. Tell with which noun the verb agrees.

1. His directions (leads, lead) straight into the lake!
2. The first day of summer (was, were) June 21.
3. This watch (doesn't, don't) need to be wound.
4. Nobody (want, wants) to go and turn off the basement light.
5. Red and yellow (is, are) both primary colors.
6. Popcorn (is, are) a healthy and delicious snack food.
7. Each of these pieces (fits, fit) in the puzzle somewhere.
8. A zonkey (is, are) a cross between a donkey and a zebra.
9. (Was, Were) there any telephone calls for me today?
10. Everyone in our family (finish, finishes) dinner by seven o'clock.
11. Carla and Molly (collect, collects) old wooden toys.
12. Someone (is, are) bringing records to the party.
13. (Don't, Doesn't) you want to stay up until midnight?
14. There (was, were) a parking place on this side of the street two minutes ago.
15. Ricardo (ride, rides) his unicycle everywhere he goes.
16. (Is, Are) there a sports section in the newspaper?
17. The Japanese often (drink, drinks) ocha, a green tea, with their meals.
18. (Were, Was) you outside when it began to rain?
19. Chocolate and vanilla (is, are) the most popular flavors of ice cream.
20. There (are, is) no fish in the Dead Sea.

You Are the Author

Choose one.

1. Retell the airport scene from the point of view of one member of the Nguyen family.
2. Have you ever been the new person in school, in the neighborhood, or on a team? Write a paragraph describing some of your feelings.

Chapter Challenge

Read this paragraph carefully and answer the questions.

¹Icebergs contain more than half the world's fresh water. ²Scientists have created a plan for the future to tow icebergs from the Antarctic to hot desert countries. ³The fresh water could irrigate the dry, thirsty land. ⁴Imagine it is the year 2050. ⁵The plan works this way. ⁶First, scientists choose a very large iceberg—at least five miles long and two miles wide. ⁷The iceberg itself actually becomes the ship. ⁸The crew members for the "ship" live on board the iceberg, which is driven by an engine. ⁹After the "ship" crosses the ocean, it is put into a giant plastic bag. ¹⁰The iceberg slowly melts, and water is piped into the fields to irrigate the land. ¹¹Scientists have estimated that one iceberg alone holds a supply of trillions of gallons of water. ¹²That is a big ice cube!

1. In sentence 1, is the verb singular or plural?
2. Name the auxiliary verb in sentence 2.
3. In sentence 3, name the receiver of the transitive verb *could irrigate*.
4. In sentence 5, is the verb *works* singular or plural in number? Why?
5. Name the verb in sentence 6. Give the past and past participle of this verb.
6. Name the linking verb and subjective complement in sentence 7.
7. In sentence 8, what person, number, and tense is the verb *live*?
8. In sentence 9, is the verb *crosses* transitive or intransitive? Why?
9. In sentence 10, is the verb *melts* transitive or intransitive? Why?
10. In sentence 11, which verb is present perfect tense?
11. In sentence 11, what person, number, and tense is the verb *holds*?
12. Name the linking verb in sentence 12. Does it link the subject with a noun, a pronoun, or an adjective?

Creative Space 4

Two Limericks

A fly and a flea in a flue
Were imprisoned, so what could they do?
Said the fly, "Let us flee!"
"Let us fly!" said the flea.
So they flew through a flaw in the flue.

There once was a pig that was thinner
Than the rest, so he thought, "What a winner!
They'll let me go free."
But mistaken was he.
The pig was the first to be dinner!

Exploring the Poem...

Do you recognize these poems as limericks? Most limericks are humorous. They are fun to read and write.

Read the limericks aloud. Can you hear the rhythm? In each limerick, which lines have the same rhythm?

Which lines rhyme? In these poems, the rhyme pattern is a-a-b-b-a. How are the rhythm and the rhyme connected to each other?

★ Try writing a limerick of your own. You can use one of the opening lines below to get started. As you write your limerick, the rhythm and rhyme pattern should help you to focus your ideas.

> There once was a shoe that went walking...
> There once was an elephant so thin...
> A robot and its friends had a party...
> Hot pizza's my favorite treat...
> There once was a _____ in sixth grade...

Chapter 5

Adverbs

Bellerophon and Pegasus

by Nathaniel Hawthorne

from "The Chimaera," in *A Wonder-Book*

Once, in the old, old times (for all the strange things which
I tell you about happened long before anybody can remember),
a fountain gushed out of a hill-side, in the marvelous land of
Greece. And, for aught I know, after so many thousand years,
it is still gushing out of the very selfsame spot. At any rate, there
was the pleasant fountain, welling freshly forth and sparkling
adown the hill-side, in the golden sunset, when a handsome
young man named Bellerophon drew near its margin. In his
hand he held a bridle, studded with brilliant gems, and adorned
with a golden bit. Seeing an old man, and another of middle
age, and a little boy, near the fountain, and likewise a maiden,
who was dipping up some of the water in a pitcher, he paused
and begged that he might refresh himself with a **draught.**

"This is a very delicious water," he said to the maiden as he
rinsed and filled her pitcher, after drinking out of it. "Will you
be kind enough to tell me whether the fountain has any name?"

"Yes; it is called the Fountain of Pirene," answered the
maiden.

"And this, then, is Pirene? I thank you, pretty maiden, for
telling me its name. I have come from a far-away country to find
this very spot."

A middle-aged country fellow (he had driven his cow to drink
out of the spring) stared hard at young Bellerophon, and at the
handsome bridle which he carried in his hand.

"The water-courses must be getting low, friend, in your part
of the world," remarked he, "if you come so far only to find the
Fountain of Pirene. But, pray, have you lost a horse? I see you

Pegasus: Horse on the Rock by Odilon Redon

carry the bridle in your hand; and a very pretty one it is with that double row of bright stones upon it. If the horse was as fine as the bridle, you are much to be pitied for losing him."

"I have lost no horse," said Bellerophon, with a smile. "But I happen to be seeking a very famous one, which, as wise people have informed me, must be found here-abouts, if anywhere. Do you know whether the winged horse Pegasus still haunts the Fountain of Pirene, as he used to do in your forefathers' days?"

But then the country fellow laughed.

Some of you, my little friends, have probably heard that this Pegasus was a snow-white steed, with beautiful silvery wings, who spent most of his time on the summit of Mount Helicon. He was as wild, and as swift, and as buoyant, in his flight through the air, as any eagle that ever soared into the clouds. There was nothing else like him in the world. He had no mate; he never had been backed or bridled by a master; and, for many a long year, he led a solitary and a happy life.

But, of late years, he had been very seldom seen. Indeed, many of the country folks, dwelling within half an hour's walk of the fountain, had never beheld Pegasus, and did not believe that any such creature existed. The country fellow to whom Bellerophon was speaking chanced to be one of those **incredulous** persons.

And that was the reason why he laughed.

"Pegasus, indeed!" cried he, turning up his nose as high as such a flat nose could be turned up—"Pegasus, indeed! A winged horse, truly! Why, my friend, are you in your senses? I don't believe in Pegasus. There never was such a ridiculous kind of horse-fowl made!"

"I have some reason to think otherwise," said Bellerophon, quietly.

And then he turned to an old, gray man, who was leaning on a staff, and listening very attentively, with his head stretched forward, and one hand at his ear, because, for the last twenty years, he had been getting rather deaf.

"And what say you, **venerable** sir?" inquired he. "In your younger days, I should imagine, you must frequently have seen the winged steed!"

"Ah, young stranger, my memory is very poor!" said the aged man. "When I was a lad, if I remember rightly, I used to believe there was such a horse, and so did everybody else. But,

nowadays, I hardly know what to think, and very seldom think about the winged horse at all."

"And have you never seen him, my fair maiden?" asked Bellerophon of the girl, who stood with the pitcher on her head, while this talk went on. "You certainly could see Pegasus, if anybody can, for your eyes are very bright."

"Once I thought I saw him," replied the maiden, with a smile and a blush. "It was either Pegasus, or a large white bird, a very

Pegasus by Odilon Redon

367

great way up in the air. And one other time, as I was coming to the fountain with my pitcher, I heard a neigh. Oh, such a brisk and melodious neigh as that was! My very heart leaped with delight at the sound. But it startled me, nevertheless; so that I ran home without filling my pitcher."

"That was truly a pity!" said Bellerophon.

And he turned to the child, whom I mentioned at the beginning of the story, and who was gazing at him, as children are apt to gaze at strangers, with his rosy mouth wide open.

"Well, my little fellow," cried Bellerophon, playfully pulling one of his curls, "I suppose you have often seen the winged horse."

"That I have," answered the child, very readily. "I saw him yesterday, and many times before."

"You are a fine little man!" said Bellerophon, drawing the child closer to him. "Come, tell me all about it."

"Why," replied the child, "I often come here to sail little boats in the fountain, and to gather pretty pebbles out of its basin. And sometimes, when I look down into the water, I see the image of the winged horse, in the picture of the sky that is there. I wish he would come down, and take me on his back, and let me ride him up to the moon! But, if I so much as stir to look at him, he flies away out of sight."

And Bellerophon put his faith in the child, who had seen the image of Pegasus in the water, and in the maiden, who had heard him neigh so melodiously.

Now you will, perhaps, wish to be told why it was that Bellerophon had undertaken to catch the winged horse. And we shall find no better opportunity to speak about this matter than while he is waiting for Pegasus to appear.

If I were to relate the whole of Bellerophon's previous adventures, they might easily grow into a very long story. It will be quite enough to say that, in a certain country of Asia, a terrible monster, called a Chimaera, had made its appearance, and was doing more mischief than could be talked about between now and sunset. According to the best accounts which I have been able to obtain, this Chimaera was nearly, if not quite, the ugliest and most poisonous creature, and the strangest and unaccountablest, and the hardest to fight with, and the most difficult to run away from, that ever came out of the earth's inside.

The wisest thing he could do, therefore, was to get the very best and fleetest horse that could anywhere be found. And what other horse, in all the world, was half so fleet as the marvelous horse Pegasus, who had wings as well as legs, and was even more active in the air than on the earth? But, wonderful as it appeared, Bellerophon believed that Pegasus was a real steed, and hoped that he himself might be fortunate enough to find him; and, once fairly mounted on his back, he would be able to fight the Chimaera at better advantage.

And this was the purpose with which he had traveled from Lycia to Greece, and had brought the beautifully ornamented bridle in his hand. It was an enchanted bridle. If he could only succeed in putting the golden bit into the mouth of Pegasus, the winged horse would be submissive, and would own Bellerophon for his master, and fly wherever he might choose to turn the rein.

Well was it for Bellerophon that the gentle child had grown so fond of him, and was never weary of keeping him company.

But, when he least thought of it, Bellerophon felt the pressure of the child's little hand, and heard a soft, almost breathless, whisper.

"See there, dear Bellerophon! There is an image in the water!"

The young man looked down into the dimpling mirror of the fountain, and saw what he took to be the reflection of a bird which seemed to be flying at a great height in the air, with a gleam of sunshine on its snowy or silvery wings.

"What a splendid bird it must be!" said he. "And how very large it looks, though it must really be flying higher than the clouds!"

"It makes me tremble!" whispered the child, "I am afraid to look up into the air! It is very beautiful, and yet I dare only look at its image in the water. Dear Bellerophon, do you not see that it is no bird? It is the winged horse Pegasus!"

Bellerophon's heart began to throb! Bellerophon caught the child in his arms, and shrank back with him, so that they were both hidden among the thick shrubbery which grew all around the fountain.

Nearer and nearer came the aerial wonder, flying in great circles, as you may have seen a dove when about to alight. Downward came Pegasus, in those wide, sweeping circles, which grew narrower, and narrower still, as he gradually

approached the earth. At last, with so light a pressure as hardly to bend the grass about the fountain, or imprint a hooftramp in the sand of its margin, he alighted, and, stooping his wild head, began to drink.

At length—not that he was weary, but only idle and luxurious—Pegasus folded his wings, and lay down on the soft green turf. But, being too full of aerial life to remain quiet for many moments together, he soon rolled over on his back, with his four slender legs in the air.

Finally, when he had had enough of rolling over and over, Pegasus turned himself about, and, **indolently,** like any other horse, put out his forelegs, in order to rise from the ground; and Bellerophon, who had guessed that he would do so, darted suddenly from the thicket, and leaped astride of his back.

Yes, there he sat, on the back of the winged horse!

The Writer's Craft

1. Myths were told to help people understand human behavior and the forces of nature. Many times gods and goddesses played important parts in these stories. What are the mythical elements in this tale?
2. What are the differences in the personalities of the people Bellerophon meets at the well? Who was of the greatest help in Bellerophon's quest to capture Pegasus? Why do you think he was?
3. As Pegasus was getting up from the ground, Bellerophon "darted suddenly from the thicket, and leaped astride of his back." The adverb of manner in this sentence is *suddenly*. Find other examples of this type of adverb that you think were well chosen by the author.
4. The child wants Pegasus to take him up to the moon. *Up* is an adverb of place. Use another adverb of place in this sentence: *The slithering monster reached ____ to strike the snow-white steed.*

Adverbs of Degree

Adverbs of degree answer the question *how much* or *how little*.

Julia has *almost* finished the long novel. (*Modifies a verb*)
Steve drank the cold water *too* quickly. (*Modifies an adverb*)
Carol's handwriting is *scarcely* readable. (*Modifies an adjective*)

Adverbs of degree modify verbs, adjectives, or other adverbs.

almost	greatly	merely	quite	sufficiently
barely	hardly	much	rather	too
fully	little	partly	scarcely	very

Exercise 4

Complete each sentence with an adverb of degree.
1. This coffee is _____ hot to drink.
2. Kathryn, approach the fawn _____ slowly.
3. A dragonfly _____ landed on the end of my fishing pole.
4. It was _____ warm enough to go out without a jacket— and they were swimming!
5. The goats had _____ finished one stack of hay when they began on the other.
6. Stamps with errors are _____ rare and so are valuable.
7. I don't _____ understand the atom model.
8. The electric eel is a _____ long and skinny fish.
9. Jon has rehearsed _____ for the trombone solo.
10. Marie had _____ smothered the hamburger with pickles.
11. The history students were _____ happy that their test was postponed.
12. We came _____ close, but we did not finish the three-legged bag race.
13. To take a picture, you _____ press the red button.
14. The forecast is for a _____ cloudy day.
15. After getting braces, I could _____ chew gum.

Adverbs of Affirmation and Negation

> Adverbs of affirmation or negation tell whether a statement is *true* or *false*.

Alice will *not* go.   *Yes*, Neil is here.

Adverbs of affirmation are *yes, indeed, undoubtedly*.

Adverbs of negation are *no, not, never*.

Exercise 5

Find the adverbs in each sentence. Tell whether each shows *affirmation* or *negation*.

1. Yes, I have finished reading the sports page.
2. We do not know the answers to any of those trivia questions.
3. Shelby's advice to rub the plant leaves with milk was indeed strange.
4. Undoubtedly, baked potatoes have fewer calories than french fries.
5. Van's father never allowed him to mow the lawn without wearing safety glasses.
6. Mark Twain was indeed the inventor of suspenders.
7. No, I did not see the sand dollar.
8. Yes, a speleologist is a scientist who studies caves.
9. The peanut butter cookies are not ready yet.
10. We'll never know how that grand piano got through the door!

Exercise 6

Find the adverb or adverbs in each sentence. Tell whether each is an adverb of *time, place, manner, degree, affirmation*, or *negation*.

1. Scarlett tied the bow on her lace dress very neatly.
2. Yes, the sea is exceedingly rough, Meg.
3. There are too many hot peppers in these chimichangas!
4. Here are the dog biscuits Blue has been stashing away.
5. The astronauts float around weightlessly in space.
6. Do turtles walk slowly because their shells are heavy?
7. Two volunteers stepped forward for the magic trick.
8. The Senate sometimes hears rather long speeches.
9. Above, we could see the banner announcing a street fair.
10. There was barely enough birthday cake for everyone.
11. The audience immediately sat down when the music began.
12. Hearing the clock chime, I looked up.
13. We always keep a supply of cherry preserves in the pantry.
14. Pansies are quite hardy and grow well in cool temperatures.
15. I promise to count the bags of bagels very carefully.
16. The crowd laughed heartily at the bear's antics.
17. We did not know that the tire was flat.
18. Blue whales are the largest animals that have ever lived.
19. I almost knocked the ant farm over.
20. News travels fast!
21. We quickly wrote a menu for our hot-dog stand.
22. He secured the loose objects on deck and climbed below.
23. Mrs. Kellog complains that she seldom sees a blue jay at her bird feeder.
24. They were fully prepared for a sensational air show.
25. Searching for her photograph, Kelly flipped through the magazine rapidly.

Practice Power

Next to each verb in the list below is an adverb that modifies it.
Write at least one synonym for each adverb. Write a sentence
with the verb and the new adverb.

VERBS	ADVERBS
answer	immediately
gallop	briskly
sing	merrily
speak	honestly
drive	cautiously
act	courageously
move	quietly

Lesson 2 Comparison of Adverbs

Many adverbs can be compared. Like adjectives, they have three degrees of comparison: positive, comparative, and superlative.

Regular Comparison

Some adverbs form the comparative degree by adding *er* to the positive, and they form the superlative degree by adding *est* to the positive.

POSITIVE	COMPARATIVE	SUPERLATIVE
high	higher	highest
fast	faster	fastest
hard	harder	hardest
late	later	latest
soon	sooner	soonest
early	earlier	earliest

Adverbs ending in *ly* generally form the comparative degree by adding *more* or *less* to the positive, and they form the superlative degree by adding *most* or *least* to the positive.

POSITIVE	COMPARATIVE	SUPERLATIVE
swiftly	more swiftly	most swiftly
	less swiftly	least swiftly
bravely	more bravely	most bravely
	less bravely	least bravely
gracefully	more gracefully	most gracefully
	less gracefully	least gracefully

Irregular Comparison

Some adverbs are compared irregularly. It is necessary to learn the comparative and the superlative degrees.

POSITIVE	COMPARATIVE	SUPERLATIVE
badly	worse	worst
far	farther	farthest
late	later	latest, last
little	less	least
much	more	most
well	better	best

Most adverbs indicating time and place (*here, now, then, when, where, again, always, down, above*) and adverbs expressing completeness (*eternally, universally, never, forever, continually, entirely*) cannot be compared.

Exercise 1

Find the adverbs in these sentences. For those adverbs that can be compared, tell the degree of comparison: *positive, comparative*, or *superlative*.

1. We searched everywhere for the missing car keys.
2. The winner must stay on the bronco the longest.
3. During the thunderstorm, George acted more bravely than the rest of us.
4. The dog barked furiously at the passing cars.
5. Andy dove most courageously from the high diving board into the pool.
6. With the sudden gust of wind, the kite soared higher into the sky.
7. Our fire died sooner than we had expected.
8. That detective gathered clues the least patiently of all.
9. Read the poem in French slowly, Carole.
10. The carpenters need to work faster to meet their deadline.
11. This burro walks more steadily than a horse across rocks.
12. I always comb my hair this way.
13. Of all the rivers, the Amazon flows most swiftly.
14. October was an unusually warm month.
15. Henri arrived latest.

Exercise 2

One degree of the adverb is given below. Write out the complete comparison of each adverb.

POSITIVE	COMPARATIVE	SUPERLATIVE
quietly	_____	_____
_____	more slowly	_____
early	_____	nearest
_____	_____	most sincerely
_____	less harshly	_____
sharply	_____	most happily
_____	less accurately	_____
anxiously	_____	most probably
_____	_____	_____
_____	less kindly	least firmly
well	_____	_____
_____	_____	soonest
sorrowfully	_____	_____
_____	more willingly	_____
late	_____	hardest
_____	_____	

Practice Power

From exercise 2, choose two adverbs in the positive degree, two in the comparative, and two in the superlative. Write sentences showing the correct use of each adverb.

Lesson 3 Using Adverbs Correctly

Adverbs and Adjectives

An adjective describes a noun or pronoun.
An adverb modifies a verb, an adjective, or an adverb.

Adverbs are often confused with adjectives that follow and complete verbs. Study the following examples.

The gymnast stood on the beam (unsteady, unsteadily).
The gymnast on the beam looked (unsteady, unsteadily).

The correct form for the first sentence is *unsteadily*: The gymnast stood on the beam *unsteadily*. *Unsteadily* modifies the verb *stood* and tells *how*.

The correct form for the second sentence is *unsteady*: The gymnast on the beam looked *unsteady*. *Unsteady* follows the linking verb *looked* and describes the subject *gymnast*.

To tell whether you use an adverb or adjective, try this: If some form of the verb *be* can be used in place of the verb in the sentence, the verb is a linking verb, and an adjective should follow it.

This peach tastes *good*. (= *This peach* is *good*.)

The adjective form *good* correctly follows a linking verb.

These peaches grow *well* in Georgia.

Well is an adverb. It tells *how* the peaches grow. If a form of the verb *be* is used in place of the verb *grow*, the sentence does not make sense.

Chapter Challenge

Read this paragraph carefully and then answer the questions.

¹Two pioneers of the American West were Lewis and Clark, explorers of the Louisiana Territory. ²Asked by President Jefferson, these men organized a party and bravely undertook a difficult mission. ³They suffered many hardships on the extremely dangerous trip through unknown land. ⁴Very slowly and patiently they pushed up the Missouri to its source. ⁵Each day they traveled farther into the wild. ⁶The men often lost the way, but with the aid of a kind Indian woman they crossed the mighty Rockies. ⁷They descended the Columbia River and finally sighted the Pacific Ocean. ⁸Courageously, the explorers continued on until they reached their goal.

1. In sentence 2, name the adverb and tell what kind it is.
2. In sentence 3, which adverb of degree modifies *dangerous*?
3. In sentence 3, what part of speech does the adverb of degree modify?
4. Find two adverbs of manner in sentence 4.
5. In sentence 4, find an adverb that modifies another adverb.
6. Give the comparative and superlative degrees of the two adverbs of manner in sentence 4.
7. Name an adverb of place in sentence 5.
8. Write the positive and superlative degrees of the adverb in sentence 5.
9. In sentence 6, what kind of adverb is *often*?
10. In sentence 7, name the adverb of time.
11. Can the adverb in sentence 7 be compared?
12. Give the comparative and superlative degrees of the adverb of manner in sentence 8.

Creative Space 5

Noise

I like noise.

The whoop of a boy, the thud of a hoof,
The rattle of rain on a galvanized roof,
The hubbub of traffic, the roar of a train,
The throb of machinery numbing the brain,
The switching of wires in an overhead tram,
The rush of the wind, a door on the slam,
The boom of the thunder, the crash of the waves,
The din of a river that races and raves,
The crack of a rifle, the clank of a pail,
The strident tatoo of a swift-slapping sail—
From any old sound that the silence destroys
Arises a gamut of soul-stirring joys.
I like noise.

J. Pope

Exploring the Poem...

Do you like noise as much as this person does? Some people might describe noise as sounds that are *too* loud. Do you think the person in the poem would agree? What noises in the poem have you heard? What noises have you not heard? Use your dictionary if there are words in the poem you do not know.

What words in the poem rhyme? When two lines that follow each other have the same rhyme, the two lines are called *couplets*. Can you find a word in *couplet* that gives a clue to its meaning?

How does the poet begin and end his poem? Do you get a positive feeling from this sentence?

★ Think about some things that *you* like. Talk with a friend and see if you can agree upon a thing that you both like. Work together to write a group of *couplets*. Remember to begin and end your poem with "I like . . . ." Here is an example.

I like names.

The beauty of Mary, the sound of a Jim,
Peter and Jonathan, Susan and Kim.
A strong name like Sarah, a neat name like Matt,
Carolyn, Janet, Cornelius, and Pat.
I like names.

Chapter 6

Prepositions, Conjunctions, Interjections

Rude Awakening

by Ouida Sebestyen

from *Words by Heart*

". . . the **Insular** Cases of nineteen aught one," Mr. Doans was saying. "Part of our colonial policy which enabled the United States to enact legislation for the government of backward people."

Elsie raised her hand delicately. "Teacher, is that what was meant by the 'White Man's Burden'?"

Mr. Doans experimentally cleared his throat. "Since the Spanish-American War, the United States has taken eight million less-advanced people under its **jurisdiction,** in Cuba, Puerto Rico, Guam and the Philippines. Yes, Elsie, throughout history the superior races have necessarily shouldered the burden of ruling the inferior ones."

A question lodged sideways in Lena's mind. She raised her hand uncertainly. "But what makes us a superior race?" Mr. Doans looked at her a long time. Back in the corner the singsong voices trailed off as Mr. Doans turned to stare too. Somebody giggled. Maybe she had said something funny.

"It is obvious from its achievements, Lena, that the Anglo-Saxon race is superior to any other."

She still didn't understand. "What's Anglo-Saxon?"

She thought that meant English.

"Caucasian."

"What's that?" The giggles were growing.

"White," Mr. Doans said.

Elsie sat primly, holding back an angelic smile.

"Sir?" Winslow's voice rose out of the giggles. "How do you explain Jack Johnson? He's a Negro, and he's heavy-weight champion of the whole world."

"I couldn't attempt to explain why brute strength should be thought of as remarkable."

Winslow said steadily, "Booker T. Washington got an honorary degree from Harvard. Don't you admire that?"

"I admire the abilities passed down to him by his *white* father. And now, Winslow, we have digressed enough. Back to government."

Lena eased a glance over her shoulder. Winslow was smiling. A fixed, championship kind of smile. With a jolt she realized that the country had just fought another small war over the White Man's Burden. Her. She was not sure who had won, but she knew her friend from her foes now. Only who else was fighting? And which way?

With all her heart she wished she could leap out through the hole in the screen that the cat had made and run down the road after Papa's wagon. But she knew she couldn't catch up with it now. It was gone, like the trust she had felt for the people in that room.

Tuesday started strangely. Lena and Claudie were up in the dark to get Papa's chores done so that Lena could take the milk to Mrs. Chism before school. No one answered her knock, so she left it on the porch.

At noon she climbed the mulberry tree again. The day before, they had all eaten in the schoolhouse because of the drizzle, but she was sure that Winslow would come this time. Maybe even with the poetry book.

He didn't. She saw him standing for a moment at the corner of the building, looking at the tree with the kind of careful, indrawn look that Sammy had had.

He stayed after school to clean the blackboard. She waited until everyone had gone, to catch him alone before he started home. She wanted to thank him for standing up for her. Or for loving justice. Or for trying to flatten Mr. Doans and Elsie. Or whatever he had done. But shyness seized her instead, and she said, "Have you learned any more new poems?"

He was startled. His eyes didn't quite meet hers.

"Listen," he said awkwardly, "I can't lend you that book we were talking about." He shrank into himself, still scrubbing away with an eraser.

"Why?" She glanced around as he had, out of sympathy for him.

"My father said I couldn't."

"Oh." Embarrassment, like raw gusts of wind, came off him, chilling her heart.

"I'm not even supposed to talk to you anymore."

She was as embarrassed as he was. "Why?"

"I don't know. I think Mr. Doans talked to my father or something." He laid the eraser down. "I've got to get home."

Tillie Taggart
by Andrew Wyeth

She almost reached out her hand to stop him, but she held her fingers stiff at her sides.

Winslow said, "My father says if you all keep filling up the country out here, you'll have to go to your own schools." He began to erase again without noticing.

"Why?" Her mouth kept making that same word like a gate creaking.

"I don't know. Because you don't need to know the same things we do, I guess." He went on rubbing a spot on the blackboard that was already clean. Did he think he could take the color off? "He says you first ones, you're like a wedge—and the more that comes, the more trouble there'll be, and it would just be better if it all stopped right now."

His perplexed eyes looked off beyond her. What did he want? Did he believe all that, or was he just trying to believe it because his father had said it? She was quivering inside, the way water skittered when a cold wind blew over it. Winslow laid down the eraser again. Quicker than he could move to leave first, she flung herself around and fled out the door.

The Writer's Craft

1. Lena's teacher refers to various peoples whom the United States has aided. What is your attitude toward immigrants? How does the author suggest that Mr. Doans may be prejudiced?

2. After Winslow defends African Americans in class, what is Lena's reaction? In the paragraph beginning "Lena eased a glance . . . ," how does the author's description of Winslow convey his attitude? Discuss your own reaction to Winslow—his support of Lena and then his change of attitude.

3. The scene between Lena and Winslow is very emotional. What role does punctuation play in conveying the emotion to the reader? Refer to specific examples.

4. Conjunctions join sentences and parts of sentences. In Lena's encounter with Winslow, the author uses conjunctions in conveying Winslow's embarrassment and Lena's confusion. Identify the conjunctions in this section and tell how they are used.

Recalling What You Know

1. Prepositions relate nouns or pronouns to other words. What word does the underlined prepositional phrase modify?
   Lena fled out the door.

2. Recall that coordinate conjunctions such as *and, but, yet, or,* and *nor* connect words, phrases, or clauses in a sentence. Give an example of each use.

3. Interjections convey strong or sudden emotions. Think of three interjections: one that expresses *pain,* one *greeting,* and one *surprise.*

Lesson 1 Prepositions

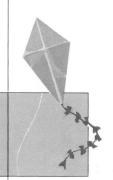

A preposition is a word placed before a noun or a pronoun. The preposition shows the relation of the noun or pronoun to some other word.

In each of these sentences, the preposition shows the relation between a noun or pronoun and some other word in the sentence.

Lena's family moved *from* Scattercreek.

From shows the relation between *moved* and *Scattercreek.*

The people *of* their new town did not accept them.

Of shows the relation between *people* and *town.*

Now Lena was treated *like* a burden.

Like shows the relation between *was treated* and *burden.*

The word *preposition* means "placed before." The noun or pronoun that follows the preposition is called its object.

The most commonly used prepositions are

about	around	by	in	through
above	at	down	near	to
across	before	during	of	toward
after	behind	except	off	under
against	beside	for	on	up
among	between	from	over	with

Exercise 1

Complete each sentence with an appropriate preposition.
1. Lena's father worked _____ Mrs. Chism's farm.
2. The Haneys, a white family, lived _____ the field.
3. When Mr. Haney was fired, his job was given _____ Lena's father.
4. One night, young Tater killed Lena's dog _____ their house.
5. _____ class one day, Lena experienced prejudice.
6. No one _____ Winslow defended African Americans.
7. _____ the teacher told his dad, Winslow's attitude changed.
8. Lena's family decided that she would not return _____ school but would help _____ Mrs. Chism's house.
9. That night, _____ the farm, Tater shot Lena's father.
10. Ouida Sebestyen wrote _____ prejudice and its effects.

Prepositional Phrases

> **A preposition and the noun or pronoun that follows it are separate words, but they do the work of a single modifier. This group of related words is called a *phrase*. Since it is introduced by a preposition, it is called a *prepositional phrase*.**

Washington, D.C., lies *on the Potomac River*.

In the sentence above, *on the Potomac River* is the prepositional phrase. It is introduced by the preposition *on*. The proper noun *Potomac River* is the object of the preposition. The entire phrase modifies the verb *lies*.

Exercise 2

Write a prepositional phrase for each preposition listed below.
Then name the object of each preposition. Follow the example.

PREPOSITION	PHRASE	OBJECT
through	through the fields	fields

1. with
2. for
3. down
4. across
5. in
6. between
7. of
8. around
9. during
10. about

Exercise 3

Find the prepositional phrases in each sentence. Name the
preposition in each phrase.
1. William Penn first landed at New Castle in Delaware.
2. The pear trees were white with blossoms.
3. Robin Hood lived in Sherwood Forest.
4. The field, with its rows of pineapples, was well kept.
5. Angry waves crashed over the dunes.
6. Farmers on nearby plantations supplied Savannah with
   cotton.
7. Books were once written on long rolls of parchment.
8. Tarzan clung to the vine above the thrashing reptiles.
9. What kind of animal made those strange tracks through the
   fresh snow?
10. There are no vitamins or minerals in sugar.
11. We heard the sound of trumpets.
12. *Treasure Island* was written by Robert Louis Stevenson.
13. With every step, she was growing thirstier.
14. The orphan had been living among wolves since infancy.
15. Watching for the hotel sign, the cabdriver slowed down.

Exercise 4

Complete each sentence with a prepositional phrase.

1. A laundry worker must have put too much starch _____.
2. When it began to hail, the picnickers ran _____.
3. We left our dog _____.
4. The silly cow just tried to jump _____.
5. In first-aid class, we will wrap gauze bandages _____.
6. That photograph _____ is very old.
7. Jonathan Earnestly likes to tell jokes _____.
8. The biggest mosquito I ever saw just flew _____!
9. Our class is saving money _____.
10. I can't believe that Vickie brought a monkey _____!
11. The ruins _____ are in Athens.
12. In the fairy tale, the witches cast a spell _____.
13. The first astronaut just stepped _____.
14. One cricket after another jumped _____.
15. The hikers place the log _____.

Practice Power

Use prepositional phrases to write a poem like the one below.
Think of an interesting topic.

A shadow
Slyly
Skipped
   across my window
   under my chair
   around my walls.
Should I try to catch it?

Lesson 2 Using Prepositions Correctly

Some sets of prepositions can be confusing. Each preposition may have a slightly different meaning and suggest a different idea. Carefully study the troublesome prepositions in this lesson. Learn how to use each one correctly.

At and *To*

> *At* **shows presence in.**
>
> *To* **shows motion toward.**

Toby and Tanya were *at* the party. (*Presence in*)
Toby and Tanya went *to* the door. (*Motion toward*)

Exercise 1

Choose the correct preposition to complete each sentence.
1. Vinnie is going (at, to) dinner.
2. About a hundred onlookers were (to, at) the farm auction.
3. Zod's pet stegosaurus comes (to, at) him when he whistles.
4. Yes, we were (to, at) the oyster roast.
5. The mummy couldn't come (at, to) the party because it was all wrapped up!
6. Were you (to, at) the last festival meeting?
7. Pedro sauntered (at, to) the gate.
8. The children are feeding apples (at, to) the horses.
9. Ricardo is (to, at) Robin's house working on the solar energy project.
10. Hazel is not (at, to) home right now.

Between and *Among*

> Use *between* to speak of two persons or objects.
>
> Use *among* to speak of more than two.

The king divided his fortune *between* the two princesses.
The king divided his fortune *among* his four children.

Exercise 2

Choose the correct preposition to complete each sentence.
1. There is an agreement (among, between) the two secretaries.
2. It might slither away (between, among) the many people in the crowd.
3. A music stand stood (between, among) the duo.
4. Watch for the helicopters (between, among) all of those dark clouds.
5. A ten-foot-tall sunflower stood (among, between) the twins.
6. Estelle Corinth-Walker's picture was (between, among) the two windows.
7. (Between, Among) the three, there was not one who knew how to say "hello" in Greek.
8. Many chestnuts are (among, between) the fallen leaves.
9. Skip a line (between, among) answers.
10. (Between, Among) the four students, there was a secret.

Beside and *Besides*

> *Beside* means *at the side* of or *next to*.
> *Besides* means *in addition to*.

Lisa walked *beside* me. (*Next to*)
Besides Lisa, Carla was also there. (*In addition to*)

Exercise 3

Choose the correct preposition to complete each sentence.
 1. Who is that (beside, besides) the traffic officer?
 2. Have you anything to drink (beside, besides) milk?
 3. Sit here (beside, besides) me.
 4. That railroad runs (besides, beside) the river for miles.
 5. Gwen has five dogs (beside, besides) this one!
 6. (Beside, Besides) french fries, we had fried onion rings.
 7. (Beside, Besides) the beaker sat a Bunsen burner.
 8. (Beside, Besides) birds, did you know that some kinds of butterflies also migrate?
 9. Mavis grows kale and turnips, (beside, besides) spinach.
 10. A small shark suddenly appeared (besides, beside) the shrimp boat.

In and *Into*

> Use *in* to show location within.
>
> Use *into* to show motion toward a place or change of position.

There are five students *in* the room. (*Location within*)
Five students ambled *into* the room. (*Change of position*)

Exercise 4

Choose the correct preposition to complete each sentence.

1. The storekeeper put the artichokes (in, into) the basket.
2. A cuckoo prefers to move (into, in) another bird's nest, rather than to build its own.
3. I'll put Arnie's books (in, into) my briefcase.
4. The clock (into, in) the kitchen keeps good time.
5. I can throw the paper (in, into) the basket from six feet away.
6. The ancient Incan civilization developed (into, in) South America.
7. She pushed the envelope (into, in) the mailbox.
8. Ray fell (in, into) the goldfish pond.
9. They have been (into, in) the hobby shop for an hour.
10. The game requires you to drop clothespins (into, in) the bottle.

Words Used as Prepositions and Adverbs

A preposition shows the relation between its object and some other word in the sentence.

An adverb tells *how*, *when*, or *where*.

Some words may be used either as prepositions or adverbs.

Below us lay the beautiful valley. (*Preposition*)
The captain went *below*. (*Adverb*)

HINT: A preposition is followed by an object—usually a noun.

Exercise 5

Tell whether the italicized word in each sentence is an *adverb* or a *preposition*.

1. All explorers left the Himalayas soon *after*.
2. I shall see you *after* the dance competition.
3. A couple skated *down* the ice-covered river.
4. The sun went *down*, leaving a dull red sky.
5. Weeds were springing *up* uncontrollably.
6. Sheep climb *up* the mountainside often.
7. Our school flag flies *above* the stadium.
8. What message was written *above*?
9. Ellen's Seeing Eye dog never has to wait *outside*.
10. The quarterback stood *outside* the huddle.
11. Have you visited this optometrist *before*?
12. Chi barely finished the assignment *before* school.
13. The bottom of a snail's body is a foot to help it get *about*.
14. Minstrels wrote songs *about* Princess Ella's long silver hair.
15. Jana wrote a paper *about* the explosion of Mount Vesuvius.

Practice Power

Use each one of the troublesome prepositions in a sentence. Underline the prepositional phrases in your sentences.

Lesson 3 Conjunctions

A conjunction is a word used to connect words, phrases, or clauses in a sentence.

The bicycle *and* the car are in the garage. (*Connects words*)
Phil could not go to the game *nor* to the picnic. (*Connects phrases*)
The sky is blue, *and* the sun is shining. (*Connects clauses*)

Conjunctions that connect words and word groups of equal importance are called *coordinate conjunctions*. The principal coordinate conjunctions are *and, but, yet, or*, and *nor*.

Conjunctions Connecting Words

Coordinate conjunctions connect words that have the same *use* or *function* in a sentence. These words may be
  nouns (subjects, objects, subjective complements)
  verbs (predicates)
  adjectives
  adverbs

Subjects

Rita *or* Clare will play left field during the game.
Toothpaste *and* ice cream contain seaweed!

Objects

Brass is a mixture of copper *and* zinc.
Have you eaten the ham *or* the cheese?

Subjective Complements

Last Friday evening was bright *but* cool.
Was the painter of the *Mona Lisa* Leonardo da Vinci *or* Michelangelo?

Predicates

Sara tried *but* failed to stand up on her skis.
A telescope gathers *and* focuses light into a tiny, sharp point.

Adjectives and Adverbs

Bamboo plants make very light *and* strong building material.
Fill out the registration form quickly *but* accurately.

Exercise 1

Find the conjunction in each sentence. Tell what *words* each
connects.
1. Mowers and pens were patented by black inventors.
2. The United States sends cooking oil and powdered milk to
   third world countries.
3. Goodwin, the magician, needed a black cape and a rabbit.
4. On his tombstone was a long but interesting epitaph.
5. Ms. Garretto sells ponchos and serapes.
6. Children clapped and laughed at the puppet show.
7. The skillful but careless chess player lost her game.
8. Early peoples made ornaments and weapons of bronze.
9. Luciano finished the third plate of linguini surely but slowly!
10. Would you like lemon or milk in your tea?
11. The contestants worked quickly and quietly on the quiz
    questions.
12. Maybe a box of candy will surprise and please Mom.
13. Sailors steer their ships by the direction of the sun, moon,
    and stars.
14. Athletes walk or run around the larger track.
15. Agent 505's assignment is dangerous but important.
16. The White Sea, north of the Soviet Union, is covered with
    snow and ice.
17. Mexican food is tasty but spicy.
18. Water and wind do not exist on the moon.
19. Lucius whistles or sings in the shower.
20. Beth seems excited but nervous about moving to a new
    neighborhood.

Conjunctions Connecting Phrases

Coordinate conjunctions connect prepositional phrases. These phrases may be adjectival or adverbial.

Adjectival Phrases

Carvings of ivory *and* of wood are for sale here.
Pineapples from the Philippines *and* from Hawaii are sold throughout the world.

Adverbial Phrases

The stream flowed across the field *and* under the bridge.
The cat ran under the bush *or* up the tree.

Exercise 2

Find the conjunction in each sentence. Tell which *phrases* each connects.

1. Shall I sit with you or with him?
2. Porcupines ran out of the field and into Mrs. Barrett's jeep.
3. Wild ponies on Assateague Island play happily on the beach and in the water.
4. There are strawberries in the refrigerator and in the cooler.
5. Silk from China and from Japan is imported through Western ports.
6. A honeysuckle vine is growing around the porch and across my window.
7. Will you send the package by parcel post or by express mail?
8. Flags of many colors and of many designs fly above the UN.
9. Huckleberry's raft swirled down the river and into the bay.
10. The Burmese child wore earrings of gold and of silver.
11. Our principal handed good citizenship awards to Denise and to Ollie.
12. We searched in the drawers and in the closet for my key.
13. You may play on the porch or in the yard.
14. We'll visit the zoos in New York and in San Diego.
15. A dog with a collar but without a name tag has been found.

Conjunctions Connecting Clauses

Coordinate conjunctions connect independent clauses. An independent clause has a subject and a predicate and expresses a complete thought.

California is on the West Coast, *and* New York is on the East Coast.

Synonyms are words of similar meanings, *but* antonyms are words of opposite meanings.

You may take the package with you, *or* we will deliver it.

Each conjunction in the above sentences connects a pair of independent clauses. Each clause contains a subject and a predicate, and it expresses a complete thought. Notice how the two independent clauses in the first example can each stand as a separate sentence.

California is on the West Coast.
New York is on the East Coast.

Exercise 3

Find the conjunction in each sentence. Tell which *clauses* each connects.

1. The curtain rose, and the tumblers rolled onto the stage!
2. You may come on the camping trip, but you'll have to carry your own gear.
3. Erase a file from the computer disk, or use a blank disk.
4. The water was icy cold, but many people were swimming.
5. Sam must pass the lifesaving test, or he will have to take the class again.
6. The human arm has thirty-two bones, and the leg has thirty-one bones.
7. I got up at 6:00 A.M., but I didn't see the sun rise.
8. The band warmed up, and an audience gathered.
9. I thought I wrote a haiku, but it had too many syllables.
10. We must buy the tickets today, or they will be completely sold out.

Exercise 4

Find the coordinate conjunction in each sentence. Tell whether the conjunction connects *words*, *phrases*, or *clauses*.

1. Artemis and Jay are basketball guards.
2. I tossed the hook into the water, and something big jerked the cork under.
3. Rita laughed and cried at the same time.
4. Neil Armstrong and Edwin Aldrin took a walk on the moon.
5. His bike was in the attic, but Ed didn't know it.
6. Beth sells newspapers in the morning and in the evening.
7. The planets are divided into two groups—the inner and the outer planets.
8. Chalk or crayons were used in many famous pictures.
9. We were wary but curious in the laboratory.
10. Every country has a flag, and most have a national anthem.
11. A doomed egg rolled off the table and onto the brick floor.
12. I dropped the mirror on the floor, but it didn't crack!
13. Unicorns might have run through these woods or across this meadow.
14. Halley's Comet came into view, but then it quickly disappeared.
15. Will the craft fair be in the auditorium or in the gymnasium?
16. The construction crew worked quickly but carefully.
17. The dalmatian in front of the fire station leaped and barked.
18. Japan has a huge population but very little farmable land.
19. Diamonds are the most valuable and the strongest gems.
20. Did they run around the houses or through the park?

Practice Power

Write sentences that contain a coordinate conjunction to connect each of the word classes below. First, write six sentences with the examples given. Then write six sentences with examples of your own. Vary your choice of conjunctions.

1. nouns (muffins/rolls)
2. verbs (collects/labels)
3. adjectives (quick/easy)
4. adverbs (slowly/confidently)
5. phrases (from the country/to the city)
6. clauses (Mark read the map/Teresa drove the jeep)

Lesson 4 Interjections

An interjection is a word that expresses a strong or sudden emotion.

Oh! We are too late to enroll in the swimming class.
Sh! The baby is finally asleep.

The word *interjection* means "thrown in." What emotion do you think is expressed by the word *Oh?* It is not directly connected with any other word in the sentence, but from the idea of the sentence we understand that it expresses disgust or disappointment. The word *Sh* calls for silence.

Interjections may express *delight, disgust, pain, agreement, joy, impatience, surprise, sorrow, wonder,* and so on. They are not grammatically related to other words in the sentence. An interjection is usually set off from the rest of the sentence by an exclamation point. An entire sentence, however, may be exclamatory. If the sentence is exclamatory, the interjection is followed by a comma and the exclamation point is put at the end of the sentence. If the interjection expresses a mild feeling, a comma follows it.

Ah, there she goes again! (*Entire sentence is exclamatory.*)
Well, what should I do? (*Milder feeling*)

Some common interjections are

Ah!	Good!	Hooray!	Oh!
Aha!	Good-bye!	Hush!	Ouch!
Beware!	Hello!	Indeed!	Sh!
Bravo!	Hey!	O!	Well!

411

O and *Oh*

The interjection *O* is used only before a noun in direct address. It is not directly followed by an exclamation point.

Oh is used to express surprise, sorrow, or joy. It is followed by an exclamation point unless the emotion continues throughout the sentence. If the emotion continues, *oh* is followed by a comma, and the exclamation point is put at the end of the sentence.

> *O Helen*! I like your new bike. (*Direct address*)
> *Oh!* What do you think caused the trouble? (*Emotion does not continue.*)
> *Oh,* how happy I am! (*Emotion continues—milder feeling.*)

Exercise 1

Tell what idea or feeling is suggested by the interjection in each sentence.

1. Hooray! We won!
2. Oh! That can't be true.
3. Bravo! You passed the exam.
4. Oh! Have you heard the news?
5. Hey! It's raining again.
6. Hush! Wasn't that a sleigh bell?
7. Indeed! You did not know that a sponge was actually an animal.
8. Sh! We finally got the triplets to sleep.
9. Ah, what a close call!
10. Well, my homework is finally finished!
11. Hey! You should have seen the size of that bass!
12. Oh, I just used my last wish!
13. Ouch! I twisted my ankle.
14. Beware! The curve is dangerous at high speeds.
15. Hello! We're glad you made it!

Exercise 2

Write sentences using the following interjections. Tell what feeling each expresses.

Good! Whew! Hey! Oops!

Write sentences using interjections that express

joy annoyance wonder pain

You Are the Author

Choose one.
1. Injustice is still a reality in our society. What are some examples of social injustice? Have you experienced injustice personally or read about it? Write a paragraph expressing your thoughts on this topic.
2. Do research (alone or in a group) on an African American who advanced civil rights (Frederick Douglass, Harriet Tubman, Sojourner Truth, Booker T. Washington, Dr. Martin Luther King, Jr., Shirley Chisholm). Write a summary of his or her achievements. Illustrate it if you wish.

Chapter Challenge

Read this paragraph carefully and answer the questions that follow.

¹The trails were lined with redwood trees as we headed toward Indian Moccasin Lake. ²Ms. Hally, our guide, told us that these trees were the tallest and largest in the world. ³Some are so big," she said, "people put holes into them and drive cars through their centers." ⁴"Hooray!" we soon heard her exclaim. ⁵She had just found a soap plant beside a thick clump of bushes. ⁶Slowly and carefully, she pulled it from the ground. ⁷Its white, onionlike root made it look like real soap. ⁸"Sh!" whispered Ms. Hally as we neared the lake. ⁹She pointed to a turtle digging a hole in the mud to lay her eggs, and then we spied a water snake sunning itself on the rocks. ¹⁰What other wonders would Ms. Hally be able to show us before the day would come to an end?

1. In sentence 1, name two prepositional phrases.
2. In sentence 2, the conjunction *and* connects what two words?
3. These two words are what part of speech?
4. In sentence 3, the conjunction *and* connects *put* and *drive*. These two words are what part of speech?
5. Name any two interjections in the paragraph. What feeling or emotion does each express?
6. In sentence 5, name two prepositional phrases.
7. In sentence 6, what two words does the coordinate conjunction connect?
8. These two words are what part of speech?
9. Name a prepositional phrase in sentence 6.
10. In sentence 9, does the coordinate conjunction connect words, phrases, or clauses?

Chapter 7
Phrases, Clauses, Sentences

The Circuit

by Francisco Jiménez

It was that time of year again. Ito, the strawberry sharecropper, did not smile. It was natural. The peak of the strawberry season was over and the last few days the workers, most of them **braceros,** were not picking as many boxes as they had during the months of June and July.

As the last days of August disappeared, so did the number of braceros. Sunday, only one—the best picker—came to work. I liked him. Sometimes we talked during our half-hour lunch break. That is how I found out he was from Jalisco, the same state in Mexico my family was from. That Sunday was the last time I saw him.

When the sun had tired and sunk behind the mountains, Ito signaled us that it was time to go home. **"Ya esora,"** he yelled in his broken Spanish. Those were the words I waited for twelve hours a day, every day, seven days a week, week after week. And the thought of not hearing them again saddened me.

As we drove home Papá did not say a word. With both hands on the wheel, he stared at the dirt road. My older brother, Roberto, was also silent. He leaned his head back and closed his eyes. Once in a while he cleared from his throat the dust that blew in from outside.

Yes, it was that time of year. When I opened the front door to the shack, I stopped. Everything we owned was neatly packed in cardboard boxes. Suddenly I felt even more the weight of hours, days, weeks, and months of work. I sat down on a box. The thought of having to move to Fresno and knowing what was in store for me there brought tears to my eyes.

That night I could not sleep. I lay in bed thinking about how much I hated this move.

Overhanging Cloud in July by Charles Burchfield

A little before five o'clock in the morning, Papá woke everyone up. A few minutes later, the yelling and screaming of my little brothers and sisters, for whom the move was a great adventure, broke the silence of the dawn.

Papá parked the car out in front and left the motor running. **"Listo,"** he yelled. Without saying a word, Roberto and I began to carry the boxes out to the car. Roberto carried the two big boxes and I carried the two smaller ones. Papá then threw the mattress on top of the car roof and tied it with ropes to the front and rear bumpers.

As we drove away, I felt a lump in my throat. I turned around and looked at our little shack for the last time.

At sunset we drove into a labor camp near Fresno. Since Papá did not speak English, Mamá asked the camp foreman if he needed any more workers. "We don't need no more," said the foreman, scratching his head. "Check with Sullivan down the road. Can't miss him. He lives in a big white house with a fence around it."

When we got there, Mamá walked up to the house. She went through a white gate, past a row of rose bushes, up the stairs to the front door. She rang the doorbell. The porch light went on and a tall, husky man came out. They exchanged a few words. After the man went in, Mamá clasped her hands and hurried back to the car. "We have work! Mr. Sullivan said we can stay there the whole season," she said, gasping and pointing to an old garage near the stables.

The garage was worn out by the years. It had no windows. The walls, eaten by termites, strained to support the roof full of holes. The dirt floor, populated by earth worms, looked like a gray road map.

That night, by the light of a kerosene lamp, we unpacked and cleaned our new home. Roberto swept away the loose dirt, leaving the hard ground. Papá plugged the holes in the walls with old newspapers and tin can tops. Mamá fed my little brothers and sisters. Papá and Roberto then brought in the mattress and placed it in the far corner of the garage. "Mamá, you and the little ones sleep on the mattress. Roberto, Panchito, and I will sleep outside under the trees," Papá said.

Early next morning Mr. Sullivan showed us where his crop was, and after breakfast, Papá, Roberto, and I headed for the vineyard to pick.

Around nine o'clock the temperature had risen to almost one hundred degrees. I was completely soaked in sweat and my mouth felt as if I had been chewing on a handkerchief. I walked over to the end of the row, picked up the jug of water we had brought, and began drinking. "Don't drink too much; you'll get sick," Roberto shouted. No sooner had he said that than I felt sick to my stomach.

I still felt a little dizzy when we took a break to eat lunch. It was past two o'clock and we sat underneath a large walnut tree that was on the side of the road. While we ate, Papá jotted down the number of boxes we had picked. Roberto drew designs on the ground with a stick.

After lunch we went back to work. The sun kept beating down. The buzzing insects, the wet sweat, and the hot dry dust made the afternoon seem to last forever. Finally the mountains around the valley reached out and swallowed the sun. Within an

Mountain Farm
by W. Victor Higgins

hour it was too dark to continue picking. The vines blanketed the grapes, making it difficult to see the bunches. **"Vámonos,"** said Papá, signaling to us that it was time to quit work. Papá then took out a pencil and began to figure out how much we had earned our first day. **"Quince,"** he murmured.

When we arrived home, we took a cold shower underneath a waterhose. We then sat down to eat dinner around some wooden crates that served as a table. Mamá had cooked a special meal for us. We had rice and tortillas with **"carne con chile,"** my favorite dish.

The next morning I could hardly move. My body ached all over. I felt little control over my arms and legs. This feeling went on every morning for days until my muscles finally got used to the work.

It was Monday, the first week of November. The grape season was over and I could now go to school. I woke up early that morning and lay in bed, looking at the stars and savoring the

Cows in Meadow, Texas
by W. Victor Higgins

thought of not going to work and of starting sixth grade for the first time that year. Since I could not sleep, I decided to get up and join Papá and Roberto at breakfast.

Two hours later, around eight o'clock, I stood by the side of the road waiting for school bus number twenty. When it arrived I climbed in. Everyone was busy either talking or yelling. I sat in an empty seat in the back.

When the bus stopped in front of the school, I felt nervous. I looked out the bus window and saw boys and girls carrying books under their arms. I put my hands in my pants pockets and walked to the principal's office. When I entered I heard a woman's voice say: "May I help you?" I was startled. I had not heard English for months. For a few seconds I remained speechless. I looked at the lady who waited for an answer. My first instinct was to answer her in Spanish, but I held back. Finally, after struggling for English words, I managed to tell her that I wanted to enroll in the sixth grade. After answering many questions, I was led to the classroom.

Mr. Lema, the sixth-grade teacher, greeted me and assigned me a desk. He then introduced me to the class. I was so nervous and scared at that moment when everyone's eyes were on me that I wished I were with Papá and Roberto picking cotton. After taking roll, Mr. Lema gave the class the assignment for the first hour. "The first thing we have to do this morning is finish reading the story we began yesterday," he said enthusiastically. He walked up to me, handed me an English book, and asked me to read. "We are on page 125," he said politely. When I heard this, I felt my blood rush to my head; I felt dizzy. "Would you like to read?" he asked hesitantly. I opened the book to page 125. My mouth was dry. My eyes began to water. I could not begin. "You can read later," Mr. Lema said understandingly.

For the rest of the reading period I kept getting angrier and angrier with myself. I should have read, I thought to myself.

During recess I went into the restroom and opened my English book to page 125. I began to read in a low voice, pretending I was in class. There were many words I did not know. I closed the book and headed back to the classroom.

Mr. Lema was sitting at his desk correcting papers. When I entered he looked up at me and smiled. I felt better. I walked up to him and asked if he could help me with the new words. "Gladly," he said.

The rest of the month I spent my lunch hours working on English with Mr. Lema, my best friend at school.

One Friday during lunch hour Mr. Lema asked me to take a walk with him to the music room. "Do you like music?" he asked me as we entered the building.

"Yes, I like **corridos,**" I answered. He then picked up a trumpet, blew on it and handed it to me. The sound gave me goose bumps. I knew that sound. I had heard it in many corridos. "How would you like to learn how to play it?" he asked. He must have read my face because before I could answer, he added: "I'll teach you how to play it during our lunch hours."

That day I could hardly wait to get home to tell Papá and Mamá the great news. As I got off the bus, my little brothers and sisters ran up to meet me. They were yelling and screaming. I thought they were happy to see me, but when I opened the door to our shack, I saw that everything we owned was neatly packed in cardboard boxes.

The Writer's Craft

1. Were you surprised by the ending of the story? What events might have led you to think that the story would end happily? What clues do these events (and the title) provide?
2. What are the things in Panchito's life that you would find most difficult to deal with? Discuss some of the effects Panchito's experiences might have on him.
3. Name the verbs that form the compound predicate in this sentence: *I walked over to the end of the row, picked up the jug of water we had brought, and began drinking.* Express these actions in three separate sentences. Why do you think the author chose to combine them?
4. Recall that sentences can be in natural or inverted order. Identify the order of these sentences: *"Vámonos," said Papá, signaling to us that it was time to quit work. I had not heard English for months. Beyond the stables was the old garage.*

Recalling What You Know

1. A subject and a predicate are essential to a sentence. Identify them: *With both hands on the wheel he stared at the road.*
2. An adjectival phrase describes a noun or a pronoun. What does the underlined adjectival phrase describe? *She went through a white gate, past a row of rose bushes.*
3. Is this a compound sentence? *I looked out and saw boys and girls carrying books under their arms.* Why or why not?

Lesson 1 Adjectival Phrases

A phrase is a group of words used as a single part of speech.

A prepositional phrase, which may be adjectival or adverbial, consists of a preposition and a noun or pronoun.

Even Panchito, although he was just a child, picked bunches *of grapes.*
(Adjectival phrase)

In November he began sixth grade in a school that he had never before attended.
(Adverbial phrase)

Each group of italicized words in these sentences takes the place of a single part of speech. In the first sentence the phrase *of grapes* modifies the noun *bunches* and explains *what kind* of bunches they were. The phrase *In November,* in the second sentence, does the work of an adverb by answering the question *when.*

Adjectival Phrases

> **An adjectival phrase is a phrase used as an adjective.**

The peak *of the strawberry season* was over.

The phrase *of the strawberry season* tells what peak. *Of the strawberry season* is an adjectival phrase modifying the noun *peak*.

Note how adjectives can be replaced by phrases.

Mamá asked the *camp* foreman if he needed workers.
Mamá asked the foreman *of the camp* if he needed workers.
Papá was a *Mexican* migrant worker.
Papá was a migrant worker *from Mexico*.

Exercise 1

Find the adjectival phrase in each sentence. Tell the noun that each phrase modifies.

1. The last days of August ended the strawberry season.
2. June and July had produced many boxes of strawberries.
3. Workers welcomed the setting of the sun.
4. The noise of the children awoke the dogs.
5. Migrant workers usually move when the harvest of a crop is over.
6. The workers' standard of living is low.
7. When fruits are ripe demand for pickers is high.
8. Workers harvest crops of grapes.
9. Long hours of work are common.
10. Migrant workers in the United States have low literacy rates.
11. Francisco Jiménez writes stories about Mexican people.
12. Jiménez was a janitor in the high school he attended.
13. At his graduation from high school he received three college scholarships.
14. He earned a doctorate from Columbia University.
15. Jiménez has been recognized for his contributions to education.

Exercise 2

Change each italicized adjective to an adjectival phrase.

Example: *Courageous* sailors sailed the ship.
        Sailors *with courage* sailed the ship.

1. *Spring* blossoms are a welcome sight!
2. The *river* bank was steep and rocky.
3. We want an *intelligent* dog.
4. Lee trimmed the *garden* hedge carefully.
5. We watched a *cowboy* film.
6. *Musical* sounds could be heard across the lake.
7. Half the world's fresh water is in *Antarctic* icebergs!
8. *Dirt* roads wind between the squash and watermelon fields.
9. Many salmon are found in *Alaskan* waters.
10. This summer we are going to start a *bug* zoo.

Exercise 3

Complete each sentence with an adjectival phrase.
1. The postcard _____ took four weeks to arrive.
2. The first game _____ was played in this stadium.
3. Batteries _____ can be expensive.
4. A bowl _____ was placed in front of the cat.
5. We need two people to help carry this basket _____.
6. Many fans collect souvenirs _____.
7. That girl _____ is my cousin.
8. We took photographs _____.
9. Rugs _____ will be displayed.
10. A troop of kangaroos followed the path _____.
11. The center _____ is hot.
12. Aunt Jeanette keeps a vase _____ in the hall.

Practice Power

Use the following as adjectival phrases in sentences.

with curly red hair	of different sizes
in our path	with green skins
behind the orange sunglasses	of stones and twigs

Lesson 2 Adverbial Phrases

An adverbial phrase is a phrase used as an adverb.

The car crept *through the safari park.*

The phrase *through the safari park* tells *where* the car crept. *Through the safari park* is an adverbial phrase modifying the verb *crept.*

In the following examples, adverbs have been replaced by adverbial phrases.

At the assembly, Ben spoke *sincerely.*
At the assembly, Ben spoke *with sincerity.*
Carol waited in the line *patiently.*
Carol waited in the line *with patience.*
The meteor fell *there.*
The meteor fell *into the wheat field.*

Exercise 1

Find the adverbial phrase in each sentence. Tell the *verb* that each phrase modifies.
1. Pine logs blaze in the old fireplace.
2. On the steps stood a large black hog.
3. One twilight star glowed in the darkening sky.
4. On every corner, balloon vendors gathered.
5. The ice fishers made a hole in the thick ice.
6. Louis Braille was born in 1809.
7. We strolled through the Dutch tulip fields.
8. Early settlers came from many countries.
9. Sam's arrow whistled through the air swiftly.
10. In the tropics, the evenings are short.
11. The folded paper boat moved swiftly down the stream.
12. Leroy slid the muffins into the oven.
13. A baby cottontail scampered across the clover field.
14. Inside Mexican jumping beans wiggle tiny caterpillars.
15. The grapevine's tendrils coiled tightly around the fence post.

Exercise 2

Change the italicized word in each sentence to an adverbial phrase. An example has been done for you.

Example: Orchids bloom *there*.
Orchids bloom *in the greenhouse*.

1. Our group built the model city *carefully*.
2. The ballet dancers leap *gracefully*.
3. He erased the pencil marks *hastily*.
4. *Faultlessly*, Keenan recited his poem.
5. She handed me the Swedish krona *immediately*.
6. Those chipmunks will disappear *instantly*.
7. *Formerly*, the Aztecs used chocolate beans as money.
8. Rain clouds travel *fast*.
9. Put your math books away *now*.
10. The audience listened *attentively* to the French fairy tale.

Exercise 3

Complete each sentence with an adverbial phrase. Tell whether each expresses *time, place*, or *manner*.
1. The dolphins leaped _____.
2. We shall leave _____.
3. A jogger ran _____.
4. The two toddlers swim _____.
5. _____ stands a very old barn.
6. The extinct pterodactyl once glided _____.
7. Carved vases were placed _____.
8. The art club will meet _____.
9. Carry the skateboard _____.
10. _____ the sun peeked.
11. Greyhounds race _____.
12. _____ the leaves fell.
13. Every book fell _____.
14. _____ the flag floated.
15. Jeremy walked _____.

Exercise 4

Find the phrase or phrases in each sentence. Tell whether it is *adjectival* or *adverbial*.

1. A baby robin with a broken wing fell to the ground.
2. Another name for the Eskimos is the Inuits.
3. Gary drives the bus with great care.
4. The checker rolled under the rocking chair.
5. The surface of the pond froze during the night.
6. My grandfather saw many deer among the hills.
7. After the spelling bee, Colleen sank into a chair.
8. Mr. Pernelli's building was destroyed in the fire.
9. I wanted to release the monkeys from their cages.
10. The strange color of the sky came from the sunset.
11. The largest signature on the Declaration of Independence was written by John Hancock.
12. The mice saw the cheese and climbed into the trap.
13. At the signal of the referee, the game began.
14. Dana keeps her cactus garden on a sunny shelf.
15. Usually each line of poetry begins with a capital letter.
16. The air was filled with the fragrance of pine.
17. A long line of covered wagons moved slowly into the valley.
18. Cleopatra was a powerful queen of Egypt.
19. Hungry bears waded through the stream.
20. Will Kelly climb to the top of the lighthouse?
21. Collections of coins were started many years ago.
22. Bumblebees were flying through the open window.
23. Ornaments of paper dangle from the reindeer's antlers.
24. Shadows of planes pass over our house.
25. The mobile of driftwood pieces was very unusual.

430

Exercise 5

Complete each sentence with a phrase. Tell whether each phrase is *adjectival* or *adverbial*.

1. A large lion prowled _____.
2. We listened to the noise _____.
3. _____ all contestants should walk quietly.
4. Long blue feathers were found _____.
5. A crate _____ is on our front porch.
6. _____ flew three squawking chickens.
7. The young knights searched thoroughly _____.
8. A small red car rolled _____.
9. Orange and red leaves danced _____.
10. The daisies _____ look like tiny stars.
11. I am carving a statue _____.
12. A giggling child sat _____.
13. _____ were jugglers, dancers, and singers.
14. The bottoms _____ were covered with mud.
15. Ralph, the dog, always jumps _____.

Practice Power

Use the following as adverbial phrases in sentences of your own.

on a T-shirt
into the knapsack
through the open window

from outer space
across the boundaries
over the doghouse

Lesson 3 The Essential Elements of a Sentence

Subjects and Predicates

> **The subject names the person, place, or thing about which a statement is made.**

To determine the subject of a sentence, place *who* or *what* before the verb to form a question.

> *Annabelle* picked flowers from our garden. (*Names a person*)

"Who picked flowers?" The answer is *Annabelle*, the subject of the sentence.

> The *garden* has many colorful flowers. (*Names a place*)

"What has many colorful flowers?" The answer is *garden*, the subject of the sentence.

> Those *flowers* are very beautiful. (*Names things*)

"What are beautiful?" The answer is *flowers*, the subject of the sentence.

The person, the place, or the thing about which a statement is made is called the *simple subject.*

> **The predicate states a fact about the subject.**

> The icicles on the roof *dripped*.

The subject of this sentence is *icicles*. What does this sentence state about the icicles? It states that the icicles *dripped*. The predicate of this sentence, therefore, is *dripped*.

The word that states what the subject is or does is called the *simple predicate*.

A simple predicate may contain more than one word. It may contain an auxiliary verb and a principal verb.

> Few low plants *can grow* in a rain forest.

A sentence is a group of words that expresses a complete thought. A sentence contains a subject and a predicate.

Complete Thought	Incomplete Thought
The scientist designed a telescope.	The designer of the telescope
The sky is blue.	Blue as a summer sky
Sally went there.	There in the country

Exercise 1

Find the simple predicate and then the simple subject in each sentence.

1. Marbles bounced.
2. Multicolored marbles bounced noisily.
3. Marbles of many colors bounced all around the room.
4. The leaves rustled.
5. Dry amber leaves rustled occasionally.
6. Leaves of a reddish hue rustled in the breeze.
7. Anthony rode the subway into the city.
8. The city has many interesting museums.
9. These museums attract thousands of visitors every year.
10. My family visited the Parthenon in Athens, Greece.
11. Greece is home to many temples and statues.
12. The ancient temples appear particularly beautiful at dusk.
13. A blustery wind had disturbed the papers.
14. The last plums in the orchard are ripe.
15. A teaspoon of water has 120 drops!
16. Frogs jump with their strong hind legs.
17. Strange symbols blinked on the computer screen.
18. The Chinese invented the wheelbarrow.
19. The frosting stuck to my hands like glue!
20. Long yellow strips of flypaper hang from the ceiling.
21. White blocks of ice drifted nearer and nearer.
22. The quartet sang a song about a bicycle for eight.
23. A red stagecoach full of passengers creaked down the road.
24. An excited horse pranced in time to the music.
25. I will owe you a favor.

The Parthenon

Exercise 2

Tell if each group of words expresses a complete or an incomplete thought.

1. A flock of sparrows rose from the flowering thicket.
2. The musical but high-pitched laugh of the actress.
3. Two attempts at winning the election.
4. Cathryn wrote clues for the scavenger hunt.
5. Tinkling noises of small bronze bells.
6. I spotted a figure moving through the empty house!
7. Someone should help Lewis with his graphics program.
8. About the worst day in my diary.
9. A distinguished gentleman with a bowler hat and a cane.
10. All the postmasters had assembled.
11. On an unusual day with no wind.
12. The water of the Dead Sea is salty enough to keep you afloat on its surface.
13. Rose-colored castle turrets rose above the trees.
14. Clear across the yard and onto the street!
15. The Himalayas are the highest mountains in the world.
16. Five ballet dancers, already best friends.
17. One hundred centimeters equals one meter.
18. Bamboo serves many purposes for the people of the Orient.
19. To the sky without thinking twice.
20. On the next transit bus!

A bamboo forest

Exercise 3

Each group of words below does not express a complete thought. Add words or phrases to each to make a complete sentence.

1. A laughing hyena
2. Reeked of the skunk's scent
3. The pieces of the puzzle
4. A museum with exhibits
5. Clapped to the music
6. Will grow in desert regions
7. In a sailboat
8. Miles and miles of flooded plains
9. Stretching their branches skyward
10. Over a wooden bridge
11. Bright orange tents in rows
12. Amid the rolling waves
13. A shiny new penny
14. The telltale sign
15. Had scattered confetti everywhere

Practice Power

Read this short paragraph. Rewrite this paragraph so that each sentence expresses a complete thought. You can combine ideas into one sentence.

The trampoline was invented by a man named George Nissen. He had fun jumping up and down on a big bed. As a child. During high school. George began to work on designs. He experimented. And used old springs, rubber inner tubes, and scraps of iron. He tried out his invention at a YMCA camp. Kids loved it. An exciting activity. Now a person can jump high. As high as a kangaroo!

Lesson 4 Working with Subjects and Predicates

> **The subject with all its modifiers is called the *complete subject*.**

Marbles rolled across the pavement.

In this sentence, *marbles* answers the question *what rolled? Marbles* is the simple subject.

Large multicolored marbles rolled across the pavement.

In this sentence, the subject, *marbles*, is modified by the adjectives *Large* and *multicolored*. The subject with all its modifiers is the *complete subject*. The complete subject in the sentence is *Large multicolored marbles*.

Study the following examples. The simple subjects are underlined. The complete subjects are italicized.

The athletes on our team exercise.
The longest bridge is outside of New Orleans.

> **The predicate with all its modifiers and complements is called the *complete predicate*.**

The word that tells something about the subject is the simple predicate. The simple predicate may contain an auxiliary.

Summer has arrived!

In this sentence, the simple predicate is *has arrived*. It contains the auxiliary verb *has*.

The simple predicate may be modified by an adverb or an adverbial phrase. It may also have an object or complement to complete its meaning.

Look at the following sentences. The simple predicates are underlined. The complete predicates are italicized.

The caterpillar _moved gracefully_. (_Adverb_)
Tad _hid in the tree house_. (_Adverbial phrase_)
Pete _played the xylophone_. (_Object_)

In the sentences below, each simple subject and each simple predicate is underlined. Each complete subject is separated from the complete predicate by a vertical line.

Our choir | sings beautifully.
The archaeologists | had unearthed the fossils in the desert.

Exercise 1

In each sentence, separate the complete subject from the complete predicate by a vertical line. Then underline the simple subject and the simple predicate.

1. A pink ribbon fluttered in the breeze.
2. Broken shells cover the beach.
3. The Declaration of Independence was signed in the city of Philadelphia.
4. A large dragonfly whirled around the flowers.
5. The rusty key fit perfectly into the lock.
6. A snail's pace is actually about three hundredths of a mile an hour!
7. The sky darkened suddenly.
8. The chair fell with a crash.
9. Gertie joined the ostrich owners' club.
10. Waiters in the Alaskan restaurant were dressed as penguins.
11. This puzzle has two missing pieces.
12. Tall trees swayed in the warm tropical breeze.
13. The right side of the brain controls the left side of the body.
14. Workers heard the news of the holiday.
15. Jorge waxed the fiberglass surfboard eagerly.
16. A panel of students will test new games for the toy manufacturers.
17. Ms. Carlyle writes music scores with a computer.
18. The cover of the magazine showed a photograph of the newborn quintuplets.
19. You inhale about a gallon of air each minute of rest.
20. The Manx is a cat with no tail.

Compound Subjects and Predicates

> A *compound subject* consists of more than one noun or pronoun.
>
> A *compound predicate* consists of more than one verb.

Aldrin and *Armstrong* walked on the moon.
(*Compound subject*)
The astronauts *trained* and *planned* for their landing.
(*Compound predicate*)

In the first sentence, *walked* has two subjects, *Aldrin* and *Armstrong*. In the second sentence, *astronauts* is the subject of two verbs, *trained* and *planned*.

> A sentence may have a compound subject, a compound predicate, or a compound subject and a compound predicate.

Jean and *Mike* enjoy poetry. (*Compound subject*)
Jean *reads* and *writes* poetry. (*Compound predicate*)
Jean and *Mike* read and write poetry. (*Compound subject and compound predicate*)

Exercise 2

Find the compound elements in each sentence.
1. I made sandwiches and put them into a picnic basket.
2. Gina and Gary told us a story, "How the Duck Got Its Bill."
3. The holidays came and went.
4. Football and baseball are my favorite sports.
5. Minneapolis and St. Paul are called the Twin Cities.
6. The wolf pups jumped and barked.
7. The photographer shoots and develops her own prints.
8. Oranges or lemons will make refreshing summer drinks.
9. Francis and Rosie are twin calves.
10. Dandelions and clover have overrun the herb garden.
11. In the Ice Age, people lived and hunted together.
12. Mosquitoes and bees come with the warm weather.
13. I read and reread *Romeo and Juliet*, a tragedy by William Shakespeare.
14. Sarah cracked the eggs and beat them with a fork.
15. Stevie Wonder composes his own music and performs it too.

Exercise 3

Complete each with a compound predicate to form a sentence.
1. The fireworks
2. My aunt and uncle
3. The trained seal
4. At the seventy-fifth floor, the window washers
5. For exercise, my friends and I

Complete each with a compound subject to form a sentence.
6. pedaled and pushed the tandem uphill
7. climbed to the top of the tower
8. will go to the street fair tomorrow
9. need oxygen and water
10. can tell time

Natural and Inverted Order in Sentences

> **A sentence is in the natural order when the predicate verb follows the subject.**

NATURAL ORDER   A fresh, cool breeze swept through the house.

In this sentence, the predicate verb is *swept.* You can find the subject by asking the question *who or what swept?* The answer is *A fresh, cool breeze* swept. The subject *breeze,* and all its modifiers, comes before the predicate verb. Therefore, this sentence is in the natural order.

   Who went with him?

The subject *Who* comes before the predicate verb *went.* This sentence is also in the natural order.

> **A sentence is in the inverted order when the predicate verb or an auxiliary verb comes before the subject.**

INVERTED ORDER   Through the house swept a fresh, cool breeze.

In this sentence, the verb *swept* and the adverbial phrase *Through the house* come before the subject *breeze* with its modifiers. This sentence is in the inverted order.

   Did you go with him?

In this sentence, the word *Did* in the verb phrase *Did go* comes before the subject *you.* This sentence is also in the inverted order.

Exercise 4

Change each sentence from the inverted order to the natural order.

1. Beside the lake stands a beautiful cottage.
2. In what state is Seattle located?
3. Did the audience applaud the performance?
4. Under the porch was a scared rabbit.
5. Had the woman seen the car crash?

Exercise 5

Change each sentence from the natural order to the inverted order.

1. Loaves of bread were on the counter.
2. Trinkets from around the world were in the glass cabinet.
3. The child has ridden her bicycle through the garden.
4. On the mountain a black bear appeared.
5. Through the open gate a Shetland pony trotted.

Exercise 6

Tell if each sentence is in the *natural order* or the *inverted order*.

1. Around the tiger's tail, the zoologists tied a small bell.
2. Coach Bremer planned a new line of defense.
3. Onto the yellow primrose climbed a ladybug.
4. Noah Webster published the first dictionary in America.
5. In the Torrid Zone, the climate is extremely hot.
6. Laurie will stop at the secondhand bookstore.
7. Under which tree did you find the four-leaf clover?
8. Delicately carved statues line the sides of the fountain.
9. In 1513, Ponce de Leon reached Florida.
10. Up the giraffe's neck crawled the green inchworm.
11. The missing ticket lay in the top drawer.
12. Ezra dragged the crate of chickens up the long hill.
13. The cheetah is the fastest animal on land.
14. In an orchestra, there are about one hundred musical instruments.
15. Through the ocean, currents race.

Practice Power

Make up three questions using information from social studies or science. Write your answers, first with a sentence in the natural order, and then with a sentence in the inverted order.

Where does the baby kangaroo hide?
The baby kangaroo hides in its mother's pouch.
In its mother's pouch hides the baby kangaroo.

Lesson 5 Sentences Grouped according to Use and Form

Division according to Use

> A *declarative sentence* is a sentence that states a fact.

Niagara Falls is on the border between the United States and Canada.

> An *interrogative sentence* is a sentence that asks a question.

Have you ever visited Niagara Falls?

> An *imperative sentence* is a sentence that expresses a command.

Look at this old painting of Niagara Falls.

In an imperative sentence, often the subject is not expressed. It is understood to be *you*.

> An *exclamatory sentence* is a sentence that expresses strong or sudden emotion.

How magnificent is Niagara Falls!

Exercise 1

Tell whether each sentence is *declarative, interrogative, imperative,* or *exclamatory.*

1. Southern Europe has mild winters.
2. Why did the chicken peck at you?
3. What a long snake that is!
4. Look in the yellow pages.
5. Was the rain dance successful?
6. Little League players wear safety hats.
7. Are we having spinach noodles for lunch?
8. Take the cat for a walk.
9. The peacock stared at its tail in the mirror.
10. *Shalom* in Hebrew means "hello" and "good-bye."
11. How many eggs does a sea turtle lay?
12. Oh, I can really see the craters on the moon clearly!
13. Avoid that dangerous road, Jerri.
14. Who broke the teapot?
15. Some weeds are just as beautiful as flowers.

Division according to Form

Sentences are divided according to form. Many sentences are *simple* or *compound.*

Simple Sentences

A simple sentence contains a subject and a predicate. Either or both may be compound.

A simple sentence expresses one complete thought.

The bicycle had a flat tire.

This sentence contains a subject, *bicycle*, and a predicate, *had*. Neither the subject nor predicate is compound.

The elephant raised its trunk and lifted one foot.

This simple sentence contains a subject, *elephant*, and a compound predicate—*raised*, *lifted*.

The cymbal and the triangle are simple instruments.

This sentence contains a compound subject—*cymbal*, *triangle*—and a simple predicate, *are*.

The wheels and the gears on the fantastic machine whirled and hummed.

This sentence contains a compound subject—*wheels*, *gears*—and a compound predicate—*whirled, hummed*.

Exercise 2

Find the subject and the predicate in these sentences.
1. The panda and its cub clutched bamboo leaves in their paws.
2. A quart of snow will not become a quart of water.
3. Ella and Warren designed and built a bird house for us.
4. Mares and their foals ran through the barn door.
5. White tables and chairs were under the yellow tents.
6. Licorice is made from the root of a plant.
7. Gymnasts run and somersault on a narrow beam.
8. Tony and I took photographs at the soapbox derby.
9. The *Iliad* tells the story of the war between the Greeks and the people of Troy.
10. Stephanie, your pencil fell and broke.

Compound Sentences

> **A compound sentence contains two or more independent clauses.**

Tara decorated the gym, and Kelly helped with the food.

In this sentence, there are two complete thoughts. The first is *Tara decorated the gym.* The second complete thought is *Kelly helped with the food.* Each thought could be used as a separate simple sentence. These complete thoughts are called *independent clauses.*

An independent clause contains a subject and a predicate and expresses a complete thought. Any part of an independent clause may be compound.

Independent clauses usually are connected by a *coordinate conjunction.* The commonly used coordinate conjunctions are *and, but, or, nor,* and *yet.* When the clauses of a compound sentence have no connecting word, the connection is then indicated by a semicolon.

We often sail on Lake Michigan, but we never fish there.
There are five Great Lakes; the largest is Lake Superior.

Exercise 3

Find the subject and the predicate in each independent clause of these compound sentences.

1. I like stories of adventure, but Marian prefers biographies.
2. Miska jiggled the weeds with a stick, and fireflies appeared.
3. He has not come, nor has he sent an excuse.
4. Wildflowers were abundant, and we decorated the house with them.
5. An inky blackness settled over the field, and we hurried for shelter.
6. Leonardo da Vinci was a man of many talents, but we remember him most as an artist.
7. The cage was open; the animal had escaped!
8. The little boy whistled, and the dog followed.
9. Charlemagne was a wise king, and during his reign his territories flourished.
10. Those mountains contained valuable timber, and the settlers found many uses for it.
11. The Phoenicians made dye from shellfish, and their traders carried the dye to the ports of the Mediterranean.
12. He opened the box, and a letter fell into his hands.
13. Tulips grow in many parts of the world, but we associate them most with Holland.
14. Tourists arrived at the wharf, and the guide was waiting there.
15. I take violin lessons, and my sister takes karate lessons.

Punctuation of Compound Sentences

1. The clauses of a compound sentence connected by the simple conjunctions *and, but, nor, yet* and *or* are usually separated by a comma.

> Fog and rain made driving difficult, but the flood made it impossible.

2. If the clauses are short and closely related, the comma may be omitted.

> The whistle blew and work began immediately.

3. Sometimes the clauses of a compound sentence have no connecting word. The connection is then indicated by the use of a semicolon.

> These are our duties; they are serious responsibilities.

Exercise 4

Add the correct punctuation to each of these compound sentences.

1. The dance-skating competition ended and the happy fans cheered the winners
2. Joseph had time but he didn't finish weeding the garden
3. King Arthur had many knights Galahad was the bravest
4. Betty is busy but she will help you
5. The yellow dress was pretty but Juanita didn't really like it
6. Bowling is an ancient sport cave people played it
7. Run quickly or you will miss the bus
8. The box held many old coins but they were unfamiliar to the collector
9. A sailor told exciting stories Mike eagerly listened to them
10. A snail weighs half an ounce but it can pull a pound of weight
11. The tourists were tired but they wanted to see the old fort
12. We had a heavy frost and the fruit was spoiled
13. Where did you go on your trip and would you recommend that place to me
14. No two snowflakes are alike but each has six sides
15. Madeline washed her father's car her sister waxed it

Exploring the Poem...

Haiku is a kind of Japanese poetry. Each of the poems on the opposite page is a haiku. In pattern and content, what do each of these poems have in common?

These poems talk about clouds, the wind, rabbits, earth, winter, and trees. All these things are part of nature. A haiku poem usually describes or comments about some part of nature.

Haiku follows a specific pattern. Did you notice that there are five syllables in the first and third lines, and seven syllables in the second?

Which haiku is your favorite? Why?

★ Think of something in nature that you would like to write about. It could be something enormous like the sea, the sky, or a mountain. It could be something tiny like a grain of sand, a pebble in your shoe, or an ant crawling on your leg. First write one descriptive sentence. Break this sentence into three lines. Move words around and rearrange ideas until you have a 5-7-5 syllable pattern. Write your haiku in the present tense.

Chapter 8

Punctuation and Capitalization

The Depths of Despair

by L. M. Montgomery

from *Anne of Green Gables*

It was dark when supper was ready, and still no sign of Anne, coming hurriedly over the log bridge or up Lovers' Lane, breathless and repentant with a sense of neglected duties. Marilla washed and put away the dishes grimly. Then, wanting a candle to light her down cellar, she went up to the east gable for the one that generally stood on Anne's table. Lighting it, she turned around to see Anne herself lying on the bed, face downward among the pillows.

"Mercy on us," said astonished Marilla, "have you been asleep, Anne?"

"No," was the muffled reply.

"Are you sick then?" demanded Marilla anxiously, going over to the bed.

Anne cowered deeper into her pillows as if desirous of hiding herself for ever from mortal eyes.

"No. But please, Marilla, go away and don't look at me. I'm in the depths of despair and I don't care who is head of class or writes the best composition or sings in the Sunday school choir any more. Little things like that are of no importance now because I don't suppose I'll ever be able to go anywhere again. My career is closed. Please, Marilla, go away and don't look at me."

"Did any one ever hear the like?" the mystified Marilla wanted to know. "Anne Shirley, whatever is the matter with you? What have you done? Get right up this minute and tell me. This minute, I say. There now, what is it?"

Anne had slid to the floor in despairing obedience.

"Look at my hair, Marilla," she whispered.

View of New Glasgow, Prince Edward Island

Accordingly, Marilla lifted her candle and looked scrutinizingly at Anne's hair, flowing in heavy masses down her back. It certainly had a very strange appearance.

"Anne Shirley, what have you done to your hair? Why, it's *green*!"

Green it might be called, if it were any earthly color—a queer, dull, bronzy green, with streaks here and there of the original red to heighten the ghastly effect. Never in all her life had Marilla seen anything so grotesque as Anne's hair at that moment.

"Yes, it's green," moaned Anne. "I thought nothing could be as bad as red hair. But now I know it's ten times worse to have green hair. Oh, Marilla, you little know how utterly wretched I am."

"I little know how you got into this fix, but I mean to find out," said Marilla. "Come right down to the kitchen—it's too cold up here—and tell me just what you've done. I've been expecting something queer for some time. You haven't got into any scrape for over two months, and I was sure another one was due. Now, then, what did you do to your hair?"

"I dyed it."

"Dyed it! Dyed your hair! Anne Shirley, didn't you know it was a wicked thing to do?"

"Yes, I knew it was a little wicked," admitted Anne. "But I thought it was worthwhile to be a little wicked to get rid of red hair. I counted the cost, Marilla. Besides, I meant to be extra good in other ways to make up for it."

"Well," said Marilla sarcastically, "if I'd decided it was worthwhile to dye my hair I'd have dyed it a decent color at least. I wouldn't have dyed it green."

"But I didn't mean to dye it green, Marilla," protested Anne dejectedly. "If I was wicked, I meant to be wicked to some purpose. He said it would turn my hair a beautiful raven black— he positively assured me that it would. How could I doubt his word, Marilla? I know what it feels like to have your word doubted. And Mrs. Allan says we should never suspect any one of not telling us the truth unless we have proof that they're not. I have proof now—green hair is proof enough for anybody. But I hadn't then and I believed every word he said *implicitly*."

"Who said? Who are you talking about?"

"The peddler that was here this afternoon, I bought the dye from him. The peddler said it was warranted to dye any hair a

Green Gables Museum,
Cavendish, Prince Edward Island

beautiful raven black and wouldn't wash off. In a **trice** I saw myself with beautiful raven black hair, and the temptation was irresistible. But the price of the bottle was seventy-five cents and I had only fifty cents left out of my chicken money. I think the peddler had a very kind heart, for he said that seeing it was me, he'd sell it for fifty cents and that was just giving it away. So I bought it, and as soon as he had gone I came up here and applied it with an old hairbrush as the directions said. I used up the whole bottle, and oh, Marilla, when I saw the dreadful color it turned my hair I repented of being wicked, I can tell you. And I've been repenting ever since."

"Well, I hope you'll repent to good purpose," said Marilla severely, "and that you've got your eyes opened to where your vanity has led you, Anne. Goodness knows what's to be done. I suppose the first thing is to give your hair a good washing and see if that will do any good."

Accordingly, Anne washed her hair, scrubbing it vigorously with soap and water, but for all the difference it made she might

as well have been scouring its original red. The peddler had certainly spoken the truth when he declared that the dye wouldn't wash off, however his **veracity** might be **impeached** in other respects.

"Oh, Marilla, what shall I do?" questioned Anne in tears. "I can never live this down. People have pretty well forgotten my other mistakes—the liniment cake and getting Diana drunk and flying into a temper with Mrs. Lynde. But they'll never forget this. They will think I am not respectable. Oh, Marilla, 'what a tangled web we weave when first we practice to deceive.' That is poetry, but it is true. And oh, how Josie Pye will laugh! Marilla, I *cannot* face Josie Pye. I am the unhappiest girl in Prince Edward Island."

Anne's unhappiness continued for a week. During that time she went nowhere and shampooed her hair every day. Diana alone of outsiders knew the fatal secret, but she promised solemnly never to tell, and it may be stated here and now that she kept her word. At the end of the week Marilla said decidedly:

"It's no use, Anne. That is fast dye if ever there was any. Your hair must be cut off; there is no other way. You can't go out with it looking like that."

Anne's lips quivered, but she realized the bitter truth of Marilla's remarks. With a dismal sigh she went for the scissors.

The Writer's Craft

1. How would you describe the character Anne? Discuss why you would—or wouldn't—like to be a friend of hers.
2. Have you ever purchased something and not been satisfied? Were the results of your purchase as disastrous as Anne's?
3. L. M. Montgomery cleverly uses dialogue to present the tone of her work. Reread Marilla's responses to Anne. Describe how punctuation marks help the reader perceive Marilla's changes of tone in her conversation with Anne.
4. This excerpt demonstrates the author's ability to use punctuation effectively as she creates natural-sounding dialogue. In a small group, list as many punctuation marks from the dialogue as you can and tell why each is used. Compare your group's findings with those of other groups.

Recalling What You Know

1. Review some of the uses of the period and the comma by punctuating this sentence.
   "Anne I cannot believe that Mrs Allan would have bought hair dye from a peddler" said Marilla impatiently
2. Recall that an exclamation mark is used at the end of an exclamatory sentence. When else can it be used?

Lesson 1 Periods and Commas

The purpose of punctuation and capitalization is to make the meaning of what you write clear. In speaking, the tone and inflection of your voice allow the listener to understand your thoughts. In writing, it is the use of punctuation marks and capital letters that help the reader to understand your thoughts.

If what you write is to be easily understood by your readers, you should learn how to use the marks of punctuation correctly. The rules taught in this chapter are the ones you will need to make your writing clear.

The Period

Use a period
1. at the end of a declarative or an imperative sentence

   Anne tried to wash out the dye.
   Wash your hair, Anne.

2. after an abbreviation or an initial

   Sept.   L. M. Montgomery   Mr. Matthew Cuthbert

Study the following abbreviations:

B.C.	before Christ
A.D.	*anno Domini* (in the year of the Lord)
P.S.	postscript
N.B.	*nota bene* (note well)
U.S.A.	United States of America; United States Army
U.S.N.	United States Navy
Gen.	General
Dr.	Doctor
M.D.	Doctor of Medicine
Lt.	Lieutenant
D.D.S.	Doctor of Dental Surgery
gal.	gallon
qt.	quart
pt.	pint
l*	liter
g*	gram
m*	meter
Blvd.	Boulevard
E.	East
W.	West
C.O.D.	collect on delivery
Mt.	Mount, Mountain

*The symbols used in the metric system are *not* followed by periods.

Exercise 3

Give the number of the rule that applies to the use of the comma in each sentence.

1. Nina played volleyball, Ping-Pong, and soccer yesterday.
2. The witch warned her class, "You should never fly off the handle."
3. *Robinson Crusoe*, a novel by Daniel Defoe, was based on the real-life story of a shipwrecked sailor.
4. Come here, Spot!
5. Yes, I heard the owl call in the night.
6. A famous toy duck of the eighteenth century ate, drank, quacked, and walked.
7. It was too stormy to hunt, and so Tuk stayed inside the igloo.
8. The first person walked in space on March 18, 1965.
9. The limerick, a five-line poem, is often funny.
10. "The lettuce for the salad," said Mother, "is in the bin."
11. There is a circus-wagon museum in Baraboo, Wisconsin.
12. No, the fish aren't biting.
13. Contestants in the log-rolling contest balance on a floating log, and the winner is the one who stays on the longest.
14. A special dish of the South is gumbo, a thick soup.
15. The genie's address is 1705 Wishful Avenue, Brass Lamp, Land of Imagination.
16. "Enjoy yourself at the ball," said the fairy godmother, "but be back by midnight."
17. Umbrellas, bird cages, and tennis balls filled the hall.
18. Contact lenses were invented in the 1880s, but they became widespread only in the 1960s.
19. "Pita is a flat bread of the Middle East," explained Yul.
20. "Wake up, girls!" shouted Gail.

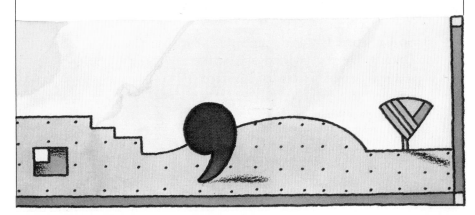

Exercise 4

Add commas and periods where they are needed in these sentences.

1. The flamenco dancers are from Madrid Spain
2. Benjamin Franklin said "A penny saved is a penny earned"
3. No I don't want to throw those magazines away
4. Orange green and purple stripes covered the toy zebra
5. We're going to ride the Ferris wheel the roller coaster and the bumper cars
6. Here is the answer Bruce
7. Thin air wind and wide temperature ranges make life on mountaintops difficult for insects
8. The ripe melons were picked and the workers carried them to the truck
9. Water from the cracked goldfish bowl had leaked onto the floor and Reba mopped it up before her parents got home
10. Charles P Tobias my great-great-uncle flew across India in a hot-air balloon
11. Yes our English papers are due today
12. Your cartoons are great Julie
13. The lion is a strong wild and ferocious cat
14. Icicles were forming on his eyebrows on his mustache and on his beard
15. "Please explain how the satellite works" requested Ann
16. Bruno went up the stairs but Thomas took the elevator
17. A baseball player on third base sang "There's no place like home"
18. Mr Carter shook the tree and the plastic ball fell out
19. The address on the envelope was 933 E Mayflower Blvd Decorah IA
20. No Christine I didn't watch the television last night
21. Thick white fog swirled across the lawn and I couldn't see my hand in front of my face

22. Buy cinnamon cloves and allspice for the pumpkin pies
23. Dr Erg's unusual invention the robot cat is shaking hands with a rat
24. Abraham Lincoln was born in Larue County Kentucky
25. The Declaration of Independence was signed on July 4 1776

Practice Power

Write one sentence to illustrate each rule for the use of a comma. Try to write a few sentences that would include abbreviations.

Lesson 2 Exclamation and Question Marks

The Exclamation Mark

Use an exclamation mark
1. at the end of an exclamatory sentence

    Here comes the parade!

2. after an exclamatory word or phrase

    Hurrah! The work is finished.
    Oh my! My pencil broke.

Exercise 1

Add exclamation marks where needed, and give the number of the rule that applies
1. What a noisy pet shop this is
2. Halt Who goes there
3. How blue your eyes are
4. How unusual that lizard is
5. Ready, set, go
6. O Matt Don't step on that flower
7. Wow Look at that ice-cream sundae
8. Listen
9. Hurry The bacon is burning
10. What a nice surprise this is

The Question Mark

Use a question mark at the end of every interrogative sentence.

> Is their flight on time?
>
> Where can you find elephant seals?

Exercise 2

Add the correct mark of punctuation to end each sentence: an exclamation mark, a question mark, or a period

1. Do you know how the badger got its name
2. We will make spinach lasagna
3. How tired I was after cleaning the boat
4. How many pretzels have you eaten
5. At the age of fourteen, boys in the Middle Ages began training for knighthood
6. From whom did the United States purchase the Louisiana Territory
7. What a silly joke I heard
8. What does a milliner make
9. Many sheep are raised in Ireland
10. Can you name the largest insect in the world
11. What a convincing argument Tanya made for a bigger allowance
12. Where is the girls' softball team playing
13. How time flies
14. The geranium is a hardy plant
15. Look out the window at the snow

Practice Power

As a contest winner, you may spend fifteen minutes in the store of your choice selecting anything you would like. There will be no charge for any item! Write a short paragraph naming some of the things you would choose. Include an interrogative and an exclamatory sentence.

Lesson 3 Semicolons and Colons

The Semicolon

Use a semicolon
>
> to separate the clauses of a compound sentence when they are not separated by *and, but, or, nor,* or *yet*

Al played the violin; Eileen played the piano.

Exercise 1

Add semicolons where they are needed in these compound sentences.

1. Vanessa cooked the spaghetti Michael made the sauce.
2. They followed every direction the experiment succeeded.
3. Angel Falls in Venezuela is the highest waterfall in the world it is about twenty times higher than Niagara Falls.
4. The sand was firm and not too wet it was perfect for building sandcastles.
5. Jean is a talented guitarist she also writes her own songs.
6. The people of India chewed pieces of Arāk roots a substance in the root whitened their teeth.
7. The first traffic signals appeared in London they were put up for horse-drawn buggies.
8. It would take much cheese to make a twelve-foot pizza it would also take many people to eat it.
9. Harry cut the wood he then built a fire.
10. New Guinea is the home for many birds of paradise these birds have magnificently colored feathers.
11. Two eyes appeared at the window my heart stopped.
12. Mount Vesuvius is an active volcano in Italy it erupts occasionally.
13. One of the stray cats disappears often it must have a secret hiding place.
14. The tickets for the finals went on sale at nine o'clock they were all sold by noon.
15. The book is new it even smells new.

Exercise 2

Below are simple sentences. Make each into a compound sentence by adding an independent clause and correctly using a semicolon.

Example: The old jalopy was sitting at the side of the road.

> COMPOUND SENTENCE: The old jalopy was sitting at the side of the road; it had run out of gas.

1. The path on the right leads to the lake.
2. Alice goes to ballet class on Tuesday after school.
3. We ordered fish soup at the Chinese restaurant.
4. At the carnival, many people tried to knock over the stack of bottles with a ball.
5. Wendy brought a camera to the parade.
6. Asparagus are in season in the spring.
7. The dark clouds gathered quickly.
8. The elephant went down the street on roller skates.
9. The Statue of Liberty stands in New York Harbor.
10. Fred likes ketchup on his french fries.

The Colon

Use a colon

1. after the salutation of a business letter

   Dear Ms. Lee: Dear Sir or Madam:

2. before a list of items

   We ordered the following articles: charts, books, paper, pens, and rulers.

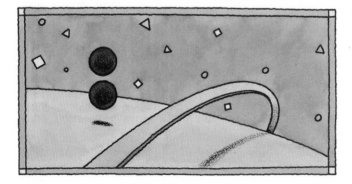

Exercise 3

Give the number of the rule that applies to the use of the colon in these items.

1. Dear Mrs. McKenna:
2. The dragon listed these items on the menu: fried leaves, rock candy, plates of armor.
3. Arrange these names in alphabetical order: Mozelle, Marcelle, Macelle, Estelle, Harry.
4. Dear Sir:
5. Provide the following: one bag of marshmallows, one box of graham crackers, ten chocolate bars.

Exercise 4

Add colons where they are needed in the following items.

1. We glued these together to make the nut ring pecans, peanuts, almonds, hickory nuts.
2. Dear Dr. Ray
3. Gwen wants to use these colors in her computer program turquoise, cyan, ocher, magenta.
4. The following beings just stepped off the UFO Zappies, Orks, Biddles, Urches.
5. The florist will use these flowers in the arrangement roses, pansies, carnations.

Practice Power

Write a short paragraph about your trip to a zoo. Make use of at least one semicolon and one colon to show that you understand how to use those marks of punctuation.

Lesson 4 Quotation Marks, Apostrophes, and Hyphens

Quotation Marks

Use quotation marks

1. before and after every quotation and every part of a divided quotation

    The teacher said, "The field day will be held next Friday."

    "Luke," questioned his friend, "have you ever seen a flying squirrel?"

2. to enclose titles of short stories, poems, songs, newspaper and magazine articles, television shows, and radio programs

    I read Mona Gardner's short story "The Dinner Party," in which a snake is an unwelcome visitor at a dinner.

    Ogden Nash wrote the humorous poem "The Hippopotamus."

Titles of books, magazines, newspapers, movies, and works of art are usually printed in italics. In typing or handwriting, italics are indicated by underlining.

Wilderness Journey is an exciting adventure story.

<u>Wilderness Journey</u> is an exciting adventure story.

Exercise 1

Explain the use of the quotation marks and underlining in these sentences.

1. "My new neighbors," said Sally, "have three dogs, two cats, and a pet chameleon named Arnold."
2. "Let's go for a dip," said one potato chip to the other.
3. "The Lapps were probably the first skiers," replied Britta.
4. I've just finished "I, Hungry Hannah Cassandra Glen...," a clever short story.
5. An old proverb says, "Well begun is half done."
6. "Bob," he asked, "where did you put my tie?"
7. Who wrote the book The Wizard in the Tree?
8. "Who has my copy of the New York Times?" asked Dad.
9. "When I was a baby," explained John Henry, "I had a hammer instead of a rattle."
10. "The Pit and the Pendulum" is a classic short story.

Exercise 2

Add quotation marks and underlining where needed in these sentences.

1. Jackie, he called, why don't you answer?
2. On Friday afternoon, said the class president, we'll have a popcorn party.
3. Going out tonight? one candle asked the other.
4. Indeed, replied Rosa, that story is very interesting.
5. Be prepared is the motto of the Boy Scouts of America.
6. Please pass the hot sauce, said Gary.
7. I thought, remarked Tex, you were going to get TV Guide.
8. His hearing is fine, declared the doctor.
9. Browning wrote the poem The Pied Piper of Hamlin.
10. I enjoyed the biography Emma and I, the story of a girl and her Seeing Eye dog.

Change each direct quotation into a divided quotation.

11. "Please leave by the rear door," announced the usher.
12. "Henry, where are you?" shouted the upset parents.
13. "What is in your hand?" Agnes asked suspiciously.
14. "Don't move an inch," warned Todd.
15. "The trees are full of hungry vultures," said Brent.

The Apostrophe

Use an apostrophe
1. to show possession

John's uncle has a butterfly collection.

2. with *s* to show the plural of letters

a's   *d*'s   *i*'s

3. to show the omission of a letter, letters, or numbers

I'll   class of '90   o'clock

Study these contractions and note the letter or letters that have been omitted to form each contraction.

they're—they are	he'll—he will
let's—let us	don't—do not
there's—there is	we've—we have
mustn't—must not	aren't—are not

Exercise 3

Add apostrophes where needed in these sentences.
1. Ill take this tomato soup next door to Mrs. Garza.
2. Mens straw hats are on sale here.
3. Wasnt Thomas Edisons most famous invention the electric light bulb?
4. Shell help you put the horse costume on.
5. My grandfather is a member of the class of 44.
6. You mustnt make wishes carelessly; they might come true.
7. The train pulled out of the station promptly at five oclock.
8. The class of 60 donated this megaphone to the school.
9. Eds *g*s look like *q*s.
10. In one unusual contest, a contestants task is to ride down a 153-foot hill on a coal shovel.
11. Theyve not yet returned.
12. Arent the Jataka tales from India?
13. Changs brother taught us to write our names in Chinese.
14. Its so hot outside you could fry an egg on the sidewalk!
15. Five-foot-tall cartoon characters decorate the childrens wing of the hospital.

The Hyphen

Use a hyphen
1. to divide a word at the end of a line whenever one or more syllables are carried to the next line

> Many unusual facts can be found in an encyclo-pedia, whether of one volume or of many volumes.

The dictionary shows how a word is correctly divided into syllables. Check the entry for a word in a dictionary when you have to divide the word at the end of a line.

2. in compound numbers from twenty-one to ninety-nine

> The ball cost ninety-five cents.

3. to separate the parts of some compound words

> brother-in-law   bright-eyed   self-respect

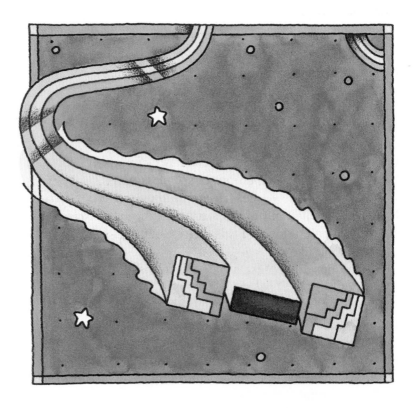

Exercise 4

Locate each of the following words in your dictionary. Use hyphens to show where the words could be divided at the end of a line.

Example: disorganize   dis-or-ga-nize

1. forgetful
2. lavender
3. parrot
4. affection
5. ingredient
6. hedgehog
7. unemployed
8. trustworthy
9. stepladder
10. catastrophe
11. embarrass
12. locomotive
13. needle
14. carousel
15. mosaic
16. sausage
17. dandelion
18. reverence
19. preparation
20. enlargement

Exercise 5

Add hyphens where needed in these sentences.
1. I can't believe my brother is twenty five years old.
2. That's a well known card trick.
3. The thirty one days of January often seem like a hundred.
4. Those guitar picks are seventy five cents each.
5. The cream colored pony was the one I wanted.
6. The baby seems good natured.
7. Farmer McGraw owns sixty five acres of prime farmland.
8. Just twenty four hours and school will be out for the summer.
9. Her mother in law owns the grocery down the street.
10. Purple forget me nots are embroidered across the quilt.

Practice Power

Add the correct punctuation to these sentences. Use any of the
marks of punctuation taught in this lesson.

1. Are you going to your sister in laws cottage
2. The ladder just fell Ill need help to get down from the roof
3. Sue Ling enjoyed the unusual words in the poem
   Jabberwocky
4. Josefina signed this parchment on March 15 1818
5. Ms Iarusso are there enough peppermint sticks
6. Graham turned the yard light off and the skunks trotted
   toward his trash can
7. Our orchestra needs these instruments a harp a clarinet a
   tuba and a comb kazoo
8. All in a Summer Day by Ray Bradbury is a short story set in
   an imaginary world but its lesson applies to the real world
9. Lukes friend called Come to lunch
10. Members of an otter family tie seaweed around themselves
    and this keeps them from being separated
11. Help me said Gilberts dad gather pinecones for the
    wreath
12. Theyll learn how to use a hammer saw drill and planes
13. How hot the biscuits are
14. The scolded dog dashed around the corner down the alley
    and into the shed
15. Weve promised to return before eight oclock
16. The Black Sea is between Europe and Asia a deadly gas
    makes its seafloor black
17. Auguste the nimble French actor memorizes his lines
    standing upside down
18. Eunice Morgan bought sixty five acres of land near Salt Lake
    City Utah
19. Liza what a long shortcut this is
20. He makes his ss very carelessly

Chapter Challenge

Below is part of a story about the day two legendary characters met: Pecos Bill and Paul Bunyan. Pecos Bill wanted the land for the grazing of his cattle, and Paul Bunyan wanted the mountain for its trees. Pecos Bill thought Paul Bunyan wanted the land, and Paul Bunyan thought Pecos Bill wanted the trees. Read about the battle that occurred. Then rewrite the selection on a separate sheet of paper, adding the correct marks of punctuation and capitalizing words correctly. Some punctuation is already given.

with the hundred men watching, the fight started. paul bunyan picked up his axe and hit at pecos bill so hard that he cut a huge gash in the earth people call it the grand canyon of the colorado river.

then pecos bill swung his red hot iron missed paul bunyan and scorched red the sands of the desert that was the beginning of the painted desert out in arizona.

again paul bunyan tried to hit pecos bill and again he hit the ground instead the scores of strange shaped rocks that are piled up in the garden of the gods in colorado were split by paul bunyans axe in that fearsome fight.

pecos bills iron, instead of cooling off, grew hotter and hotter, until with one swing of his iron he charred the forests of new mexico and arizona these trees, burnt into stone by the heat from pecos bills running iron, are now the famed petrified forest.

neither man could get the better of the other for the first and only time, pecos bill had met his match. . . . it was the first and only time that paul bunyans crew had seen a man that could stand up to him.

finally they paused to get their breath and paul bunyan suggested lets sit down a minute.

all right agreed pecos bill and they sat down on nearby rocks.

—From *Pecos Bill and Lightning* by Leigh Peck

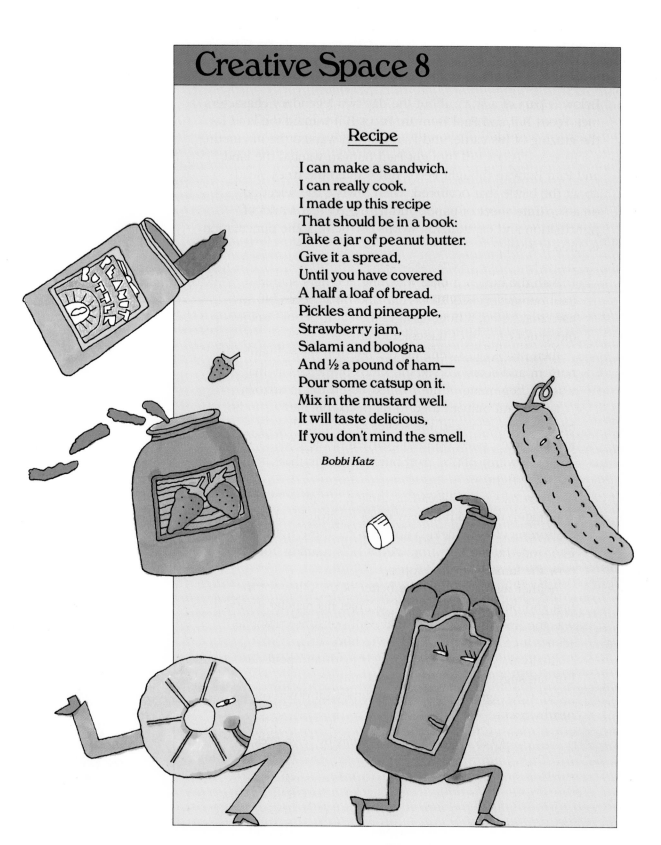

Creative Space 8

Recipe

I can make a sandwich.
I can really cook.
I made up this recipe
That should be in a book:
Take a jar of peanut butter.
Give it a spread,
Until you have covered
A half a loaf of bread.
Pickles and pineapple,
Strawberry jam,
Salami and bologna
And ½ a pound of ham—
Pour some catsup on it.
Mix in the mustard well.
It will taste delicious,
If you don't mind the smell.

Bobbi Katz

Exploring the Poem...

Do you think you would like to eat the sandwich described in the poem? Which ingredients do you like in the recipe? Which don't you like? Why do you think some foods taste good together and some don't?

Name the sets of words that rhyme. Notice how the second and fourth lines rhyme. What other lines in the poem rhyme?

★ The title of the poem, "Recipe," is very simple, but the recipe itself is very original. Now work with a partner to write your own original recipe for a sandwich or a dish you both like. Start with the *same first four lines* that this poem uses, although you can change the word *sandwich*. Then use different ingredients for the next eight lines. Try to make your lines rhyme. Finally, end with the *same last four lines*, but change the words *catsup* and *mustard* to something else.

Would you like to eat what you just described? Would you serve it to anyone else?

487

Chapter 9

Model Diagrams

Diagrams show the relationships among the words in a sentence. Since there are simple sentences and compound sentences, and because sentences may contain various kinds of modifiers, no one form of diagram will serve for every type of sentence. The diagrams given here are those that will help you most in your work. When asked to diagram a sentence, look here for a sentence of the same kind and see how the diagram is made.

Nouns in Simple Sentences

Nominative Case

Subject: *Molly* will train for the marathon.

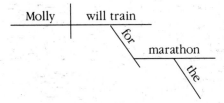

Subjective Complement: A junk is a wooden *sailboat*.

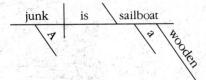

What do you see in this picture? Let your words help
make this picture clearer.

489

Direct Address: Close the door, *Peter*.

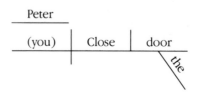

Appositive: Ms. Pucci, an *engineer*, designed a modern bridge.

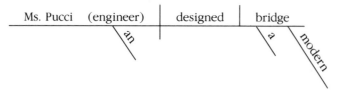

Possessive Case

Sally's mother works at a radio station.

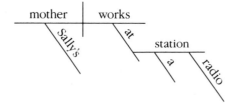

Objective Case

Direct Object: The hikers discovered an ancient *cave*.

Object of a Preposition: The spacecraft landed on the *moon*.

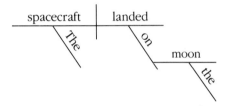

Indirect Object: The geologist showed *Chet* the limestone.

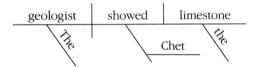

Appositive: We cannot see oxygen, a colorless *gas*.

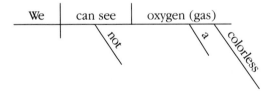

Kinds of Simple Sentences

Declarative Sentence

In the ocean, an aquanaut wears a wet suit.

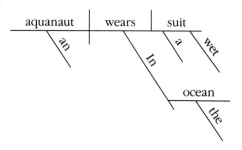

Interrogative Sentence

Have you read *Superfudge*?

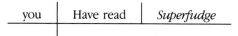

Imperative Sentence

Name two African countries.

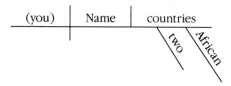

Exclamatory Sentence

How exciting the raft ride was!

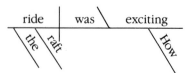

Compound Elements in Simple Sentences

Compound Subject: Laurie and Lynn take their own pictures.

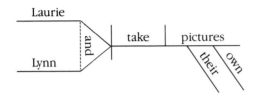

Compound Predicate: Laurie takes and develops her own pictures.

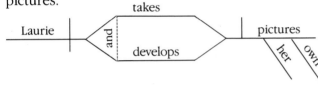

Compound Subject and Compound Predicate: Laurie and Lynn take and develop their own pictures.

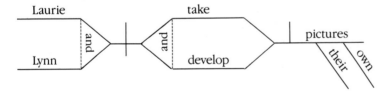

Compound Sentence

Max likes adventure stories, but Marian prefers biographies.

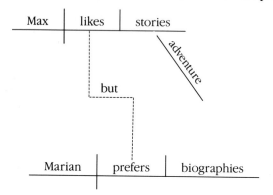

Index

Acknowledgments

Text

50 "Fourth of July Night" from *Hop, Skip and Jump!* by Dorothy Aldis. Copyright © 1934, 1961 by the author. Reprinted by permission of G. P. Putnam's Sons.

51 "Stop-Go" from *I Like Automobiles* by Dorothy W. Baruch. Reprinted by permission of Bertha Klausner International Literary Agency, Inc.

51 "Autumn Woods" from *A World to Know* by James S. Tippett. Copyright © 1933 by Harper & Row, Publishers, Inc.; copyright renewed © 1961 by Martha K. Tippett. Reprinted by permission of the publisher.

59 From *The Black Stallion* by Walter Farley. Illustrated by Keith Ward. Copyright © 1941, 1969 by the author. Reprinted by permission of Random House, Inc.

67 Excerpts totaling approx. 175 words from pp. 27 and 29 from *Sounder* by William H. Armstrong. Copyright ©1969 by the author. Reprinted by permission of Harper & Row, Publishers, Inc.

93, 94 From *Across Five Aprils* by Irene Hunt. Copyright ©1964 by the author. Reprinted by permission of Modern Curriculum Press, Inc.

99 From "May I Have Your Autograph?" by Marjorie Sharmat, from *Sixteen Short Stories by Outstanding Writers for Young Readers,* Donald R. Gallo, ed. Copyright © 1984 by the author. Reprinted by permission of Delacorte Press.

152 "Hector the Collector" (text only) from *Where The Sidewalk Ends: The Poems and Drawings of Shel Silverstein.* Copyright © 1974 by Evil Eye Music, Inc. Reprinted by permission of Harper & Row, Publishers, Inc.

155 "It Couldn't Be Done" from *Collected Verse* by Edgar A. Guest. Copyright © 1934 by Contemporary Books, Inc. Reprinted by permission of the publisher.

156 "Velvet Shoes" from *Collected Poems of Elinor Wylie.* Copyright © 1921 by Alfred A. Knopf, Inc.; copyright renewed © 1949 by William Rose Benet. Reprinted by permission of Alfred A. Knopf, Inc.

158 "Stopping by Woods on a Snowy Evening" from *The Poetry of Robert Frost*, Edward Connery Lathem, ed. Copyright © 1923 by Holt, Rinehart and Winston; copyright © 1951 by the author; copyright renewed © 1969 by the publisher. Reprinted by permission of Henry Holt and Company, Inc.

159 "The Camel's Complaint" from *The Admiral's Caravan* by Charles Edward Carryl, in the public domain.

160 "Raccoon" from *Laughing Time* by William Jay Smith. Copyright © 1953, 1955, 1956, 1957, 1959, 1968, 1974, 1977 by the author. Reprinted by permission of Delacorte Press/Seymour Lawrence.

161 "Wind Song" from *I Feel The Same Way* by Lilian Moore. Copyright © 1967 by the author. Reprinted by permission of Atheneum Publishers, New York.

191 From *The World Almanac and Book of Facts, 1987.* Copyright © 1986 by Newspaper Enterprise Association, Inc., New York.

197 From *A Wrinkle in Time* by Madeleine L'Engle. Copyright © 1962 by the author; copyright renewed © 1990 by Crosswicks Ltd. Reprinted by permission of Farrar, Straus and Giroux, Inc.

241 From *Do Not Disturb* by Margery Facklam. Illustrated by Pamela Johnson. Text copyright © 1989 by the author; illustrations copyright © 1989 by the artist. Reprinted by permission of Little, Brown and Co.

274 "City" by Langston Hughes. Copyright © 1958 by the author; copyright renewed © 1986 by George Houston Bass. Reprinted by permission of Harold Ober Associates, Inc.

277 From *Mary Cassatt: A Portrait* by Elisabeth P. Myers. Copyright © 1971. Reprinted by permission of Reilly & Lee Books.

Fine Art

279 *During Carnival: On the Balcony,* 1873, by Mary Cassatt. Philadelphia Museum of Art, W. P. Wilstach Collection.

308 *Buffalo Chase with Bows and Lances* by George Catlin. National Museum of American Art, Smithsonian Institution, Washington, D.C.

310 *Adam's House,* detail, by Edward Hopper. Wichita Art Museum, Roland P. Murdock Collection. Photographed by Henry Nelson.

313 *High Road,* 1931, by Edward Hopper. Watercolor on paper (20 x 28 in.). Whitney Museum of American Art, New York; bequest of Josephine N. Hopper.

352 *Sunflowers,* 1888, by Vincent van Gogh. Philadelphia Museum of Art.

364 *Pegasus: Horse on the Rock* by Odilon Redon. Pastel on carton (31.5. x 23.4 in.). Hiroshima Museum of Art.

367 *Pegasus* by Odilon Redon. Lithograph courtesy of William and Jeanne Seabright.

392 *Her World* by Philip Evergood. The Metropolitan Museum of Art, New York.

395 *Tillie Taggert,* 1948, by Andrew Wyeth. Watercolor on paper (23 $\frac{1}{2}$ x 29 $\frac{1}{4}$ in.). Museum of Fine Arts, Boston; anonymous gift in memory of Nicholas Jarrott Tiffany and Lt. George Shepley Tiffany.

399 *Residence of Mr. Gottfried Walder* by Paul Seifert. Henry Ford Museum and Greenfield Village, Dearborn, Mich.

418 *Overhanging Cloud in July,* 1947-1959, by Charles Burchfield. Watercolor on paper (39 $\frac{1}{2}$ x 35 $\frac{1}{2}$ in.). Collection of the Whitney Museum of American Art, New York; purchased with funds from the Friends of the Whitney Museum of American Art, 60.23. Photographed by Geoffrey Clements, New York.

421 *Mountain Farm,* 1935-1936, by Victor Higgins. Watercolor (16 x 23 in.). The Snite Museum of Art, University of Notre Dame; gift of Mr. and Mrs. John T. Higgins.

422 *Cows in Meadow, Taos* by Victor Higgins. Watercolor (15 x 22 in.). Private collection. Photograph courtesy of the Gerald Peters Gallery, Santa Fe.

469 *Abraham Lincoln* by an unknown artist. Illinois State Museum, Springfield.

488 *Three Musicians,* 1921, by Pablo Picasso. The Museum of Modern Art, New York; Mrs. Simon Guggenheim Fund.

Photographs

Cover: Alan Shortall

i Jeff Lane. **ii, iii** Comstock. **xv** The Image Bank. **xviii–xix** Heidi Brandenburg/Minden Pictures. **xx** James L. Ballard. **2** NASA. **11** Tom Stack/Tom Stack & Associates. **21** James L. Ballard. **26** T. E. Adams /Peter Arnold, Inc. **31** Index Stock Photography. **32** Kevin Schafer/Tom Stack & Associates. **39** The Image Bank. **43** Index Stock Photography. **45** Werner Muller/Peter Arnold, Inc. **48** Ira Kirschenbaum/Index Stock Photography. **49** Stock Boston. **51** Rod Planck/Tom Stack & Associates. **69** Magnum Photos, Inc. **75** Dr. James Blinn, Jet Propulsion Laboratory. **84** Stephen J. Krasemann/Peter Arnold, Inc. **86, 87** Wells Fargo Bank, San Francisco. **119, 121, 138, 152, 153** James L. Ballard. **158** Index Stock Photography. **161** Al Satterwhite/The Image Bank. **172** NASA. **178** Index Stock Photography. **179** Peter Arnold, Inc. **191** Bettmann Archive. **194–195** Michael J. Howell/Index Stock Photography. **199** Bettmann Archive. **202** Tom Stack & Associates. **203** Larry West. **205** Peter Arnold, Inc. **211** Index Stock Photography. **236** Larry West. **238, 239** James Carmichael/The Image Bank. **240** Michio Hoshino/Minden Pictures. **273** American Foundation for the Blind, Inc. **274** Hyatt/The Image Bank. **288** The Image Bank. **289, 302** Arthur Meyerson Photography, Inc. **305** Hiroji Kubota/Magnum Photos, Inc. **319** Steve Elmore/Tom Stack & Associates. **321** Thomas Rampi/The Image Bank. **321** Pete Turner/The Image Bank. **325** Chiko/The Image Bank. **325** John Serafin/Peter Arnold, Inc. **332** Hiroji Kubota/Magnum Photos, Inc. **335** Werner Muller/Peter Arnold, Inc. **350** Ponza Scianna. **361** R & M Magruder/The Image Bank. **378** The Image Bank. **390** Bryan F. Peterson Photography, Inc. **434** The Image Bank. **435** Shinji Takama. **443** James L. Ballard. **448** Guido Alberto Rossi/The Image

Bank. **454** Richard Pasley/Stock Boston. **455** Larry West. **456** Tom Stack & Associates. **459** The Image Bank. **463** A. Mangold/The Image Bank.

Illustrations

Steve Berman, 433(B). **Mary Lynn Blasutta,** x, 2, 3(T), 4, 5, 10, 11, 29, 30(T,B), 31, 74, 75, 85, 93, 105, 106, 107, 124, 148, 149, 150(T), 151(T,M), 152, 153, 154(T), 155, 157, 158, 159, 160, 162(T), 164, 165(T), 167, 208(T), 209(T), 215, 225, 226(M), 248(B), 251(B), 252, 253(B), 255(B), 270, 284(B), 290(T), 299, 322, 323, 330, 331, 338(T), 348, 349, 404. **Frank Bozzo,** 449(T). **Nan Brooks,** 140(B), 141(B). **Ted Carr,** xvi(T), 135, 208(B), 209(B), 271(B). **Ralph Creasman,** 14, 40, 56(T), 57(T), 96, 173, 248(T), 249, 286, 287, 288, 297, 337(B), 442, 443, 444, 445, 485. **David A. Cunningham,** 3, 18, 19, 24, 25, 27, 60, 61, 67, 94(B), 95(B), 102, 103, 104, 142, 143, 147, 150(B), 151(B), 171(B), 174(M), 342(B), 343, 402(B), 403(B), 416, 417, 430(B), 431(B), 438(B). **Pat Dypold,** 378, 379, 380, 429(T). **Jean Cassels Helmer,** 8, 9, 30(M), 44(T), 88, 89, 190(M), 192(B), 193(B), 261(M), 376(B), 439(B), 446(B). **Cynthia Hoffman,** 39, 45, 53, 65, 156(T), 160(T), 221(B), 232(T), 336, 337(T), 355, 427, 448. **Paul Hoffman,** 156(B), 212(M), 228(B), 328(B), 329(B), 382(B), 383(B). **Pamela Johnson,** 243(B), 244(B). **Mary Jones,** xi, xvi(B), xvii, 16, 17, 22, 41, 46, 64(B), 65(B), 68, 69, 76, 77, 110, 113, 114(B), 166, 177, 180, 181, 188, 199, 200(M), 204, 205, 207, 230, 231, 242, 243(T), 244(T), 245, 250, 251, 253(T), 261(B), 264(B), 265(B), 277, 278, 279, 280, 281(T), 296(B), 315, 316(B), 334, 335, 338(B), 339, 354(B), 355(B), 362, 363, 408, 409, 433(T), 446, 447, 449(B), 457, 458, 459, 460, 461(T). **G. Brian Karas,** xiv(T), 34, 35, 78, 82, 97, 101, 108, 109, 118(B), 154(M,B), 165(M,B), 198, 199, 206(B), 224, 226(B), 232(B), 246, 247, 256(B), 257(B), 290(B), 291(B), 306, 307, 346, 347, 407, 410, 411(B), 440(B), 452, 453. **Carl Kock,** xii, xiii, xv(T), 1, 6, 7, 8(T), 9(T), 15, 16(T), 17(T), 18(T), 19(T), 20, 21, 22(T), 23, 26, 32, 36, 37, 42, 43, 44(B), 48, 49, 52, 55, 58(T,B), 59, 62, 63, 64(T), 65(T), 66, 70, 72, 73, 78(T), 79, 83, 90, 91, 92, 94(T), 95(T,M), 98, 99, 100, 101(T), 114(T), 115, 116, 117, 118(T), 119(T), 120, 121, 122, 123, 125, 126, 127, 128, 129, 130, 131, 132, 133, 134, 135(T), 136(T), 137, 138, 139, 140(T), 141(T), 144(T), 161, 163(T), 170, 171(T), 174(T), 175, 178, 179, 182, 183, 184, 185, 186(T), 187, 189, 190(T), 191, 192(T), 193(T), 200(T), 201, 202, 203, 206(T), 210, 211, 212, 213, 218, 219, 220, 221(T), 222, 223, 226(T), 228(T), 229, 233, 234, 235, 236, 237, 254, 255(T), 257(T), 258, 259, 260, 261(T), 263, 264(T), 265(T), 266, 267, 268, 269, 271(T), 281, 282, 283, 284(T), 285, 289, 291(T), 292, 293, 294, 295, 298, 300, 301, 317(T), 324, 325, 326, 327, 332, 333, 340, 341, 342(T), 350, 351, 352, 353, 354(T), 357, 358, 359(T), 360, 371, 372, 373, 374(T), 375, 376(T), 377, 381, 385, 398, 399, 400(T), 402(T), 403(T), 404(T), 405, 411(T), 412, 413, 414, 415, 426, 430(T), 431(T), 434, 435, 438(T), 439(T), 440(T), 441(B), 450, 451(T), 461, 463, 464, 465, 466, 467, 468, 469, 470, 471, 472, 473, 474, 475, 476, 477, 478, 479, 480, 482, 483(T), 484, 485(T), 490, 491, 492, 493, 494. **Joan Landis,** 384(B), 453. **April Uhlir Lemke,** 359(B). **Eileen Mueller Neill,** 38(T), 176(T). **Robert Post,** 33, 38, 56, 57, 71, 374, 429(B), 462, 483(B). **Phil Renaud,** xiv(B), 317(B), 400(B). **William Seabright,** 214, 451(B), 486, 487. **Lynn Westphal** (handwriting), 12, 13, 24, 25, 86, 87, 114, 115, 116, 119, 120, 121, 124, 125, 126, 129, 130, 131, 139.

Editors

First Edition: George A. Lane, S.J.; Joseph F. Downey, S.J.; Jeanette Ertel; Jane Guttman; Laura Fries. **Revision:** Pam Bernstein, Stephanie Iverson, Suzanne Mazurek, Jane Samuelson, Richard F. Weisenseel.

Production Staff

First Edition: April Uhlir Lemke, David Miller, Kristina Lykos. **Revision:** Nancy Gruenke, Mary O'Connor, Gloria Dallmeier.

The type for this book was set by Jandon Graphics, Inc.; the revised type was set on Macintosh computers; the film was made by H & S Graphics, Inc.; and the book was printed by R. R. Donnelley & Sons Company.